LEXX: Unauthorized Series 2

The Light at the End of the Universe

By

D. G. Valdron

FOSSIL COVE PRESS

LEXX Unauthorized, Series 2: The Light at the End of the Universe

Fossil Cove Publishing,
1301 - 90 Garry Street,
Wpg, Mb, Can, R3C 4J4

Issued in electronic formats
ISBN: (ebook) 978-1-7771551-0-0 / (print/trade paperback) 978-1-990860-95-9

Text set in Garamond

Dedicated to

John Dunsworth
1946-2017

LEXX: Unauthorized, Series 2
The Light at the End of the Universe
TABLE OF CONTENTS

Prologue: Beginning at the Far End of the World, or at least Halifax

"The impulse to Heroism, is the same impulse.... that sends us bumbling off a cliff," Jeff Hirschfield, LEXX writer and voice of 790, private conversation, 2003

Have you ever been to Halifax? It's a sleepy little city of a quarter of a million people, tucked in long deep harbor in the center of the Canadian province of Nova Scotia. It's a quaint place, full of rolling hills, everywhere you go is either steep uphill or fast downhill, it's full of old buildings and mementos, creaking with age. The French settled it first, or perhaps it was the English, either way, it didn't turn out so well, and they all starved. Then the French made a go of it, and the land was called Acadia. A few wars later, the British took it over, scattered the French colonists, imported a bunch of Scots and named it Nova Scotia (New Scotland). The fledgling settlement was named Halifax after some English lord.

Through the eighteenth century, as the French and English warred for North America, the British spent thirty-six years and immense treasure on an immense fortress that kept falling down as they were building. Two centuries later, that fortress is still sitting there in the center of town. Never used, but somehow, they didn't have the heart to do something useful with it. It still looms over the center of the city, green and blocky, a monument to something or other. Directly across the street, were LEXX's cutting edge 21st century CGI post-production offices. That's a nice juxtaposition.

During World War One, also known as the Great War, two ships collided in Halifax Harbor. One of them was a munitions ship. The explosion was three kilotons, leveling half the city, killing two thousand, injuring another nine thousand. This in a community of only sixty thousand. This was the largest manmade explosion in human history, until Hiroshima. Today, you can look out over the placid harbor and see sailboats and windsurfers crossing back and forth, as the big freighters lumber in. The city is rebuilt now, a quarter million people live there. But they still talk about the explosion. Lex Gigeroff once shared a joint with me on the ferry wharf as he pointed out the location of the explosion.

Halifax isn't large, but it's the largest city in the Maritimes. It's an economic hub, but not so active or frantic, literally every street is drenched with history, and somehow the pace of life is both slow and fast. Paul Donovan, the creator of LEXX lived in a house older than his country, Canada.

It's a peculiar place, both cosmopolitan and isolated, naive but somehow sly. There are bars everywhere, each of them with the quaint history that money and designers can never duplicate. It's got a rich artistic tradition, music, theater and hooked rugs, some hybrid fusion of Acadian French, hardy Scots, native wisdom, small town intimacy and big city ambition. I don't think that there's a place on earth quit like it.

It's probably the last place on earth you'd ever expect to create a television series as subversive and surreal as LEXX. And yet....maybe it was the perfect place. A place that was peculiarly its own, far from naive, but not quite cynical, worldly but practical, with a wry sense of humor that sees a little too much.

LEXX isn't your typical space opera. With its bizarre characters, anarchic sense of humor, and surrealism, it owes as much to Heavy Metal comics, **Monty Python** and experimental film makers like Jodorowsky and Bunuel as it does to **Star Trek** and **Star Wars**. There hasn't been anything quite like it before, and perhaps won't be again.

Welcome! A Quick Recap!

This is the second volume of LEXX Unauthorized. We appreciate you coming; we hope you'll hang around. We strongly recommend you check out the first volume, every bit of LEXX is unique, what happens in each season is as night and day to what came before, or comes after. So you really should read that first volume, and for that matter, the one that comes after this.

But just in case you haven't, here's a brief recap, the Cole's notes version....

It began with a quirky, awkward young man named Paul Donovan. Donovan was the son of a surveyor hailing from the city of Halifax, Nova Scotia, due north of Maine. There was no film or television industry in Halifax, back when Donovan was growing up. Of course not.

Donovan attended university, got a physics degree, but what he really wanted was to be a film maker. In Halifax in those days, that was probably like growing up and wanting to be a Martian.

But that was his dream, so off he went to the London film school in the UK. Every year, he'd come back and see Les Krizsan, a Hungarian expatriate working in the audio visual department of one of the local universities, and tell Krizsan he was going to make movies. Krizsan would laugh.

But somehow, Paul Donovan came back, and he and his brother, Michael Donovan, found enough money to make a movie. Donovan was lucky. Around the time that he and his brother decided to make their movie, the Canadian government had decided that Canada needed its own film industry - it was a culture thing. They tried to do this by creating an incredibly lucrative tax shelter to encourage local entrepreneurs to get into the business. It worked; Canada went from three movies a year to rivaling Hollywood's output. The movies were terrible of course. But for a while, there was a film industry grown up overnight, awash with money. Most of it went to the big centers, Toronto and Montreal. But somehow, the Donovan Brothers put together enough to make a feature.

The movie was South Pacific 1942. It failed disastrously. You don't need to know more.

The Tax Shelter boom was dying by that time. But the Donovan brothers managed to scratch together enough money for another, smaller project: Siege. This was an ultra-low budget movie about a gang of homophobic rednecks terrorizing a small group of apartment dwellers during a police strike, shot in the house they were living in. Despite its nonexistent budget, the film managed to be tense and gripping.

By this time, they were out of money. End of the road.

But they had a film, so they decided to try and sell it. They travelled to Los Angeles. When they got there, they were so broke; they sold their car to keep on going. They were reduced to riding the bus, carrying their heavy film cans with them, taking their film from one distributor to the next.

Finally, they found a European distributor who was interested. He asked them what they wanted. They had no idea. He suggested a million dollars, and they said "Sold!" Salter Street Films was born.

The brothers went back to Halifax to make B-movies. The tax shelter boom was over, but that was all right. Because this was the era of the video explosion. Video stores were opening everywhere, and they needed movies to stock their shelves. In short order Paul Donovan directed Defcon 4, Norman's Awesome Adventure, Buried on Sunday, and a host of other low budget direct to video or made for TV productions.

Meanwhile, Michael Donovan focused on the business side. From Newfoundland came a quirky independent comedy called The Adventures of Faustus Bidgood. Made on less than a shoestring, it starred almost everyone in Newfoundland - Andy Jones, Mary Walsh, Cathy Jones, Greg Thomey, Brian Downey, Greg Malone, Robert Joy, Brian Hennessy, and a whole bunch of people you've probably never heard of. The Donovan brothers recruited the Faustus troop, and started making local television series, CodCo, This Hour Has 22 Minutes, Daily Thoughts, Blackfly and so forth, which became staples of Canadian Content for the CBC, and for a Canadian government burned by the Tax Shelter implosion and looking for new ways to support Canadian production.

The Donovan Brothers weren't setting the world on fire, but they were developing a niche as a small regional production company that reliably produced low budget fare, sufficient to fill video store shelves or local television time slots.

There was very little here, of course, to suggest that this was going to give rise to the madness and mayhem that became LEXX. Hell, there wasn't anything. LEXX was miles bigger, stranger, more expensive, more complicated than anything the Donovan Brothers had dared touch. It was as if the local handyman had decided to build his own space shuttle

But like a pinball machine flashing to life, a series of twist and turns began to take place.

Paul Donovan decided he wanted to make a war movie. His problem was that the movie he wanted to make would be incredibly expensive, as expensive as all his prior movies put together. So he was either looking for the money to make it the way he wanted, or looking for ways to do it cheaply.

Around this time a couple of Professors at the local university were trying to persuade the government to fund a supercomputer. The government was prepared to fund them... as long as they made it available to local businesses. But who needed a supercomputer? They looked up Donovan.

Donovan became fascinated with computer generated imagery, initially as a way to make his war movie. The trouble was the technology wasn't up to it. But he was still fascinated, and started looking to make a movie based on what the technology could do. He began thinking of a science fiction project. He called up a local actor friend, Brian Downey. Together they shot a demo video. Then he began to look for money.

The cosmic pinball machine tilted again. Thousands of miles away, a giant American entertainment conglomerate called Viacom bought a Canadian Theater chain, Famous Players. That purchase sent a ripple through the Canadian government and the Canadian cultural industry. In response, it was decreed, if an American company was going to take money out of the country, they were also going to have to put it back. And so, Showtime, a subsidiary of Viacom started looking for a suitable Canadian project for its television channel.

And there was Paul Donovan.

All these little random factors, a direct to video production company, a war movie, a supercomputer, Canadian culture, corporate acquisition, all these elements, intersecting, colliding, changing new trajectories, and somehow, LEXX.

There's more to it: Brian Downey, a local Newfoundland actor, and part of the Faustus Bidgood cast, became the star, Stanley Tweedle. An Ontario actor, Michael McManus, that Donovan had worked with and liked, was recruited to play Kai, a living dead man. Les Krizsan had gone from his job at the University, to becoming Donovan's Director of Photography. Lex Gigeroff, a local writer and performer came on board. Jeff Hirschfield, a writer with an anarchic sense of humor, joined the band, and ended up playing a decapitated robot head. Actors and performers and production crew from Halifax, or from Donovan's movies. One newcomer was Ellen Dubin, who had auditioned for Zev, and ended up with Giggerotta. Multiple designers were commissioned, puppeteers, stop motion animation, everything but the kitchen sink was being thrown in. It's amazing how much this was a local production, and it's amazing how ambitious this was compared to what had gone before.

It was as if a local group of high school students had decided to put on a play down in the barn, and mounted the entire Star Wars trilogy. Or as if the local handyman had actually built his own spacecraft.

Wolfram Tichy, a German producer came on Board, and with him came a contingent of German actors and actresses, directors, and crew. Among these were the third leading role, Eva Habermann, playing Zev, and Doreen Jacobi, playing Wist.

Originally, Donovan wanted to do a television movie, and then spin that off into a series of episodes. But Showtime wanted something more. One television movie became four. Name actors - Rutger Hauer from Blade Runner, Malcolm McDowell from Clockwork Orange, and Barry Bostwick and Tim Curry, both from the Rocky Horror Picture Show. In the end, Showtime had hoped for Star Wars. That wasn't what they got, and they weren't sure what to do with it.

The name changed - initially, it was the Dark Zone. But that turned out to be the name of a laser tag company. Eventually Donovan settled on LEXX.

The movies aired on television, they didn't do so well in the United States where it ran as 'Tales From a Parallel Universe'. Showtime's management changed, the new leadership wasn't interested. Showtime bowed out, and with it, so did the American money that had made the whole thing possible.

The end.

Seriously, you should just go buy the first volume, its terrific reading.

In fact, do it now. Go ahead. We'll wait.

The Plan and Other Stuff That Went Wrong

"The plan was that we were always going to do a series. That was the plan, we'd do a movie, then we'd do a series, and every week, they'd go to a planet and weird stuff happens," Jeff Hirschfield told me during an interview.

The second season began to go off the rails almost from the start.

The plan had always been to follow up with a series. The original plan had been for a pilot movie followed by a series which would make a syndication package. Now, following up on a series of four movies, the plan was for three seasons of twenty episodes apiece, culminating in a grand slam ending.

But the LEXX movies hadn't seemed to have done particularly well in the United States where they played under the title "**Tales From a Parallel Universe.**" Showtime declined to participate further. The American money dropped out. American funders weren't interested.

That hurt. The American market is the five hundred pound gorilla of film and television production. Numbers tell the story. The American market is about three hundred and thirty million people - movie goers, ticket buyers, cable subscribers, television watchers.

English Canada is maybe thirty million. Australia twenty. Britain fifty. You might have seventy million Francophones, ninety million Japanese, forty million South Koreans. Compared to literally any place else, the American market is gigantic, and so is the money. American participation pretty much guarantees that a project will happen. And America walking away, usually guarantees a project dies.

So Showtime walking way? That probably wasn't good.

I think that someplace else, somewhere else, that would have been the end. People would have just shrugged their shoulders, gone 'it was nice while it lasted,' and then wandered off somewhere and done something else. I'm sure that's how it would have happened in New York, or Los Angeles, or Montreal or Toronto.

But Donovan was stubborn. I suppose you have to be stubborn to create a film industry from nothing in an obscure corner of the world.

Or maybe Donovan, having reached this level, wasn't willing to go back to making small local films. Maybe it there just wasn't a better more, exciting option close by, Halifax wasn't a hotbed of productions. Or maybe they LEXX crew was just wedded to its original plan, and just never reconsidered.

The German partners remained in, or were willing to go back in. According to Wolfram Tichy the first season had been successful enough that they had no trouble finding a purchaser for the second season.

It had done well in Canada, or at least parts of Canada, where the guest stars had attracted a lot of attention. That counted for something.

"It aired on CITY-TV I think they had the highest ratings ever that they had on a new show. A lot of buzz and fanfare, especially the actors, big stars, and all about the technology. There was a lot of print and publicity," Norman Denver recalls.

SPACE to the Rescue!

Paul Donovan had always been lucky. He'd started out catching the tax shelter boom, and then he rode the home video explosion, and then Canadian content funding. He'd always managed to be just at the right time to keep on making films.

Timing was with Donovan once again. On October 17, 1997, literally within months of LEXX the Canadian Sci Fi Channel, Space, went on the air, and Donovan was back in business.

It's a little bit more complicated than that. It always is. **The Space Channel** was owned by CITY-TV. CITY-TV was the flagship of a small media empire run by Moses Znaimer. Moses, one of those quirky brilliant geniuses occasionally thrown up by normally stodgy Canadian society, had gotten his start in the late seventies and early eighties producing an hourly program called **The New Music**. Partly early music videos, partly critical commentary, it was sort of like Video Hits, but with brains. It achieved a cult status of its own and Moses went on from there to pioneer the Canadian equivalent of MTV, MuchMusic.

CITY-TV had been involved in the original season of LEXX, at least as far as producing the first documentary segment by Media Television, and the first full documentary. When Paul Donovan was looking for backers, Jay Switzer of CITY-TV actually made the decision to fund LEXX, even before his company been awarded the Sci Fi Channel. CITY-TV would have supported LEXX even if they'd never have gotten their Sci Fi Channel. LEXX was exactly the sort of quirky original kind of programming that they liked to support.

Television bandwidth wasn't unlimited, particularly way back when. There's traditionally only been a certain amount of space for radio and TV signals to be heard or seen clearly before they start interfering with each other. As a result, the American government created the FCC (Federal Communications Commission) and the Canadian government created the CRTC (Canadian Radio and Telecommunications Commission).

Through the 90's, as cable expanded, the meaning of bandwidth changed. Once upon a time, the airwaves only had room for perhaps a handful of television channels. Now, with cable, you could have dozens, even hundreds. New specialty channels proliferated in both Canada and the United States. But as many specialty slots were created, there was always far more fledgling channels ready to jump into the fray. So, in Canada, the CRTC awarded channels in a sort of lottery. A round of available channel slots would come up, various proposals would be made, and the CRTC would pick the winners and losers.

Ironically, Salter Street Films, the producers of LEXX were in the running for a Sci Fi Channel. But the Toronto based CITY-TV, with its popular music station, beat them out. SPACE, Canada's Sci Fi channel was born. Ironically, it's possible that CITY's association with LEXX may have been one of the factors that helped them win the channel rights.

The CRTC when it granted its license to Space for a Canadian Sci Fi Channel imposed two conditions, the same ones it imposed on almost every new channel license that it granted.

   1) The Space Channel had to devote a certain amount of its percentage of its airtime to Canadian programming;

   2) The Space Channel had to put a certain percentage of its income into funding new Canadian programming.

The trouble was, there wasn't really a lot of Canadian content science fiction out there. There were a handful of movies, some like the **Neptune Factor**, dating back to the tax shelter days or before. Of indigenous local sci fi television there was precious little. There'd been **Space Command**, featuring James Doohan in the fifties, and then there'd been the **Starlost** in the early seventies, but the less said about them, the better. Besides, they were so old their whiskers had whiskers, and while there's a tradition of running old movies, no one wants to see old television series. Television's technology and production values usually lagged far behind even cheap films, so a film might age well, but television shows wouldn't.

There were a few modern TV series that qualified, mostly American branch plant assembly series like the **X-Files, Highlander** and **Earth Final Conflict**, which were American owned but made in Canada because it was cheap. These series were driven by American money, had American creators, stars and directors, were careful to spread the stars and stripes around and there was nary a sight of a maple leaf to be found. They'd do in a pinch.

Now, the thing is that CRTC guidelines determined whether a product was Canadian content through a points system. Thus, if your star is Canadian, you got a point. If your composer was Canadian, get another point, and so on. Shoot in Canada, get a point. Have a Canadian electrician, get a point. The way the points system is calculated, you don't have to score every point in order to be rated as Canadian content.

If you scored enough, you could be considered to have a Canadian show notwithstanding that the real creators and owners were American. And it was proportional, so your show could be scored as 20% Canadian, or 50% Canadian, if you were good enough to hire some local grips and electricians, use local actors in supporting roles. What this mean was that if the Space Channel aired your hour long program, they'd get a 15 minute or half an hour credit towards their Canadian content obligations.

LEXX on the other hand was right off the charts. Canadian creators, writers, principal actors, production crew, it was Canadian Content to the core. The way the rules were set up, it was possible to score over a hundred per cent. So, in the case of LEXX, to exaggerate slightly, you might get a 200% rating, which would mean that running an hour of LEXX counted as two hours for your Canadian content obligations. This meant that you now had a spare programming hour that you could use to put in a highly rated, slick American series like **Babylon 5** or **Star Trek** to your prime time that would help you generate revenue. It was perfect.

What this meant was that the Space Channel loved LEXX. They were going to run it endlessly, and pay to run it, and they were going to put money in to producing more LEXX, what money they actually had to give.

"With financing, I was one of the producers," Willie Stevenson told me. *"We put it together with Space Channel money, TiMe (German) film money.*

Space Channel was not involved creatively, but they had a huge impact. Literally, they were make or break in terms of allowing it to go forward."

"Without the Space channel, it would have been harder to do the funding. Space in Canada and Sci Fi in UK was instrumental," Norman Denver, the series line producer, agreed.

On the other hand, for a dissenting view...

"Space didn't have a lot of money to give us," Jeff Hirschfield recalled, *"but they were certainly our head cheerleaders. They were enthusiastic supporters, and promoted us everywhere and to everyone."*

Mark Asquith, a producer for the Space Channel, and the creator of the second and third season documentaries has a different perspective.

"LEXX was really crucial to establishing our identity. Mostly, as with all specialty channels, we were faced with rerunning a lot of old stuff that was already out there. Actually getting involved in production was an important step. We were literally out of the starting gate with our own series, and then we were involved with **First Wave**. *It took the US Sci Fi Channel years to get its own series off the ground, and then it was* **Hypernauts**.*"*

LEXX almost immediately became the flagship series of the Canadian Space Channel, running twice a week in prime time slots, the subject of documentaries and extensive promotion. If the maple leaf was nowhere to be found, at least it wasn't displaying the stars and stripes or establishing shots of the Washington monument at every opportunity the way the X-Files or Earth Final Conflict did.

Regardless of the level of financial commitment, Space was crucial to LEXX in providing a home base, a platform for the series to build an audience, and to promote itself worldwide.

Fortified by small revenue and big support from Space and by Canadian film and television funding commitments, Paul Donovan and his partners went out and sold the series around the world, in places like Australia, New Zealand, Lithuania, Denmark, Spain and so forth.

None of these places brought in big money, by any means. But collectively, between the Canadian partners, the German partners and the international sales, it was enough to put a deal together.

Of course, that took eighteen months.

The Creative Side, Shaping the New Season

Would you believe that His Divine Shadow was supposed to return in the second series, with a resurgent Divine Order, to chase the LEXX through several episodes? That Pa Golene and Wist were going to be recurring characters? That the musical episode would be on a tropical island? Or that Kai would encounter the Brunnen H, a race of ultra-feminist cousins? That there was no trace of Mantrid or Lyekka? Or that the LEXX would go to Heaven and Hell a season earlier?

Life is what happens when you're making plans. A lot happened in those eighteen months. Paul Donovan, Lex Gigeroff and Jeff Hirschfield stuck together, continuing to call themselves the Supreme Beans, or the Beans for short. The plan was still, do the movies, then the series.

They were probably kicking around ideas for episodes all the way back to the beginning before the first season had even begun shooting. By June 28, 1996, before post-production had been completed on the first season's movies, they'd done outlines for a season of twenty episodes. As post production wound down, they were already working on scripts.

But there's eighteen months between the end of the movies and the beginning of the series. Eighteen months for the series to evolve and develop. Indeed, the ideas and stories for the series had been evolving and developing going back to the beginning, to the original ideas and plans, back all the way to when Kai was alive, before they decided to make him undead.

We can actually trace the changes and evolution of LEXX through a series of benchmarks.

(1) The June 28, 1996 series outline, in the middle of post-production;

(2) The Contender DVD extras after the series from the end of 1996 after the movies were being completed, where the Beans talk about their plans'

(3) There's another series brochure from June of 1997, from the casts visit to England, announcing only thirteen episodes, suggesting they were considering a reduced season;

(4) There's yet another updated and revised series outline from December 17, 1997, back to twenty; and

(5) Finally there's the series itself airing from December 11, 1998, to April 23, 1999.

What changed? What was dropped? What was added? Who came in and who went out? We can actually trace how we got from here to there, how the series morphed into what it became.

Take it all with a grain of salt, of course. The June 1996, June 1997 and December 1997 outlines were marketing tools. They knew they wanted to go to series, they knew that the movies were going to be what sold the series. So they had to have a package for the next season ready to go.

They couldn't simply go 'Hey! You loved the movies? Give us three months and we'll have a pitch for the next year!' They had to be ready then. To sell the next season, they had to be able to tell stations what was going to be in it, which meant having a list of episodes and descriptions to hand out as selling points.

Some of the episodes written and locked in, some of the episodes they were pretty intent on, and some of them were just there to fill in the page. It can be surprising what was planned from the start, and what came out of left field.

From the June 28, 1996, outline, eight of the twenty, barely forty per cent, would in one form or another wind up in the finished episodes of season two; some like **White Trash, Lafftrack** and **Stan's Trial** would be very close to the finished product. Others like **Lament for a Love Slave/Terminal** or the **Return of His Shadow/Mantrid,** would mutate considerably. Two early proposals for stories, **Heaven** and **Hell** would form the basis of season three.

But at least, June 1996, gives us an idea of what was intended and where the series was supposed to go.

A few months later, late 1996 or early 1997, the Beans would sit down in front of a camera to create some homemade DVD content for the Contender videos. These would become known as the **LEXXtras**. They're very 'lo fi' - just the three writers sitting around talking about their plans.

The trio tip their hands on upcoming projects. Paul is going to write the first episode, about the **Return of His Divine Shadow,** Jeff's project was **Luvliner** and Lex was doing **Lafftrack.**

Then a few months after that, around June 1997, the casts visit England for a signing, a promotional flyer setting out a reduced season of thirteen episodes was circulated, mentioning **The Last Days of the Brunnen G** and renaming **Brigadoom** as **Broadway in Space,** two episodes, each telling versions of Kai's story.

German co-producer, Wolfram Tichy remembered this period as a time of ferment when ideas were bounced around at the Economy Shoe Shoppe (a local bar), and everyone was contributing ideas. He noted though, that only those of the principal writers, Donovan, Gigeroff and Hirschfield, made it as episodes. Tichy himself contributed ideas for four episodes, two of his ideas, in somewhat mutated form made it to screen.

By December 17, 1997, a new blueprint for a season, back to twenty episodes had been fashioned for the series, which was going into pre-production in January, 1998. Of those twenty, twelve episodes, or sixty per cent would make it to the screen more or less as planned, three others would appear considerably mutated, and five would disappear entirely.

So basically, we get a snapshot every six months or so - June 1996, December 1996, June 1997, December 1997, up to the finished series in 1998, that shows how LEXX is developing. A handful of episodes remained unchanged, but a vast number evolved considerably, and a larger number wound up getting dropped for one reason or another.

His Divine Shadow Strikes Back

For instance, the earliest drafts and outlines contemplated the return of His Shadow. His Shadow was going to play a significant role in at least four episodes of the June, 1996 outline, and was almost certainly going to be coming back as a recurring villain in the third season.

"Early on," Hirschfield admits, *"we thought His Divine Shadow was coming back. Definitely he was going to be back. It was only as we were going along that it changed to Mantrid."*

In a draft of **Luvliner** published on the internet, there's actually a reference to His Divine Shadow having returned and willing to pay big money to get the LEXX back. This suggests that the return was somewhat common knowledge in the LEXX universe and that His Divine Shadow was still operating on fairly conventional terms.

The events of Gigashadow had perhaps not been fully incorporated into the series, as late as 1997. The story that would bring His Shadow back eventually evolved into **Mantrid,** but more than that there was the question of why bother?

Bringing back His Divine Shadow was going to be a fairly good trick, since in the first movie, His Divine Shadow's brain had been scooped out and his body sliced by Kai. In the fourth movie, that brain had been crushed, its evil essence moving into a giant bug which was then crushed in a black hole. The population of the

League of 20,000 worlds had been killed off; the Divine Order had wiped itself out.

But the end of **Gigashadow** had shown Kai's eyes swirling with the black evil essence, so I assume the plan was that essence would escape and start the whole thing all over again. But even assuming His Divine Shadow came back through Kai, what was he going to do with his empire obliterated and the most powerful weapon in the universe in enemy hands?

This hardly seemed satisfying. Basically, it had been done and done perfectly the first time out. The new His Divine Shadow couldn't do anything but suffer by the comparison. He'd be a stripped down, paler, softer, punier version of the looming evil of the original.

After all, the original had culminated in a giant monster erupting from a planet. What was this one going to do? Pop out of a dumpster and go *"Boo!"* Chase teenagers around the halls of an empty high school at night?

Blowing up a planet was nothing; the LEXX did that all the time.

Destroying thousands of worlds? Did that last year.

Why not.... destroy them all? Toast the whole Universe? After all, we had a spare. How were you going to top a holocaust encompassing 20,000 worlds and a giant insect the size of a planet? The simple truth was that His Divine Shadow had gone as far as he could go. It was time for a new character, and an even bigger scale. Besides, Lex probably didn't want to have to wear the costume again.

Mantrid and his story arc came from Paul Donovan himself and from an abandoned idea from the first series. Originally, **Gigashadow** wasn't going to be the final movie, that was a last minute replacement. Instead, the final was going to be an almost entirely different story, called Back to the Cluster. The story of Back to the Cluster and how Gigashadow came to be is related in volume one.

But at the end of **Back to the Cluster**, His Divine Shadow escapes the LEXX in a gigantic planet destroying machine which begins to consume suns and planets. This sets up a denouement in which the LEXX and its crew are confronted by a star devouring juggernaut. This idea was abandoned, probably for a number of reasons, costs included.

But in a sense, **Mantrid,** the devouring force, if not the actual character, went way back to the original concepts for the movie. Abandoned in the first series, it was available for recycling.

In the June 1996 series outline, several episodes end with a planet devouring force that is following the LEXX eating a world, oddly, this seems to have been completely unrelated to the Divine Shadow arc, it's not at all clear why it's doing it or what it is. It's just a mysterious planet eating force. It's possible that was something intended to be developed to be resolved in a third season.

The central idea of the **Mantrid** arc, that of self-replicating machines which tear down whole worlds is actually a well established concept. What we're looking at are "Von Neumann" machines. Back in 1966, John Von Neumann published a "Theory of Self Replicating Automata." Essentially, machines which would make copies of themselves.

Then in 1974, R.N. Bracewell published a paper suggesting that these Von Neumann machines might be perfect for interstellar exploration. Essentially, all you had to do was send one out to some far star. When it gets there it turns into a factory, consuming raw materials to make copies of itself to explore the star system, with each copy making still more copies to explore and to launch to new star systems, where they would make still more copies. Eventually, the whole universe would be explored and colonized by these machines. Of course, it would take tens of millions of years, and humanity would probably be extinct, but we'd have done it.

Or possibly, someone out there had already done it, or was doing it. Keep watching the sky, boys and girls.

The idea was seized by both science theorists and science fiction writers. Frederik Pohl wrote a novel where self-replicating machines on earth solved all the world's problems, and then created new ones as they scoured the planet's resources to bedrock for a consumer society gone wrong.

Philip K. Dick, in a story called **Second Variety**, eventually made into a movie called **Screamers**, played with the idea that these self reproducing machines might evolve to replace us.

Fred Saberhagen wrote a whole series of stories and novels about '**Berserkers,**' self-replicating machines with a mission to eliminate all organic life.

More recently, David Brin ventured stories about '**Eaters**', self-replicating probes without an off switch who would literally consume an entire star system, dismantling planets and even stars to make endless copies of themselves.

The point is, the idea of self-replicating machines has been around for a long time and has spun in endless permutations. The idea seems so obvious and well ingrained that one might actually stop and wonder, if there is intelligent life in the Universe, why haven't their self-replicating probes shown up, or why aren't the stars winking out one by one.

The latest twist on Von Neumann machines is nanotechnology. Theoretical molecule sized machines which would busily make copies of themselves, and then as their numbers proliferated, would be used to literally create objects as required, literally sculpting molecules. Nano- technology's been written about extensively by SF writers such as Greg Bear, in **Blood Music**, or Kevin J. Anderson in **The Assemblers of Infinity**.

This is hardly an exhaustive list, but merely a smattering of examples to show that the concepts been out there for a while and spun off in a variety of directions. Paul Donovan was combining a leftover idea from the first season with Von Neumann machines and coming up with **Mantrid**. It was too big a story to do all at once though, it needed an arc, it needed time to build.

Gigeroff's and Hirschfield's scripts, in contrast, indicated a desire to return to the anarchic standalone format which seems to have been part of the original vision of LEXX. They wanted something free from back story and history. Their interim scripts, **Luvliner, Love Grows, Lafftrack** reflected a raw, rude sensibility, a universe of anarchy and chaos. The LEXX would come to a strange planet, weird stuff would happen to them, and then they'd leave. That was it.

But by December of 1997, His Shadow was gone. Mantrid had taken his place, and had become the author of the mysterious planet destroying force, whose story arc became the focus of the season.

Departures and Arrivals

Other problems arose that altered the plans for the second series. In particular, Eva Habermann had moved on, and would be replaced by Xenia Seeberg. Concurrently, Doreen Jacobi was no longer available to play Wist, so both her and her character had to be replaced by Louise Wischermann paying Lyekka.

In the eighteen month hiatus between series one and two, the actor's options had expired.' Downey and McManus were still ready and willing, and Hirschfield was on staff, but Eva Habermann had accepted a role in **Strand Clique**, sometimes referred to as a German version of Baywatch. She wasn't available. They had to find a new Zev and, since Eva didn't have a twin sister, they had to explain why their lead actress was changing, she had to be German for the Co-Production partner and they had to do it quickly.

They had trouble finding the new Zev, and that process dragged out. How much pressure they were under we can see in the story that Xenia Seeberg got the part largely on the basis of an interview with Paul Donovan at the New York airport, and a recommendation, if we accept it, by renegade German film maker, Jorg Buttgereit.

It's likely there was more to it than that. Donovan probably studied her resume carefully, watched her previous work, asked around about her. Wolfram Tichy contributed his input. But still, Xenia's selection seems to have been a hastier and more desperate process than either McManus or Downey went through originally.

The intention always seems to have been to bring Doreen Jacobi back as Wist. But the change from Eva Habermann to Xenia Seeberg upset the timing of those plans.

Originally, as early as June, 1996, **Lament for a Love Slave** they intended to have Zev die in one episode and reappear in the next through the benign actions of a new Wist. This seems to have been intended to sell the return of a Wist, or a new version of the character. But this was scheduled for the eighteenth and nineteenth episodes in the June, 1996, outline. It's possible that the original plan, to the extent there was one, was to have had her emerge as a recurring character for the third season, after reintroducing her late in the second.

By December of 1997, the storyline had accommodated a new Zev, with two episodes moved up to the front and devoted to killing off the old one and recreating the new one. Jacobi's Wist character had consequently expanded to appear in four episodes, though she may be used for more. Figuring more prominently in the series now, and with a continuity gap in the lead female role, Jacobi's part may have been expanded from a one shot to more of a continuing character.

Then, Doreen Jacobi backs out, or isn't available. So once again, they've got to go looking for a new actress. Unlike Zev, however, they aren't tied tightly to the character, and it would be fairly implausible to continue yet another character from one actress to the next. Instead, Wist is dumped and a new character, Lyekka is created.

Also, as the series goes into production, several of the episodes planned for Wist/Lyekka are dropped. But somehow much of the characters subplot winds up reappearing in other planned episodes.

It's not clear whether this would have occurred, or whether she's being shoehorned in because of contractual obligations.

But, by and large, the casting side of things turned out better than anyone had a right to expect. Seeberg took to the role and expanded and developed the character of Xev in new directions, introducing strength, conviction and vulnerability. In contrast, the friendly engaging Wischermann proved far more appealing than the frosty Jacobi.

Odds and Ends

There were peculiar developments. One of these was the emergency of Pa Golene as a continuing character.

Pa Golene appears in **White Trash**, of course, as he would in the final iteration of the series. But as originally written, he would survive and continue to stow away on the LEXX, coming out occasionally to meddle in the plot, before eventually getting killed in a later episode.

This is surprising; you wouldn't think a character like Pa Golene would have any sticking power. But as we saw in the first series, Paul Donovan liked to work with people he'd worked well with before. A number of his cast members in LEXX can be found sprinkled through his earlier movies, undoubtedly that has a lot to do with the fact that the Nova Scotia acting community just isn't that big.

But even so, he likes to work with the same people again and again. And he and the other writers liked to visualize their characters played by particular actors. So it's likely that the driving force of Pa Golene and his arc was Maury Chaykin, a well-known Canadian actor who had been the villain in Donovan's **Defcon IV**.

On another front, the various drafts and outlines, suggest that while the Beans wanted to do certain things... They wanted to do a musical episode, they wanted to do an episode about Kai's backstory, they wanted to do a theatrical episode, they didn't really seem to have any clear idea of where they were going with any of it. What eventually became **Brigadoom** was the result of a long process of mutation, and entire scripts were abandoned along the way.

A number of ideas in the outlines were clearly undeveloped, not even half baked. In some cases barely more than a few paragraphs. That's the case with the **Heaven** and **Hell** episodes, which oddly enough became the backbone of the entire third series. On the other hand, it's interesting to see apparently well-developed episodes abandoned.

And it's surprising to see which episodes have the deepest roots, for instance neither **Luvliner** nor **Lafftrack** are particularly extraordinary, and you could be forgiven for thinking they were late replacements. But they're some of the oldest, purest concepts.

The Production Side, Building Brave New Worlds

Official Pre-production on the second season started at the end of January, 1998. By that time, the official roster of episodes had been worked out and there were already seven or eight scripts written.

The series started formal production and principal photography around March 29 or 30 at Babelsberg Studios, near Berlin in Germany, for five episodes, until May, 1998. While this was going on, Electropolis was being prepared and the new bridge was under construction.

After that, the production moved to Halifax and Electropolis studios, to shoot the balance of the season including bridge and standing sets scenes for the early episodes, finishing November 15 and 20th.

Post-production ran until the following March, 1999. But early episodes had already begun to air on television well before post-production was completed, so they wound up racing the clock to get episodes done in time.

The estimates of the budget for second year ranged from episodes of 1.5 million to 1 million. The average episode budget was about 1.2 million. Turnaround was approximately eight days per episode. This was a significant drop from the first season, where the movies averaged about 4 million, or close to 2 million per episode hour, and fifteen to twenty days per movie.

The budget split was split 70/30 Canada/Germany. So much for the basic statistics.

On the writing side, people were pretty happy there as well. There had been complaints that the first season movies had felt stretched out, as if they were hour long episodes pumped up to movie length. Upon hearing this, Lex Gigeroff would cast his eyes at the ground and stick his hands in the pocket while he scuffed his feet and admitted, yes, it was true.

In an interview on the second series documentary, Lex talked about how much happier they were to be going to an hour long format, that he felt it was more comfortable, more appropriate to the stories they wanted to tell.

As Hirschfield said, many of the stories they wanted to tell just wouldn't work in a movie format. It was simply too long a period of time to drag a premise like **White Trash** out. They wanted to move faster, they wanted to make the hit, make their point, and move on. They didn't want to do epics.

If that's true, then the writers were a lonely voice on the show. Moving to a series of hour long episodes put more pressure on everyone else. The bottom line is that each new episode literally called for new costumes, new wardrobes, new props, new sets. And it had to be designed; each episode was a challenge for the art department.

It wasn't all that portable, the sets and costumes from **Twilight** couldn't be recycled for **Woz,** for instance. Unlike **Star Trek,** which continually recycled its Klingons and Romulans and Ferengi, LEXX had pretty much toasted its own back story. The clerics and soldiers and robots of the Divine Order were mainly history, the worlds of the League of 20,000 had been depopulated and The Cluster itself was now a collection of very small bits of space junk, there was very little available to be recycled and each episode opened on a whole new world.

In addition, the production was moving to a new location. The Volvo automobile plant on Pier 9 had been a bit of luck. But that space was now being abandoned. Much of the production work, sets and components done in the first season had to be abandoned, either as a result of the change in format or the change in location.

Instead in the time between the first and second season, the Donovan brothers had lead the movement to have an abandoned electrical generating plant rehabilitated and renovated into a first class film production space.

The building, renamed '**Electropolis,**' was a huge sprawling structure in the Halifax downtown. It would contain an immense sound stage with a sixty foot green screen, one of the largest in North America, as well as a half dozen other studios and sound stages, with office spaces, storage spaces and workshops.

Some of the first pieces were preserved and relocated. The cryochamber room, with its cryochambers, control panel and protein regenerator remained. So did the galley, which was relocated. The shower room and Stan's bedchamber were both reproduced. The full sized Moth props remained in use, as did various ganglions and wall sections which could be used for LEXX interiors. Costumes and smaller props were simply put in storage, to be dragged out again, when the opportunity arose. The blackpacs, for instance, were reused in both **Luvliner** and **Woz**. Kai's colorful costume was dragged out for **Brigadoom**.

But the old bridge went the way of all flesh. The bottom line there was that it had proven awkward and inconvenient to shoot on, difficult to enter and exit, and there'd been constant problems with shooting off the bridge. There seemed to be little support for going through the trouble and expense of moving and reconstructing the old bridge, when ultimately, it might pay off to build a new one. The decision was made to invest in the construction of a new permanent bridge which would be used for the second and subsequent seasons. This bridge remained in use for all three seasons and was only torn down in November, 2001.

Mark Laing was assigned to design the new bridge. Studio 2 a room that was 60 x 60 feet was assigned. Paul Donovan and Bill Fleming required that the base contain His Shadow's logo. Story requirements meant that they had to look up and see a screen. There had to be exits and entrances consistent with story geography."

"Arguably," Laing recalls, *"it didn't fit. We had to achieve depth... The bridge is on a pedestal, way up between the eyeballs of the LEXX, in this great chamber. You can fall off the bridge, from a great height. The optic channel, the central nerve of the LEXX, it branches off dendrites up at the top, that's what Stan sits in to command the universe. You had to have that, and a sense of depth in all directions in a room that's only 60 by 60. That's basically what I came up with."*

Laing is correct; the new bridge is a fairly claustrophobic space. The original concept was always that the bridge would be an island or a balcony floating in a vast space. But by and large, this kind of imagery didn't appear very often, which is a shame. The best portraits of it actually came only in the fourth year, when CGI began to give us shots of the vast spaces outside the bride.

Laing's bridge is much more enclosed than the previous webwork of stretched membranes, the color scheme is darker, there's much more of a feeling of mass and weight to this new Bridge. In a way, it actually works. The massive steel girders, the dark tunnels, the vaulting cathedral like ceiling gives it more of a feeling of space than it deserves.

Also lost in the move was the Predecessors chamber. There seemed to be no reason to keep it in terms of either practical issues or the logic of the series. It no longer had a function, the Predecessors were all long dead as of Gigashadow, and it had been established that their chamber could only be reached from the bridge by a moth flight. There was no reason to go there.

The loss of the old Bridge and the Predecessors chamber brought to an end the unique look of stretched fabrics and membranes of Nigel Scott that had given the first season some of its distinction. From now on, LEXX's organic components would be much fleshier.

However, the essential format of the series: Travels to different worlds where bizarre things would happen, meant that they'd have to continually build new sets, perhaps several for each episode. The first season, after all, took place through four movies entirely on three worlds: The Cluster, Klaagya and Brunnis, with a limited number of sets built for them. The second season would amount to twenty episodes, and involve demand endless sets.

Terminal, for instance, is set on a space station called Medsat One, but that station wasn't a single room, there was a corridor, an operating room, Stan's recovery room, Kai's furnace room, Zev's torture room the lava lamp restaurant. Going to any world often called for several sets, interiors and exteriors.

Even episodes which took place primarily on the LEXX would demand at least some additional construction. **White Trash** involved a full sized spaceship prop for Norb, the abandoned field of Norb's ship, and the last fortress of the Vermals. **Wake the Dead** required that an interior be constructed for the teenager's ship. **Lyekka** required an interior set for the eagle one, as well as at least a couple of minimal additional sets or locations for the dream sequences.

All of this, of course, was going to cost money, quite a lot of money. And all of this had to be planned, the props, costumes and sets had to be constructed, which meant you needed time as well as money to do it, and both of these were in short supply, which would get shorter as the season went on.

You could try to compensate for this with extensive CGI backgrounding, which in fact is what LEXX did. This is one of the reasons why the ratio of special effects is so high. On the other hand, this sort of approach sometimes didn't do much more than shift the problem around. It was still going to cost money, and it was still going to take time, it was just that the hope was it would be less of either or both.

Donovan also tried to shake things up with experimental film directors. Rather than look for local directors or experienced television directors, he raided Indy film. Stephan Wagner was an independent film maker that he and Bill Fleming met at a film festival. Srinivas Krishna had made his mark with a film festival hit called **Masala**. Jorge Buttgereit was considered the most wicked film maker in Germany for films like **Nekromantic** and **Schramm**. Stephan Ronowicz was a documentary film maker, who'd been one of Paul's teachers at film school. The thought was that by going outside the normal channels, by bringing in fresh independent talent, he could again give the episodes a more unique look and feel.

The results were mixed. Ronowicz's **Luvliner** is at best, average fare. Krishna's **Terminal** is visually disappointing. Buttgereit and Wagner scored with **791** and **Lyekka**, but in each case, credit tended to go to the creative producer.

"The young Germans..." Norman Denver reflected, *"Jorg and Stephan, they come from a different space than we do. It's just a different world, making TV is more a business. They weren't used to the demands, more interested in making independent films. Episodic television, you have seven days, gotta know your craft, you have to shoot seven or eight pages a day and you have to do it on time, you have to know how to make the shots."*

The truth was that the pace and circumstances of independent film - marginal budgets, unlimited time and the flexibility to improvise simply didn't mesh well with the rigorous demands of a television schedule.

The principal successes among the new directors were Chris Bould, a British director who had worked for Salter Street on **Emily of New Moon**, Christoph Schrewe, a former East-German who had worked with Wolfram Tichy, and Bill Fleming, a pivotal LEXX person who made the leap from design and producing to directing.

But in the second season, Donovan's watchwords were experimentation and diversity. He wanted to try different things, he wanted to shake things up to get more interesting results. To try and encourage creativity, Donovan decided that each show would have a separate creative producer, and each would have a separate production designer and a separate creative producer.

This seems to hark back to **Defcon 4** where he wanted three production designers, one for each principal set, **or I Worship His Shadow**, where he unleashed a battalion of designers, each going off in their own direction in order to create a wildly diverse universe.

The hope was that with a different designer on each episode, they'd avoid the monotonous sameness of series like **Star Trek**, where every episode looks pretty much like every other episode. Rather, each episode would go off on its own direction, with a different visual look each time out. After all, these were different planets the LEXX crew was visiting; it wouldn't make sense for them to all be buying out of the same catalogue.

This experiment received an unwanted boost when the sheer volume of CGI effects overwhelmed local resources. Effects for some episodes had to be contracted out to Cage Digital, or Blink or other companies. Effectively, different companies, as well as different designers and creative producers were assigned to distinct episodes.

To some extent that worked. Certainly a number of episodes went off in their own surreal directions, producing startling images or odd visuals. Ingolf Hetscher did **Mantrid**, but left shortly thereafter. After that, the work primarily got divided up between Mark Laing and David Haackl, with Laing eventually moving on. Frank Wieman, Alexander Knopf from the first season returned. Gerry Kunz, a new designer, also came on board for episodes.

Cordell Wynne distinguished himself as a creative producer on **Lyekka** and **Woz.** Bill Fleming was creative producer on **Mantrid.** Andrea Raffaghello was creative producer on **Brigadoom.** But not all combinations worked well. Wynne and director Stephan Wagner, by multiple accounts, didn't get along. The creative producer system tended to break down; Willie Stevenson wound up with creative producer credits on ten episodes, and almost certainly contributed to more.

Despite it all, I think that looking at the season as a whole, Donovan's idealistic experiments, with Indy directors, with multiple designers, with creative producers and even different CGI was successful. The series achieved a breadth of look and style, a diversity and a texture that was largely unmatched. From one week to the next, LEXX consistently surprised you with where it would go and what it would do.

Backstage, for reasons partly financial and partly political, the art department tended to naturally consolidate itself. Up on the screen, increasingly limited resources tended to undercut this drive for visual diversity. The LEXX interior sets existed, they were easier to plan around, and you didn't have to go through the time and cost of designing and constructing new ones, so there was an increasing pressure to confine stories to the interior of the LEXX itself.

The fact of the matter was that without Showtime or an entry into the American market, LEXX was financially a delicate proposition.

Half way through production, Jeff Hirschfield was shocked when Paul Donovan told him that they'd be able to finish the series. He hadn't realized that things were that tight or that the financing was that delicate.

It was a revealing comment which shows us just how close to the edge the series was skirting. They'd started without being quite sure they could finish.

The series turned into a race against its budget. Episodes were abandoned because they were too expensive to do. Instead, new episodes were written to take place almost exclusively on the ship on existing sets, often with minimal or even nonexistent guest casts. The production quality looks good throughout, but as the

series goes on, you can almost hear the squeaking as its belt is tied tighter and tighter.

Of the twenty episodes planned in December, 1997, two of them had been created or extensively revised to allow for the change of Zev's, subsequently, another eight of them were either abandoned entirely or so extensively revised as to barely resemble their original versions. That's forty to fifty per cent of your series out the window, which implies a certain amount of chaos occurring behind the scenes.

Of course, although many of the episodes fell by the wayside or mutated substantially, the major storylines of the season, the **Mantrid** arc, the **Lyekka** subplot, and even some of the **White Trash** Golene's family saga remained basically intact, with bits and pieces of these being lifted from abandoned episodes, and transplanted into other episodes.

Still, the first season of eight hours or four movies had taken about six months to put together, and it had been anarchy backstage. The second season was twenty episodes, equivalent to about ten movies, made in about the same time frame with less money. Clearly, they'd moved up an order of magnitude in logistics and organization. Yes, they'd gone through cast changes and dumped whole episodes and scrimped wherever they could, but on the other hand, they managed to ride every wave. The main plotlines held together throughout, the new episodes were generally as interesting as the ones that got bumped and as a whole, the series turned out quite well.

Although some fans felt that the second series dropped in quality in comparison to the first, episodes like **Mantrid, Lyekka, Wake the Dead, Woz** and **Brigadoom** certainly matched or exceeded the standards of that first year.

It wasn't perfect, but by god, they were getting the hang of it.

Lost LEXX, the Return of His Shadow Trilogy

The original vision for the second season was a very different show. His Divine Shadow would reappear as a returning nemesis; Eva Habermann would continue as Zev, Wist would become a recurring character, as would Pa Golene. The series arc would be different. All of these were episodes that were planned and conceived. These were episodes that, had things gone differently, could have been made. These were a version of LEXX that you never got to see.

The show would open with a trilogy of episodes...

Part One: Motivation

For some strange reason, Kai becomes motivated to cross the dimensional barrier into the Light Universe. After a lot of investigation, our heroes manage to find another fractal core.

(Handwritten note - Kai should have to force Stan to return. Stan does not think it is a good idea to go back to the scene of so much trouble. Kai threatens his life. Zev, 790 and Stan realize that something is very wrong.)

We soon learn that during his battle with the Gigashadow in the last picture of the pilot cycle, Kai received and still has a little of the insect's essence. The essence lay dormant in Kai, but is now acting up like a kind of malaria. In fact, it is even starting to exercise some control over him.

Under the subtle influence of the insect essence, Kai takes the LEXX into the Light Zone and seeks out Gigashadow eggs that may have survived the insect's destruction. He argues, again showing strange motivation, that the Gigashadow was the source of protoblood, and therefore its eggs would likely contain or be able to produce the substance. If they can find one or more, Kai's protoblood supply problem will be forever solved.

They eventually do find one well developed larvae. The dark essence slips out of Kai and into it.

(Handwritten note - They try to thwart Kai going to the Larvae, but at the last minute, Kai makes the connection he wanted. Then we see the Gigashadow grow and our crew fail to stop it. Kai, drained of the dark force realizes what he has done... too late)

A smaller version of the Gigashadow soon hatches and attacks the LEXX. (Handwritten note – The new Gigashadow zips to other planets to muster his Shadows forces and then turns to attack our crew. LEXX comes up with the ancient defenses of using the new Gigashadow's force to defeat itself... I.e., the LEXX retreats just further than the new Gigashadow can shoot it down, the new Gigashadow keeps on shooting, the LEXX keeps on retreating just in front of the charge and eventually the Gigashadow uses up all its resources, shrivels and implodes.) Kai and company have to battle it, and after much drama, are ultimately successful in destroying it.

(Handwritten note - As the wreckage spins out into space, we focus on a tiny escape bubble amid the debris. We know that something has survived!)

But unbeknownst to our crew.... The new Gigashadow is able to pass its essence to an unsuspecting human... Thus creating a new His Shadow... Who hooking up with directionless clerics, founds a new Divine Order.... And starts the whole cycle over again....

Part Two: Time Loop

The new incarnation of His Shadow is having a rough time. Its host brain was not 'vacced' (wiped clean), and is causing serious interference with the insect essence and its agenda. And, on a more crucial note, it turns out that Kai did not pass all of the essence into the larval Gigashadow. His Shadow is therefore missing the thousands upon thousands of memories he should possess. He is unable to properly know himself and his role without them, and is determined to get them back.

He sends several dispossessed clerics who are charged with getting the memories from Kai. Most meet their deaths trying to obtain them. But one is eventually successful in retrieving the missing memories on a disk. The disk is returned to His Shadow, who transfers his essence through the ritual of 'the kiss' to a clean, fully vacced host before incorporating them. This new His Shadow quickly realizes that he should have instructed the clerics to destroy Kai, as he becomes aware of the prophecy again.

Meanwhile, without his memories, Kai has turned into a form of vegetable. He reverts back to being a mindless assassin in waiting. His only reply to every question being "Who would you like me to kill, Divine Shadow?"

With the help of 790, Zev and Stan are able to locate the planet of the Time Prophet. As it is incredibly small, they have to leave the LEXX, taking Kai with them, and approach in a moth. Zev asks the Time Prophet what is going to happen now, but the ancient seer is senile, cantankerous and drunk.

Her answers to Zev's questions are obtuse and contradictory, and she proves to be no help at all. However, when Zev asks her what their fate will be, the Time Prophet replies, "His Shadow is going to kill you all in about five minutes."

They look to the LEXX in the distance and see one of His Shadow's ships approaching. Zev and Stan grab Kai and race towards the LEXX in their moth, but they are too late. His Shadow gets on board and targets them in the LEXX's sights. He commands the great ship to blow them up... And the LEXX obliges.

The Moth is destroyed and our heroes are all killed!

His Shadow then turns the LEXX against the planet of the Time Prophet, with her on it, and blows it apart. But this accidentally breaks open a TIME LOOP. It is suddenly one hour earlier, and our heroes are alive again.

They are able to use this second chance to avoid being blown up and to disable the LEXX before His Shadow can steal it. However, His Shadow manages to escape and returns to the New Cluster. None of their actions are able to save the Time Prophet. She is destroyed forever, an event she saw coming and was anxious to get to....

Part Three: Dog Fight

Zev, Stan and 790 having successfully disabled the LEXX are now unable to get it up and running again. They are stuck drifting in the Light Universe, sitting ducks, should His Shadow come after them again, and with Kai in no better shape than he was the last time we saw him.

And His Shadow is definitely planning to come after them. He has his minions scour the universe for any surviving Gigashadow eggs. They manage to return to the New Cluster with several. The eggs are soon hatched and some of His Shadow's essence is passed to each of the insects within, developing them into living weapons. This army takes off to attack the LEXX.

Zev and Stan learn of their approach and become rightly afraid. In usual circumstances an attack like this would be no big deal, as a healthy LEXX could easily defeat such an enemy. But now their only hope is to outfit moths with home-made weaponry and engage in a dogfight. Each of the crew members (including any temporary crew members) pilots their own moth. Even 790 is able to fly one, using his eye light to affect the control panel. Only Kai is left on board, useless to them in his coma like state.

This rag-tag group of fighters enjoys some initial success against the attackers, but it is obvious that they will soon be overwhelmed.

Stan forces one of the insects to crash into the LEXX where it sticks into the hull. He is able to extract some of its brain from it, board the LEXX and bring it to Kai. The essence from the piece of brain matter is passed to Kai...

....and the gamble pays off. The insect's aura contains enough of His Shadow's essence and memories to 'reactivate' Kai. The last of the Brunnen G is in fighting form again, and he is able to turn the tide of battle. The insects are defeated, the LEXX repaired and our heroes able to escape back into the Dark Zone.

But His Shadow survives, becoming more powerful and knowing that he must, above all, destroy the last of the Brunnen G. *(thanks to Brian Downey)*

Commentary

This trilogy of episodes dates back to the June 28, 1996, draft. In the Contender DVD LEXXtras around 1996 and 1997, Paul Donovan notes that he's writing the **Return of His Divine Shadow**, so these episodes, or some of them, probably exist in script form in a filing cabinet somewhere. His Shadow also emerged as a 'behind the scenes' adversary in a fourth episode **LoveLine**, which mutated into **Luvliner**.

The first episode in the trilogy would clearly evolve into **Mantrid** by December of 1997. All the basic elements are there; this is just an initial version of Mantrid with some different hats.

Oddly, there are apparently unrelated signs of the **Mantrid** story arc in the June 1996 series outlines. Several episodes, including **My Bonnie** which apparently was intended to come before His Shadow's revival, but also **Sniff the Bliss, Dorkadia** and the original **Brigadoom** conclude with a PLANET EATING FORCE which sweeps in after the LEXX to devour the world. This doesn't seem to have anything to do at all with His Divine Shadow.

This force is never explained nor does it resolve through the June, 1996 outline. Neither its origins, nor its motivation. Whatever it is, it's following the LEXX, which may suggest that in some way it's derived from the menaces of the first season, possibly the Gigashadow, possibly Wist. Or it might have been the original form of the planet eater in the final episode of the fourth series. The four teaser appearances, possibly more, and their lack of ultimate resolution suggests that it was being set up to come into play as the major story arc for the third season.

This is ironic, considering that **Heaven** and **Hell** were to be disposed of midway through the 1996 outline for the second season. What seems to have happened is that the series inverted, the **End of the Universe** arc developed and concluded in the second season, and a two episode **Heaven** and **Hell** idea expanded to fill a reduced third season.

The big complaint about the trilogy is that we've seen it all and done it all before in the first season. This Divine Shadow is a pale copy of the original god/emperor of 20,000 worlds, ensconced on a new Cluster' with an army of leftover clerics. The new generation of Gigashadows are merely runty larvae, rather than a planet crushing monster. And we already know the big secret about the essence, the Divine Order and the insects. That didn't necessarily mean its bad, merely a diminished kind of threat by its nature.

Still, the episodes seem to have potential in and of themselves. **Time Loop** appears rushed, it seems to incorporate a lot of plot development, while **Dog Fight** appears to feature braver and more capable and resourceful versions of Stan and Zev than we're really used to.

Still, the real reason why this didn't happen is that a better idea shouldered its way forward. Already present in the end of **Back to The Cluster**, and revived as a sub-plot/arc in the June 1996 outline for the season, the Divine Shadow idea was married to the planet destroying force thread. In the end, the first episode of the trilogy would become **Mantrid**, and the source of the planet destroying force which would constitute the season's overarching arc.

LEXX 2.01, Mantrid

Story

"Many thousands of years ago, we were defeated by humans in the Great Insect Wars. Our human enemies thought they had destroyed all Insects, but I escaped to live on. I hid myself by burrowing deep into a small planetoid and there I waited," voice of the Gigashadow.

An opening flashback scene tells the story of the last Insect, fleeing the Insect wars and burying itself in the asteroid that will become The Cluster, home of the Divine Order. Sometime later, a geological crew comes along, at the bottom of a test shaft; the Insect pours its essence into a human host - the first Divine Shadow.

Present day - In the Dark Zone, on board the LEXX, Kai wakes up on his own, showing an unusual degree of motivation. He insists that they must return to the Light Universe for more protoblood, the alien fluid that animates his dead body. But the Cluster has been destroyed, and the last Insect is dead, and there is no more protoblood. Undaunted, Kai takes them back through the fractal core to the ruins of the Cluster, where they locate a dormant larval insect. Secretly, Kai tries to revive the creature, but the Insect is too damaged to be of use.

Kai then leads the crew of the LEXX to Mantrid, the exiled Bio-Vizier of the Divine Order, a man who is reduced to a head atop a floating glass jar of organs, living on a swamp world. Mantrid hasn't been doing much; he floats around with his jar, using a pair of free floating drones for arms, and has a weird S&M relationship with his henchman, Vigl. After some persuasion, Mantrid agrees to help revive the Insect Larva. But both Kai and Mantrid have their own secret agendas. Kai wants to reanimate the creature. Mantrid wants to use the Insect's essence to power a machine to host his soul after his body dies.

Kai betrays Mantrid, smashing his jar. As he is dying, his henchman, Vigl transfers Mantrid's head into his machine. It works, but the revived Mantrid kills Vigl. Kai pours the insect essence he has been carrying since Gigashadow, into the Larva, reanimating it, and then collapses. The revived Insect pursues Zev, but Stanley Tweedle arrives in the moth just in time. The three escape back to the LEXX where Stanley blows up the planet, killing the Insect. The crew flies off, not noticing that Mantrid's machine, accompanied by a few drones, is following them.

Review & Commentary

"Who is Mantrid?" Zev asks.

"He was once the Divine Order's greatest Bio-Vizier. No man ever had a more insatiable hunger for knowledge and experience. A brilliant scientist and a truly dangerous human being, so dangerous he was imprisoned by the Divine Order," Kai responds.

You can't watch this episode, without being overwhelmed by the character himself. Visually, Mantrid is simply mind boggling. Armless, legless, bodiless, a floating ribbed transparent jar filled with the shadows of organs, with a human head on top of it, crowned by that strange helmet. He's a figure out of surrealist nightmares; his very existence violates logic and expectation in primeval ways.

The performance by Dieter Laser is similarly over the top; his Mantrid is a larger than life figure, arrogant and imperious. Every word is a pronouncement or a command. Historically, we're reminded of figures like Marat in his bath and Sade in his madhouse, or perhaps Napoleon in Elba. The lion in exile, impotent but imperious still.

Perhaps not surprisingly, Dieter Laser would go on to another cult vehicle as the imperious mad doctor, in The Human Centipede series.

Mantrid's weird S & M relationship with Vigl, played by Holger Kunkel, may be a nod to a particularly nasty film called **In a Glass Cage** about an Nazi concentration camp commander in an iron lung and his a sick erotic relationship with a former prisoner now nursemaid.

But subtract Mantrid and his relationship with Vigl, and it's clear that this episode is literally a remake of **Gigashadow**.

Think about it: In each, there is an establishing prologue borrowing 'stock' footage from previous episodes. In each the crew is driven from the Dark Zone back to the Light Universe by the apparent need for protoblood. Each time Stan is reluctant and Zev is the fulcrum of motivation. In each, the hidden mystery is the struggle of the Insect to reunite with its essence and awaken. In each, Kai is left helpless as the Insect rises up, leaving a despondent Zev to flee for her life with the monster emerging behind her. And, of course, each time, Stan arrives just in time to save the day. The basic storyline, shorn of sub plots, is identical.

The resemblance does not end with story thread either. The settings for each resemble each other. Both feature contrasts of space and enclosure, the action taking place in vast cathedral like spaces which are nevertheless claustrophobic and closed over. Both sets are flooded wet shallow pools, with lighting reflecting off the water to give the characters an unearthly look.

I'm not at all sure why they chose to produce what was essentially the same story back to back. I'm not even wholly sure they were fully conscious of it. If I had to guess, I'd suspect that consciously or unconsciously, the tortured production history of **Gigashadow** had left them feeling that it had failed and so they were on some level, compelled to try it again. But perhaps that's just dime store psychologizing.

The fact remains, however, **Gigashadow** and **Mantrid**, and for that matter, **Sigl's Shadow**, play off each other as three variations on a theme, and perhaps should be appreciated in that way. Each the same essential story, but handled in a different way. **Sigl's Shadow** is a mystery/suspense/thriller, **Gigashadow** is an epic, and Mantrid....

Mantrid is LEXX does gothic. In an episode filled with arresting images, one of the most recognizable is that of a white clad heroine fleeing in terror, surrounded by darkness, a barely sensed menace looming in pursuit, the archetypal image from the cover of almost every gothic romance or horror novel.

A brooding narration by the insect essence sets a tone of pervasive evil for the episode. The use of flashback footage from **I Worship His Shadow** and **Gigashadow** give us a sense of almost epic menace. The flashback to the beginning, with Rockhound being the first human to fall prey to the essence, is a tribute to gothic horror movies.

Some horror films go out of their way to establish normality at the outset, depicting ordinary people doing ordinary things, setting up our protagonists and only gradually introducing evil to the domestic paradise.

On the other hand, gothic horror films, particularly Hammer films, almost invariably have their first scenes with the monster rising up and establishing itself. Grave robbers stumble across Dracula's corpse and pull the stake out, the mummy rises from the swamp, and so forth. The intention of these scenes is to have the shadow of the monster falling over everything else in the film, a kind of subliminal taint, so that we know characters are in danger even when they don't. It's a considerably darker vision, one that implies evil as a sort of natural state.

Rockhound's closing quotes, *"I was asleep, but I'm awake now. I'm coming up, straight to the top,"* mimics the Essence's agenda in the present. Immediately after those words, we cut to Kai waking, the message is clear: Evil has been dormant, but it's woken up, and it's heading for the top.

In structure and in atmosphere, Mantrid follows the gothic closely enough that it could easily have been written by one of the Bronte sisters. All the elements are there: The dark brooding hero, Kai, whose terrible secret is at the center of the plot; the heroine, Zev, whose strength is her capacity for love; the vast decaying gothic mansion, the strange characters creeping around the edges, the sense of almost palpable decay and smothering evil.

Mantrid is also gothic for the Spartan lushness in its imagery and structure. The overall impression is one of decay and desolation, of a colossal emptiness. Excepting the trio of prospectors, the episode has only two guests to round out a cast of three, and these two are continually dwarfed by the scale of the episode. Think on it, Mantrid and Vigl are literally the sole occupants of an entire planet. Their home is an immense cavernous construct of cyclopean dimensions.

The imagery is wet, almost disturbingly so, substantially more than **Gigashadow**. And it's not a clean wetness as in the CGI effects of Cameron's **Abyss** or **Terminator II**. Rather, it's a wetness of stains and drips, of decay and leaks, of seepage, of viscous, clinging mortality. This is Cronenberg territory. Inside Mantrid's prison, the place is filled with pools or ponds. Mantrid's jar is filled with gurgling liquid, the mark of his physical decay, he splashes when he shatters. Liquid images abound, the wetness of the insect innards, the insect essence swirling around in Kai, like oil in his eyes, Vigl's transparent raincoat. The whole interior is a small lake with useable surface restricted to small islands and walkways. Somehow, subliminally even the air feels damp and muggy in Mantrid's domain, but not necessarily warm.

But this isn't a lush wetness of sensuality. This seems a cold alienated lushness. The episode is replete with sexuality, but it's a crude dark sexuality that has nothing to do with love. This is all about hunger and possession, about guilt and condemnation or unthinking animal urges, this is **Cruising** as opposed to romance. The opening scene where Vigl and Mantrid enact their passion play is creepy, creepier still is the scene where Vigl meets Zev and licks her hand. The scenes with Kai and the insect are inherently sexual ones, he seems to kiss and couple with it, a sort of parody of intercourse. Given that he wants to pass his essence into it, sexual contact isn't necessarily inaccurate.

Mantrid is one of the darkest and most claustrophobic of the episodes, much of the episode seems underlit. Even on the LEXX, shadows are omnipresent and overpowering. In Mantrid's airy sanctuary, there's little room for shadows, but nevertheless, it's as if light is simply swallowed up, leaving smothering grey. There's a fascinating trick with the lighting. Mantrid's realm is supposed to be a huge dome filled with a stagnant lake, dotted with bridges, rafts and islands. Its gothic turned inside out, with the forbidding moors being inside the decaying mansion. To reflect this, the lighting often has a flickering quality, as if the light is being reflected off the surrounding water. The effect is a constant rippling of light and shadow, subtle but creepy.

The insectoid images also abound. There's the insect Larva of course, an impressive full sized prop. Mantrid's base resembles a giant hive; the machine he's building is a kind of insect-like construction, a praying mantis or a spider, perhaps. Even the drone arms are suggestive. Finally, there's also Mantrid himself, whose rippled transparent jar, and towering headpiece resembles nothing so much as an insects pupae stage, which, provides a hint as to Mantrid's ultimate evolution. While much of this comes from Donovan, a fair amount of credit must go to production designer Ingolf Hetscher. A German illustrator, Hetscher had in the first season, designed the LEXX and the Gigashadow among others. Here, his Gigeresque sensibility is in full flower.

The episode is a tour de force of the alienated and alienating, of isolation and decay, of barren sexuality. It's a gothic nightmare, a glimpse of a vast sterile hell which repudiates even the concept of human love.

In gothic romances, it's the heroines love for the hero which redeems him from his dark secrets. There's often a neat reversal in which, temporarily, the heroine becomes strong and the hero weak and dependent, at least symbolically. This happens here, when Kai, freed of the secret essence, is left helpless in Zev's arms.

In gothic horror, its love which saves the hero or heroine, giving them that last bit of needed strength or somehow invoking a 'Deus ex Machina.' After the possessed Kai strikes, Vigl, who's fought for Mantrid's soul, returns to try again, true love riding to the rescue. Zev comes to Kai's rescue. Stan comes to Zev's rescue as a Deus ex Machina, after Zev has established her virtue by standing by Kai and ordering the destruction of Mantrid's world.

The victory of humanity is pyrrhic, however. Vigl's struggle to save his lover, Stan's rescue of Zev and Kai basically creates the new Mantrid. If Vigl had minded his own business, hadn't struggled to save his lover, if Stan had simply sacrificed his friends and blown up the planet, Mantrid's soul would never have merged with the insect and the machine and gone on to destroy the universe.

Essentially, we'll discover that love has doomed the universe. Zev's love for Kai, Vigl's love for Mantrid, Stan's love for his friends, has driven a chain of decisions which ultimately destroy everything. They've done the right things for the right reasons, but it's all turned out wrong. It's an irony that will repeat in the third season, when his love for May leads him to damnation.

In the context of most popular film and television, this message is almost heretical. In a Spielberg/Lucas universe, bad things simply aren't allowed to come out of good intentions. Good works and good people don't create horrific things.

* * * *

Mantrid was the first episode of the second season, both in chronological order and in shooting schedule. It was also the one of five episodes partially shot at Babelsberg studios in Berlin, Germany.

By partially shot, of course, we acknowledge that all the LEXX interiors were shot at the standing sets at Electropolis in Halifax after they returned from Babelsberg.

The other four shot in Berlin were **Terminal, Lafftrack, Stan's Trial** and **Nook.**

Unlike many of the other German episodes from this season, Mantrid is marked by a strong visual style, likely a confluence of Christoph Schrewe who would go on to be a regular director, Ingolf Hetscher as production designer and Bill Fleming as creative producer. Not all of these team ups worked, but in this case it all came together perfectly and the results are stunning.

According to Fleming, a lot of the stunning design of **Mantrid** was inspired by and taken from European post-industrial art and imagery. A lot of it came from the script, of course. Mantrid as a head in a jar was in the original script, and Mantrid's spider-machine is clearly a scaled down edition of the mechanical spider version of the Giga-Shadow from **Back to the Cluster.** But the script itself was probably influenced by Ingolf Hetscher's insect drawings from the first season and some of the imagery from **Gigashadow**. The actual construction of the sets and props was guided and influenced by a Berlin aesthetic.

"Just to put it in context for those who've never been to Berlin," Fleming says, *"Or looking at any European city, there are areas, of industrial decay. Just places where there is all this abandoned steel and concrete, and it's quite stunning. Some of the East German industrial areas,* **Enemy at the Gates***, were shot around there. There are incredible factory spaces littered all over East Berlin. Rudersdorf, where we shot (in third season), it had all those brick kilns. We shot at a fort dating back to 1890's. They were amazing, simply amazing. We toured Second World War bunkers, subway stations, bomb shelters. We went to one place where the wall was painted with phosphorescent paint, so that when the power went down it would glow. It was incredible. There were rich opportunities for diverse locations."*

"And the thing was, this sensibility, this stunning visual look, would find its way into the work of artists, so they would be doing these amazing stark images in steel or glass."

*"There was a bar I'd have loved to shoot at, it was all velvet and steel, incredibly textured. We were able to bring the guys who made that stuff, the guys who worked on **Mantrid** worked on that bar. The guys who made that game-thing in **Eating Pattern**. Even when we weren't able to take advantage of locations, we were able to take advantage of the type of artist created by this environment. Sets and props, Mantrid and the Insect Larvae were all built by local Berlin artists."*

I had assumed that **Mantrid's** look and design was heavily influenced by the work of Giger, and I'm not prepared to fully abandon that notion. But at the same time, it's clear that at least some of the resemblance to Giger comes from the fact that both are inspired by and developed from the same European post-modern, post-industrial sensibility.

In ironic contrast to **Gigashadow, Mantrid** was actually quite an expensive episode. Being the first up, it consumed a lot of resources. In addition to baroque sets and props, it was the only second season episode to use motion control (this is a sort of effects shot where a camera movement is recorded on a computer, the movement is then repeated several times, under normal lighting and under intense lighting, in order to create a seamless composite special effect image).

It was one of those early times, when there was the luxury of time and money to try to get it right. Dave Albiston, who had assisted on the effects and had done the model work for Rockhound's ship, and Les Krizsan, the Director of Photography, had very positive memories. In fact, everyone I spoke to in connection with the show seemed to speak well of the experience.

Notwithstanding, the episode had to have been physically uncomfortable for Dieter Laser. He had to perform without a body, without the advantage of movement or gestures, locked into an awkward neck brace. In order to get the floating jar effect, he had to hold position through several motion control passes, so that at times, he was as much prop as actor.

"To get the shot where he floats through...." Bill Fleming recalled, *"The background plate is a lock off, the motion control moves towards the fixed actor, towards his head, and the camera shifts as it's doing so. It made it look like he was floating towards the camera and turning his head. Something went wrong with the motion control and so we had this long period where Dieter was locked into the collar with nothing happening. I felt badly about it, so I went over to apologize to him. He smiled and looked at me and said 'Acting is fun; waiting is what I get paid for.' He was good."*

Patience was a good thing. He only had to endure the neck brace for one episode, but he'd be a disembodied head for the rest of his appearances. It wouldn't be until the third season that he would actually get a body. Interestingly, according to a published interview, Laser claims that he had originally been approached to appear in the first season of LEXX. I have no idea in what role.

At that time, he felt he didn't want to do Science Fiction, although he actually had at least one previous science fiction credit, **Operation Ganymede**. *(Four astronauts returning from a mission to Jupiter find that they can't raise Earth. Maybe their radio is broken. The make a landing and spend most of the movie wandering around in what they think is a post-apocalyptic wasteland arguing with each other, but it turns out they were only in Mexico. I'm not making this up.)*

I'm told by Michael McManus that Dieter Laser developed his imperious Mantrid drawl by practicing speaking with a wine cork clenched in his teeth. Perhaps this is true, perhaps McManus was only funnin' with me. Perhaps things are best left as mysteries.

Laser's sidekick in the episode, Holger Kunkel who played Vigl, had actually appeared before in LEXX. He'd been in **Eating Pattern** as the Klaagyan with the cymbal-helmet. There were a few other familiar 'faces' knocking around the episode - that's Lex Gigeroff in His Shadow's robes in stock footage **from I Worship His Shadow**, and Walter Borden, who had provided the imperious voice of His Divine Shadow and of the Gigashadow, returned to do opening narration.

"Mantrid was fun. What I remember about that episode was just being surrounded by water, shooting on all this black water," Eva Habermann remembers. *"I think of water (laughs) I think of Christoph Schrewe. I came back for two episodes in 1998. It was a strange experience. I was with my boyfriend then, married actually at that time. I was not in a very good state.. He was very jealous and possessive; he would give me such a hard time. I was psychologically not well at all during the shooting of those two episodes. I was stressed out, I was totally stressed out. It was a mistake. So, I wasn't really concentrating. I'd go home and cry at night. I think I put some of my sadness in those episodes."*

I believe she did. Watching **Mantrid** and **Terminal** again, there is a certain melancholy quality to her performance. There's mournfulness to her singing of Yo Ay Oh at the beginning of Terminal. There's an edge to her irritation, an extra quality of intensity to her moments of longing, fear and horror. But then, as in the first season, Habermann seemed to have a gift for taking the emotions going on in her real life and infusing them into her role.

Despite her memories, others saw a different picture. *"She was in good spirits,"* Fleming recalled. *"Her own performance had matured. When she worked with us originally, she'd been very young. She was always very enjoyable to work with. She steadily improved. She certainly had a quality on camera."*

"I think it was a really interesting show," Fleming concludes. *"I think in the end, we spent a bit too much time on the Rockhound thing. There was a cut of the show where we cut way back on that and focused on Mantrid."*

All in all, it was an auspicious beginning.

****

CREDITS

Creators: Writer *- Paul Donovan; Director - Christoph Schrewe; Creative Producer - Bill Fleming; Designers - Gerry Kunz, Ingolf Hetscher.*

Main Cast: Brian Downey *(Captain Stanley Tweedle); Michael McManus (Kai, Last of the Brunnen G); Eva Habermann (Zev Bellringer, Rejected Wife/Love Slave/Cluster Lizard); Jeffrey Hirschfield (Voice of 790); Tom Gallant (Voice of LEXX).*

Guest Cast: *Dieter Laser (Mantrid); Holger Kunkel (Vigl); Chris Duffy (Captain); Burgundy Code (Navigator); John Davie (Rockhound); Walter Borden (Voice of His Divine Shadow/Insect)*

Lost LEXX, Lament for a Love Slave

Story

One day, Zev starts to feel a little oddly under the weather. 790 explains to her that the Clerics on the Cluster considered variety to be the spice of life, and that with such an abundance of fresh love slaves available, it simply wasn't necessary to preserve them for any length of time. During her love slave transformation, her genetic material was altered to incorporate a self-destruct mechanism. Specifically, after her shelf life has passed, she will shortly transform into a big bag of protein. 790 informs an incredulous Zev that the sack of protein she will soon become would normally be fed into the protein bank, always a priority on the Cluster.

All efforts by the crew become concentrated on reversing Zev's inevitable slide towards protein sack-dom. Kai offers up proto-blood and Stan volunteers his semen, but neither can help her. Under 790's advice and expertise, they build their own homemade love slave transformation cylinder from found materials. However the equipment they cobble together is both unstable and unpredictable, and messing with love slave DNA is always a tricky business.

Zev climbs into the rough and ready transformation cylinder and Kai fires it up. The machinery does its work, the cylinder lifts off her....and she becomes a Cluster Lizard. Subdued with difficulty, she is put back into the machine. She is turned back into Zev, but the self-destruct mechanism is still intact. Several more attempts to counteract it yield no results.

The moment of truth arrives. Standing in a large basin, Zev bids her companions a tearful farewell. Then in the space of a few seconds, she dissolves into liquid mulch that fills the container. As we leave our heroes, 790 cries robot tears over his lost love, while Stan and Kai contemplate the future without the vivacious, beautiful heart of their crew.

(Thanks to Brian Downey)

Commentary

This is another of the very very early potential episodes from the June 28, 1996, outlines. Interestingly, Eva Habermann was still with the series at that time, so far as anyone knew. What we've got here is an early version of **Terminal.**

Originally 18th episode in order, with **Hi Wist** as the 19th episode, once Habermann departed, it was the most appropriate vehicle and the story got moved up to the 2nd episode in the December 1997 outline, and was retitled **Somebody Dies**, where it took its current form.

This initial version looks like it may have been designed originally as a 'ship in the bottle' episode. No additional cast members, no new sets, just a tight, cheap filler episode. Of course, the premise is somewhat thin and linear, so the addition of subplots in Somebody Dies/Terminal, like Stan's almost death and Kai's almost destruction, and the evil Doctors in the hospital, makes sense from a dramatic point of view. Otherwise, it might have been tough filling an entire episode.

One interesting bit is the jettisoned information about Zev's expiration date here, replaced in favor of Stan's near death experience and the trip to the medical satellite, eventually makes its way into **Woz**, replacing the plot device of the **Clizzards of Woz.**

And of course, the whole thing, with all its variants... Zev's love slave transformation malfunctioning, Zev reverting back to Cluster Lizard, goes back to the long lost sub-plot from the abandoned, **Back to the Cluster**, discussed in the first volume.

LEXX 2.02, Terminal

Story

Zev is lovelorn and sad, singing a dirge on board the LEXX as they wander through the Light Universe. Unable to take it any more, she insists on waking Kai. Stan tries to help, but unfortunately, he makes a mistake waking Kai. Reverting to Divine Assassin mode temporarily, Kai uses his brace to crush Stan's heart. Stan's 'key', a kind of glowing force that controls the LEXX transfers to Zev.

The shock fully wakes Kai, and he and Zev manhandle the dying Stan into a cryosleep chamber, and go looking for medical help. They arrive at a floating hospital, where the Doctors form their own plan to take control of the LEXX. The hospital is for profit, and unwilling to help, until they realize what's out there. Soon, Stanley Tweedle is in surgery and having his heart restored by a trio of Doctors.

Zev develops a crush on Doctor Kazan, they go to a restaurant, where she asks if they can just have sex, but he has other ideas and sedates her. Meanwhile, Kai is captured by Doctor Funz when he is frozen to sub-zero temperatures. The physicians are revealed as amoral monsters who simply want the power of the LEXX. Kazan reveals his true nature as he tortures Zev, trying to force her to give up the key to the LEXX, but this only makes her stubborn. Elsewhere, Doctor Funz prepares to disintegrate Kai.

In another part of the hospital, 790 revives Stanley Tweedle, and they go off to try and save their friends. Zev reverts to her Cluster Lizard form and goes on a rampage. She rescues Kai, knocking him out of the disintegration beam, but is caught herself. Reverting to her old form, she transfers the key back to Stan, before turning into a puddle of goo. Stan wants to blow up Med-Sat, but Kai dissuades him. Heartbroken, they return to the LEXX and fly off.

Meanwhile after they're gone, a mysterious force, like a cloud of locusts, destroys Med-Sat.

Review & Commentary

It's a bold stroke to open your season by killing off your heroine, literally in the second episode, as we've seen here. Killing the hero or heroine early seems to have been a thing with Donovan.

Whether you started with **I Worship His Shadow** or with **Mantrid**, it's a real kick in the face. The hero never dies, it's against the rules.

Fittingly, the episode doesn't spoil the tragedy at all. There's no effort to milk the tears and then pull a rabbit out of the hat and reassure us that everything is all right in the end, there's no last minute resurrection. We don't finish by rolling back to square one. In fact, it's not all right, Zev doesn't get better, she's is still dead at the conclusion and the characters have nothing but their mourning. There's nothing but sadness and regret.

There's a nice symmetry at work here. The episode opens with Zev alone singing a slow torch version of "*Yo Ay Oh*" the Brunnen G death song. Singing for Kai, it's almost a dirge for her love, one of both mourning and longing. The episode begins with melancholy and sadness and it ends with melancholy and sadness. In the end, we realize Zev was singing of her own death.

The inspiration, or at least the placement, for this episode seems to be fairly prosaic. There had been a few episodes written before Season Two actually became a going concern, these included **Lafftrack, Luvliner**, an early version of **Brigadoom** and a stripped down version of **Love Grows**. The **Mantrid** story arc had been conceived by Paul Donovan. But by and large, most of the episodes and story lines were probably planned after the series received the go ahead.

That 'go ahead' had taken 18 months. In the meantime, the actors options had expired, and they were free to take other work. McManus and Downey were available, Habermann wasn't. So when they sat down to work out the structure and stories of the second season, they knew that they'd have her for only a couple of episodes at best when her schedule permitted. They had to replace her.

So, they needed an episode to write the old Zev out and write the new one back.

Fortuitously, they'd already played with the death and rebirth of Zev in **Lament for a Love Slave** as a device for re-introducing Wist, as early as June, 1996.

It's likely that having a 'hospital' episode was already in their minds somewhere as an idea, although that wasn't in any of the plans. But in their early thinking, their approach seems to have been to deliberately select targets and skewer them. So this is at least consistent.

But so far as I can tell, **Terminal** was always intended to be the episode where Zev dies.

In fact, the previous title from December, 1997, **Somebody Dies**, is a clue to where the writers were going. Literally, through the episode, each character is killed or almost killed in an attempt to apply some misdirection as to who the true victim will be.

Somebody does die: Stan, right at the beginning, as his heart is shredded by Kai. It's a shocking moment.

Then again: Halfway through, Kai dies, sort of, as he's cryogenically flash frozen. And again:

Then it's Zev's turn, dying on the torture table. But instead of dying, she turns into a monster.

Then its Kai's turn again to be vaporized as a nuclear furnace is turned on his face. But at the last minute, Zev saves him, reverts to human for a moment, and dissolves into goo.

It's like a game of musical chairs, until finally, the music stops on Zev.

After a shocking opening, we've pretty much got a variation of the standard LEXX plot. Stan, Zev, Kai and 790 are, one by one, separated, and each disabled or endangered in a different way as the story opens up: 790 ends up in a trash bin, Stan unconscious on a hospital bed, Zev in a torture chamber and Kai about to be roasted. Then, one by one, they reunite - first 790 with Stan, then Stan and 790 with the Zev lizard, and finally to rescue Kai, who almost rescues the rest of them.

Interestingly, for such a small cast, the writers have a consistent penchant for disabling one of their characters for much of an episode. In **Terminal**, Stan is out of commission for much of the episode, more a plot device than a character. In **Woz**, it's Zev on her back with nothing much to do. As often, it's Kai taken off the board for a spell, as in **Tunnels**. In an uncomfortable number of episodes, one character or other winds up tied up or unconscious or out of commission for a large part of the episode. It's as if they don't have enough time, sometimes, to manage three at once.

It's odd, many other TV series manage to handle larger ensemble casts, but this often seems to trouble LEXX. Indeed, quite often the guest stars don't have much to do. Lyekka, Louis Wischermann's character appeared to be consistently underused. Although Dieter Laser guest starred in a half dozen episodes, many of his appearances were surprisingly brief.

Visually, this episode is one of the few that repudiates the overall LEXX look of brutal functionalism. The appearance and sensibility of the episode is high tech, with floating stretchers, clean antiseptic walls, delicate high tech equipment.

In fact, it's a little too clean, too antiseptic. Sandwiched between the gothic decadence of **Mantrid** and the lush surrealism of **Lyekka, Terminal**'s sterile production design is such a letdown it's almost like stepping off a cliff.

But then again, this is a hospital or medical station, so what do you expect?

I'm not sure.

But I've been to a few hospitals, I imagine we all have, and the thing that always strikes me is how cluttered they are. The walls are crowded with shelves and charts, outlets, fixtures, there's colored arrows on the floors, signs everywhere and exotic pieces of equipment everywhere you look. The fact of life for most hospitals is that technology and tools continually overwhelm the space available for them.

Medsat One resembles a Television hospital more than a real one. It has that clean emptiness of a soap opera hospital, or perhaps the emptiness is merely a lack of imagination.

It certainly wasn't a function of money; the hospital sets were shot at the very beginning of the season, when the resources were theoretically plentiful. In fact, Brian Downey was amazed by the distance the German set builders went.

"The script calls for a 200 foot steel corridor," Brian told me, *"now around here, that means you but up twenty or forty feet of plywood and paint it silver grey for a metallic look. The Germans actually built a 200 foot corridor and they built it with steel. They were very thorough, these Berlin craftsmen, when they made my body bag, they were so realistic that they left out air holes."* He mimes trying to take a smoke at this point.

Still, quite often the second season German sets tended to be much more 'polished' than their Canadian counterparts, as if the Germans weren't quite getting this whole grunge thing. Another example of this are the interiors of the Seles Pleasure Transport, which looks like a whole different universe from the Luvliner, and worse, looks more like a conference center than a pleasure dome. Even low tech Nook is much more pastoral than brutal. The sense of texture and density often simply doesn't appear for many of the German sets. This may have been a function a differing style, or simply poor communication.

"Germany was just more conservative," Bill Fleming recalls. *"When we did* **I Worship His Shadow**, *we did a hallway, like a row of dominos, nothing in between and just shot down it. In Germany, they did the whole hallway. More conservative I guess. It cost more and took more time, less flexibility."*

"The Germans at the time, you see, they were working under a certain aesthetic and attitude," Alex Busby concurs. *"'Who are these guys in Canada telling us what to do?' It was very kind of union. When someone said 'That's not quite it,' they said 'It's finished.' Coming from the Fritz Lang tradition, you do a set once, you do it right, you don't change it. It becomes one of those things where you had to work under their rules."*

The shooting and sets at the Babelsberg studios in tended to be substantially more expensive than in Halifax. But at the same time, Babelsberg was an extraordinary place. This was where Fritz Lang shot Metropolis (speaking of which, that scene where Zev is tied to the medical table while jolts of electricity course through her body, just before her transformation, might be a visual nod to the robot transformation scene in the earlier film... Or maybe not), where Marlene Dietrich shot her films. Several of the people I talked to raved at the storied history.

Some of the studios were huge, Les Krizsan speaks with awe about a main studio so large you could park a 747 inside it and still have plenty of room. Bill Fleming was astonished at the technical versatility and machinery available. Still, within its range, Babelsberg seems oddly conservative.

"For some reason, I can't remember, we were shooting **Stan's Trial** *and* **Terminal** *in the biggest studio in Babelsberg, which was insane. You look at those episodes, they're very tight and confined, there's nothing huge in those sets,"* Bill Fleming recalled.

But it's symbolic of the Babelsberg experience in those episodes - highly professional, expensive, very polished... and it looked like shit. Or at least, what showed on screen didn't really reflect the care and dedication that went into it.

"Terminal was technically just horrible," one crew person complained. *"The script was bad, the aesthetic was lost. The sets - the economy of the set. It*

looks like a soap opera hospital. Stainless steel set, it's cramped, it's expensive, it's hard to dress. Once a script was done, this may be unfortunately, the inexperience or tenacity of the script writer. The aesthetic was very lost. The clock is ticking, we can't rewrite it, that happens in LEXX a lot, it's not quite derelict enough."

I'm not sure I agree completely with that. Certainly, the production design fails, and even the costumes are clunky and unappealing. The only striking visual is the 'lava lamp' restaurant whose look was added in post as a CGI effect.

But I think one of **Terminal's** saving graces is its script. Written by Jeff Hirschfield, it comes tearing at you like a jagged comic book, full of lurid images and razor edges. It makes a virtue of unpredictability, consider the chutzpah of tipping off the audience with a title like **Somebody Dies** and then playing it out with so many rapid zigs and zags that no one can really tell until the end, who it's going to be. Hirschfield delights in coming at you out of left field, and this time, he's got it under control, so that it works, dragging the audience along without snapping the delicate suspension of disbelief.

He also deliberately plays characters as cartoons. Don't look for subtle characterization here, it's meant to be rude and crude. One look at the trio of Doctors, Veezra (Viscera), Funz and Kazan and their respective hairstyles tells you that they're meant to be a malevolent version of the three stooges, and that's how they play it. Simon Licht, as the evil Doctor Kazan, hams it up for all its worth. If he had a mustache, he'd have been twirling it. Kazan is not just a bad guy, but rather, he's a guy who's having a blast being a bad guy, kicking old ladies out into vacuum just for the sheer god awful fun of it.

Interestingly, Habermann doesn't play it broad. In contrast to the guest cast, her acting is very natural, and her emotions come across clearly, it's Habermann's episode after all, and her departure. Brian Downey is taken out of play very early on and stays out for much of the episode, Michael McManus' role is essentially supportive, so it's Habermann on center stage. And she does it well, her depression and irritation at the start are heartfelt, so is her horror and then desperation at the accident and even her growing resentment just before her transformation. Her swan song, her final lines, just before her characters dissolution, is genuinely touching.

Habermann was going through a difficult period in her life, as we've noted, and so she drew effectively on the negative emotions around her to feed it into her performance. It works, the only times where she plays even a little false is when she's supposed to be happy. It's a poignant performance, and a poignance that both the script and the principal cast respect.

* * * *

One of the really odd things about this episode is its premise. A money grubbing hospital quite willing to turn away the sick and injured if they couldn't pay their bills, Doctors who are merely power mad, money hungry sadists and a health care establishment more interested in emptying their patients bank accounts than in curing them.

Actually, Canada has socialized medicine, so cost is never an issue with regard to hospital admissions or emergency treatment, so the 'money grubbing hospital' thing seems entirely foreign. It's hard not to see this as a deliberate satire of the United States health system driven by profit oriented HMO's, dollar oriented hospitals and Doctors engaged in the single minded pursuit of wealth. The staff and physicians of Medsat One have no counterparts with most television Doctors and Nurses who are endlessly sincere. Rather, it seems to be a deliberate attempt to tear that down and present an exaggerated version of the operation of American health care, fine speeches, unbelievable technology and naked greed and indifference.

This leads us to another insight.

Most Science Fiction is really about America. No shock there, most of it comes out of America and therefore tends to reflect American sensibilities and issues. It reflects the American view of the universe, thus the original Star Trek was about the American frontier, but it also reflected other social and political concerns, with Klingons and Romulans standing in for Chinese and Russians. Star Wars isn't much more than a Kansas farm boy going to the big city and having derring do adventures. Even something like **Planet of the Apes** functions as American allegories about itself, a society looking into a distorted mirror.

LEXX isn't American. Inherently, it's foreign. But here's the thing. Quite often, LEXX is *about* America. It's the foreigners view. It's a Canadian perspective on this strange land to the south of us where people resemble us, but are oddly alien. LEXX often explores America itself as the alien landscape. It's not about America as it sees itself, but about America quite often as others see it, a land of erratic contrasts, strange and volatile.

So, American health care gets skewered in **Terminal**, NASA gets it in **Lyekka,** American television buys the ticket in **Lafftrack,** American youth is skewered in **Wake the Dead** and **Boomtown** and the American 'heartland' sensibility of politicians like George Bush gets nailed in both **Lyekka** and **White Trash**. In the fourth season, the examination is naked as the insanity of American society is directly explored in episodes like **Texx Lexx** and **Stan Down.**

Obviously, this 'America as the alien landscape' theme is only one theme among many in the sixty five or so hours of LEXX. There are many episodes which are preoccupied with other themes or ideas.

Still, given the overwhelming influence of American film and television on Canadian movie and TV screens, of the overwhelming presence of the American sensibility in the Canadian consciousness, it would be almost impossible for a show with LEXX's satirical aspects not to take a look at the United States. The truth is that people write what they know, and in Canada, the United States looms over the landscape.

Michael McManus, in published interviews, has repeatedly commented that he saw LEXX as ultimately a Swiftian work.

Jonathan Swift, who wrote **Gulliver's Travels** and **A Modest Proposal** was an Irishman whose works were often direct or indirect commentaries on British society and mores.

Such a comparison may be pretentious, but it may not be entirely ill founded for a surreal sci fi production from a city on the fringes of a nation on the fringes of the United States of America.

* * * *

No puppeteers were harmed in the making of this episode. The Cluster Lizard is entirely CGI; the work was outsourced to a company called Blink. This Cluster Lizard looks different from the monsters of the first series, more slender and flexible. Must be that human DNA.

■■■

CREDITS

Creators: Writer - Jeffrey Hirschfield; Director - Srinivas Krishna; Creative Producer - Stephan Wagner; Production Designers - Gerry Kunz, Frank Wieman and Alexander Knop .

Main Cast: Brian Downey (Captain Stanley Tweedle); Michael McManus (Kai, Last of the Brunnen G); Eva Habermann (Zev Bellringer, Rejected Wife/Love Slave/Cluster Lizard); Jeffrey Hirschfield (Voice of 790); Tom Gallant (Voice of LEXX).

Guest Cast: Simon Licht (Doctor Kazan); Oliver Stern (Doctor Funz); Barbara Geiger (Doctor Veezra); Eva Ebner (Mrs. Deebee); Errol Shaker (Administrator); Ian T. Dickinson (Berg); Tatjana Alexander (Nurse)

Lost LEXX, My Bonnie

Story

A vessel comes on the scanner... A young handsome man is pleading for help... Zev immediately convinces Stan, against his better judgement, to come to his aid.

The young man, Clod, has with him his girlfriend, Bonnie. But Bonnie has a problem, as she has been dead for quite some time. Clod carries her rotting corpse around strapped to his shoulder in some kind of harness, and is in total denial that she is dead. After all, they've made a great team for a long time. He carries on conversations with her that only he seems to really see and hear... Stan agrees to drop him off at the next available planet... It's all very sweet, this heartfelt guy with his poor, dead girl.

But Bonnie is actually in a kind of false dead state. Clod is the second part of the same parasitic organism. Clod dives into the bowels of the LEXX ... And Bonnie comes to. Clod releases a kind of enzyme that will make the LEXX and its contents, palatable to the new lifeform, and Bonnie starts chowing down, consuming everything and anything in her wake and growing to a massive size as she works her way through the ship...

The crew must work to defeat the invader by ensuring that Bonnie does not reach Clod, thus reuniting the pair into a single organism. Kai maneuvers Clod into a desolate area of the ship, and Clod is dispatched to the vacuum of space... which prompts Bonnie to "save her love," and she jumps ship too...

The pair tumble through the void until they land on a desolate planet... Where they are stuck until.....a mysterious planet eating force rolls through, gobbling it up....

(Special thanks to Brian Downey)

Commentary

Well, that was certainly peculiar; I'm not at all sure what to make of this one. Ultimately, this potential episode seems to have died quickly, never made it to script form, and vanished entirely after the June 1996 outlines, where it had appeared as the fourth episode.

This was the first appearance of the 'planet eating force' which appeared at the end of several other potential episodes in the June 1996 draft, and became the **Mantrid** story arc of the December, 1997, outline and ultimately the second season. But the 'planet eating force' is clearly tacked onto this episode, and gives us no clue as to its nature or origins.

It doesn't appear to fit conceptually or thematically with any other known episode or lost episode. There doesn't appear to be anything else in it which survived or was recycled in any other episode, a rarity with LEXX which otherwise never allowed any idea, good or bad, to slip away.

LEXX 2.03, Lyekka

Story

790 weeps beside the bowl of goo which is all that remains of his
Zev. Out in space, as the LEXX cruises through space, it passes
through a cloud of green swimming tadpoles, one of which enters
the LEXX. On board, Stan is dreaming of his youth, and of a girl
he had a crush on, who ended up humiliating him - Lyekka. Stan
wakes up to find Lyekka, naked in front of him, but this new
Lyekka is not anatomically correct. He wakes Kai. Lyekka tells
them she thinks she is a plant.

Meanwhile, a crew of astronauts, Boosh, Bando and Moss, from
the planet Potataho, travel for the first time beyond the cloud
barrier concealing the rest of the universe from their planet, where
they encounter the LEXX and come on Board. Unknown to them,
far behind them, the mysterious swarm devours the planet
Potataho as the inhabitants scream.

After an awkward 'first contact' encounter, the LEXX carries the
astronauts home, only to discover that Potataho has disappeared.
Later, as the occupants of the LEXX sleep, Lyekka appears in each
of the astronaut's dreams, offering fulfilment. Boosh dreams of a
'first contact' with Lyekka in the cabin of their spaceship. Bando
dreams of a restaurant date. Moss dreams of life on a farm, where
he cultivates human heads.

Stan becomes concerned, as each of the astronauts disappears.
Lyekka is on the loose. But before Kai and Stan can find her, she
drinks Zev's goo, and uses the energy to constitute a new Zev, or
Xev. The crew are reunited.

Review and Commentary

I'll be honest here; Lyekka is one of my favorite episodes. And it's not just because it features two apparently naked, beautiful women covered in slime, although frankly, I suspect that's some kind of fetishist's fondest dream.

It's not quite without shortcomings. Plot? Ha, we spit on plot! Ptooie!!!

But we don't need plot because Lyekka is one of the most visually luscious and surreal pieces of television you'll ever see. A sci fi version of **The Discreet Charm of the Bourgeoisie** the episode is structured as a series of dreams. It's a journey into a world of subconscious logic and image.

Even the waking sequences are replete with dream logic and dream images. This episode isn't science fiction at all, not in the North American sense.

Science fiction has always prided itself on its underlying rationality, no matter how bizarre the images or the story, we're always given is bordered by the premise of a rational universe. Things are supposed to make sense.

In contrast, Lyekka's real roots are found in surrealism. This is LEXX as done by Luis Bunuel or Alejandro Jodorowsky. Like Science Fiction, Surrealism takes off from the mundane concerns of the here and now. Strange things happen in Surrealism, as in science fiction, and rational people attempt to deal with it. But Surrealism isn't all that concerned with literal meanings; rather, it digs deep into symbolism and metaphor. Surrealism seeks pipelines into the unconscious and the subconscious working with obscure and hidden meanings. Science Fiction is about questions, Surrealism is about mystery.

In the United States, with only a few exceptions, Surrealism has never really caught on. Beginning with visual arts, it was one of a series of movements in the early part of the century, including cubism, dada, impressionism, which rebelled against formal art. At that time, painting was approaching a crisis. Photography had reached the stage as an art form where it could capture the world better than any 'realistic' painting. In response, artists became increasingly interested in realities that could not be captured by photographs. They explored hyper realities, unconscious realities, distorted realities. They sought the realities of consciousness and perception, the recesses of dream and emotion.

These developing artistic traditions found their way into European film of the twenties and thirties. Back then, there weren't any hard and fast rules for the developing art form. The result were strange pieces like the **Cabinet of Dr. Caligari** and **Nosferatu,** films whose sets, characters and even acting were deliberately unreal and exaggerated. Stark contrasts, odd angles and an oddly distorted logic ruled.

The thirties and the rise of Nazism, brought a flurry of refute artists and a brief import of this stylish sensibility to America, mostly emerging in Universal's horror films, particularly **Dracula** and **Frankenstein,** but visible elsewhere, even at times in **Flash Gordon** serials.

However, tastes soon shifted to a more documentary or realist form. War was looming, and newsreels offered an endless flood of riveting, fascinating, horrifying material. The real world, captured in news cameras, was bizarre enough, thank you. Film and later television shifted to trying to capture that flavor of documentary reality. The style became flat lighting, natural acting, realistic sets and props. Film and television attempted to ape newsreels, programs like the **Untouchables** or **Dragnet** brought in a newsreel-style narrator and tried for an almost documentary feel. Or they attempted to beat them at their own game, affecting a naturalness of look and feel, as if the camera was invisible.

The European traditions of expressionist and surrealist cinema more or less died out in North America, surviving only in a few genres where film or television was allowed to depart from strict realism and logic.

Children's film and television was one of these, kids stories were allowed to be exaggerated or illogical, as with the **Wizard of Oz** or **Invaders of Mars**, because children hadn't developed the strict logical viewpoints that would reject them. Lions and Tin Men talking? Flying monkeys? Sure why not. The perception was that the critical threshold was lower for children, so you could get away with being more experimental. Or perhaps you were simply allowed to be cheaper and more inept.

The other areas were Science Fiction and Horror. Science Fiction and Horror survived, however, because their distortions and exaggerations were bounded by critical lens. The images of Red Planet Mars or Forbidden Planet might be bizarre, but that was because it was an alien planet and those were monsters from outer space, so it was all right. The surreality was strictly bordered by reality. The rational was firmly in control, the forces of normality always triumphed. In fact, I've heard arguments that Sci Fi is essentially the American version of Surrealism. Restricted and confined, perhaps, but a form of Surrealism, nevertheless.

Perhaps for this reason, the genres tended to cross over. Both having roots in Surrealism, it was easy to make Sci Fi and Horror for a children's market, or for children to get into Sci Fi and Horror. To the public, the two tended to slide easily into one another, so space opera, even comparatively adult stuff for its time, was seen as 'kids' stuff.'

Over in Europe, Surrealist film was alive and well. Everyone knew it was only a movie; there was less of a drive to give the illusion of absolute reality. The sort of documentary reality of the newsreels wasn't quite as compelling. They had not been fascinated by reports of wars in far off countries and bombs dropping on strange cities... The wars had been fought in their countries and the bombs dropped on their cities, that may have been a bit too much realism.

Film makers and television producers had more freedom to pursue a visual effect or to play with ideas. Reality was optional, it was a take it or leave it situation, what mattered was the delivery. Surrealism flowered in genre productions, but it also found flower in the works of film makers like Bunuel or Jodorowsky, or even in comedy productions like **Monty Python**.

Thus at the same time American Sci Fi was producing **Star Trek** and **2001: A Space Odyssey**, European Sci Fi was producing **Barbarella.**

LEXX is inherently about surrealism. That may be a factor of the German Co-Producers influence. But it also has something to do with the Canadian character of the series. Canada stands as a kind of borderland between the United States and Europe. With longer and deeper historical and cultural connections to Europe, and more deliberately accessible to Europe to balance American influence, Canada was much more open to surrealism, especially among its small and marginal film and television producers. Cult film makers like John Paisz or Guy Madden, or more mainstream creators like Bruce McDonald, David Cronenberg, Atom Egoyan and Paul Donovan himself have all dipped their toes in the river of the surreal.

The fact that Surrealism remains a continuing underlying motif makes the series distinctive; LEXX is at its best when working with subconscious or even bizarre imagery. It's all about floating jars with imperious heads sitting on them, ringed planets with donut holes, 'Jules Verne'-style war balloons floating passing between worlds of desert and ocean, an army of severed hands dismantling the Universe, an oddly clueless Satan, incestuous cannibal hillbillies in space or a world eerily similar to but off kilter from our own. The roots are in surrealism, in an off center vision of the universe where the laws of logic and reason are arbitrary.

This applies to a series notable for its consistently strange and stunning visuals, but also to a madcap style where just about anything can happen, which thrives on the bizarre occurrences. The normal mainstays of film or television, plot or dialogue can take second place to more subtle or more madcap explorations. This is a series that might devote an entire episode to a musical in **Brigadoom**, or half an episode to watching a folk song evolve in **The Rock**. It's a series where succeeding episodes can be so different from each other in style and content, they might as well be from different series.

Is this a genuine part of the series sensibility. It's hard to say, I've discussed it with various crew members. Production designer Mark Laing picked up on it, another director said he could see it, and Willie Stevenson was doing surrealist paintings in Central America before he returned to Halifax to join the LEXX crew. Paul Donovan would have studied it in film school. There does seem to be a background and an acknowledgment there.

Others seemed to have no idea what I was going on about. Lex Gigeroff gave me a very strange look and Jeff Hirschfield simply laughed and said, *"We're just more evil."*

My take is that LEXX is not necessarily self-consciously surrealist, not in the sense of studying Luis Bunuel and then going out and copying it. But LEXX is dedicatedly anarchic. Its creators, its actors and crew aren't mainstream. They come from a variety of fields, independent film, fringe stage, art and a broad range of experiences. Most of them are aware of the surrealist traditions or surrealist works and they're equally dedicated to having fun. So whether or not they're conscious of it, they're probably drawing from the surrealist well.

Of course, in the case of **Lyekka,** with its deliberate dream-structure, it's hard to believe it's not deliberate. The sort of people who would do skewer a classic film in **Woz**, or cross **Alien** with **Cruising** in **791** must be judged capable of anything, perhaps even of Bunuel with intent.

Bunuel's **Discrete Charm of the Bourgeoisie** is a quietly beautiful little film about a dinner party that never seems to take place. The friends gather for dinner, but something odd always happens. In one case, the restaurant they go to is having a funeral. People stop and relate their dreams. There's no plot, no story, just a series of mundanely strange events, the characters are continually progressing towards a deceptively ordinary goal, lunch together, which somehow continually recedes, so they never quite get there.

I'm not sure that **Lyekka** references Bunuel's film deliberately or subconsciously. Despite this, the parallels are remarkable. **Lyekka** plays out as a series of dream scenes, odd surreal images which link up in strange ways.

The opening image itself is weird. What appear to be space-going sperm, their tails flickering, swim towards the phallic LEXX. A single specimen penetrates one of the LEXX's round eyes, which for that scene resembles an ovum, or perhaps the curve of a female breast. The opening image then, is a confused irrational vision of conception, laced with sexual ambiguity; the LEXX is at once both masculine and feminine in form and function.

Once inside, there's a series of vaginal corridors POV images as the invading force examines the inhabitants. Kai sleeps, 790 weeps, Stan dreams. The overall impression is of repose. Even the LEXX itself seems to be asleep, drifting its corridors dark and empty. The sense is that this is the realm of the unconscious.

We sink deeper into Stan's dream, a dream of sexual longing and humiliation, as the young Stan flashes back to a soft focused and idealized Lyekka, who cruelly mocks him. He's awakened, but the dream doesn't end. Instead, he wakes to the form of the girl who humiliated him, no longer cruel but welcoming, but now stripped of sexual identity.

"She's smooth right around the bend."

Her statements are nonsensical.

"I think I am a plant."

Panicked, Stan flees from this benignly sexless and unthreatening Lyekka to awaken Kai. Kai's reaction is indifferent.

"It must have been a good dream."

Lyekka is completely uninterested in Kai.

Notice how the strangeness piles up, one odd image leading to the next, filled with ambiguous sexual overtones. The LEXX is male and female, Stan desires and fears, Lyekka's inviting and then cruel, then alluring and sexless.

Even her name is oddly strange and familiar: Lyekka.... *'Like a'* ... *'Lie echo'*

Actually, according to Wolfram Tichy, it's a variation by Lex Gigeroff on Laika, the name of the first dog in space, during the early Russian space program. It's just one of those odd facts that hang around in the back of your subconscious, never really remembered, but triggering an odd unplace-able feeling of familiarity.

On the other hand, Louise Wischermann has a different recollection. *"We were all having dinner together, Wolfram, Lex and I. My character's name from my Brazilian TV show was Luca, and Lex was playing with that. Luca, Luka, Lika... Lyekka..."*

There's a complete acceptance of the situation. Neither Lyekka nor Kai express surprise or confusion, it's as if it seems natural to them, again a very dreamlike attribute. Everything is oddly familiar, but nothing is recognizable. In a very real way, there's been no waking, merely a progression through a series of dream images.

The Potataho astronauts appear. In contrast to what's gone before, the scenes with the astronauts have a hyper-realism to them. When I first saw the launch of Eagle One, I thought my television station had pre-empted LEXX in the middle of the episode. It's a whiplash turn into a dead on parody of NASA with its cramped spaceship cabins and endless monotone jargon. The super reality of these scenes contribute to the sense of the dream. Dream images are often very concrete; it's only the logic that seems to decay.

It's also dead funny, although the scenes are so startling it takes a moment to catch up. As Lex Gigeroff points out with glee, *"Notice how they're all saying 'great!' over and over. "*

This is often the key to LEXX's humor by the way. They're not self-consciously funny; usually it's not driven by dialogue or pratfalls. Rather, LEXX's humor comes from the weirdness of its situations, and the way those situations mutate.

The deadpan NASA scene slowly drifts off kilter until finally; E.J. Moss is wearing a gigantic foam rubber cowboy hat which seems to belong to someone in the crowd of a Superbowl football game. If the astronauts ever represented reality, they have somehow crossed over into surreality and are now part of the dream world, with their lazy drawls and endless reminiscing about Sally Sues and Mary Mays.

Their initial meeting with Stan and Kai, in which they try to do a classic NASA/Hard SF first contact, is so sincere and unctuous it's hilarious. Again, there's that odd lack of surprise. The astronauts simply board the ship as if walking into someone's living room. The further they go into alien territory, the more relentlessly rustic and down home they become. Space suits give way to overalls, a visit to the galley invites more down home reminiscing. The humor works both ways, when the astronauts ask Stan how his ship works, he can only stutter.

Later, Stan sees Lyekka drinking in the shower in a scene that's both sexual and disturbing.

The Potataho world simply dissolves in a flurry of locust shapes and screaming.

Kai watches and observes everything, but in the end, he says *"I have no motivation to save them from Lyekka, or Lyekka from them."*

Again, Kai's odd lack of motivation or interaction, appropriate to the character, seems more appropriate to the way people relate or fail to relate in dreams.

The characters seem to interact with each other like sleepwalkers. Except for Stan, they walk and talk, but they don't really connect. Each one seems to be off in their own impenetrable world. They speak but they don't really listen. Stan's the only one who seems concerned about what's going on. There's a strange plant woman on his ship, there's a planet that's not where it's supposed to be, there's these astronauts on the ship, he tries to be a good host, but they disappear one by one... Although Stan cares, he's completely ineffectual. No matter how hard he tries, he's just running in place, powerless to affect his surroundings.

Meanwhile, Lyekka devours the astronauts one after the other. Again, sleep is referenced. In the Astronaut Boosh's fantasy, his companions are asleep in their capsule, dressed in pajamas and slippers. Speaking but unable to wake up.

The fantasies grow stranger. Boosh's alien encounter at least bears a resemblance to what's gone on. Bando's fantasy is one of flirting as he dines with Lyekka. Bando's fantasy is an odd inversion of Stan's own dream from the beginning. Both involve sexual desire and approaches. But where Stan's is timid and uncertain reaching out, Bando's is self-absorbed although he flirts with Lyekka, he's really only concerned with his bigness. Stan's dream focused on Lyekka, Bando's focuses more and more urgently on his own swelling head.

Bando, for the record, is played by Jeff Hirschfield, one of the three principal writers of the series and the voice and lips of 790. *"I had a scene with myself. It was great. I had to hold up the head and talk to him. It was great. I really enjoyed it. Steven McHattie was excellent to work with. I love acting. I loved it, it was great, great fun. I had that wonderful scene with Louise Wischermann at the end, my head explodes and it's terrific, you know."*

I was interviewing him in a bar, and all of a sudden he got serious and started unbuttoning his shirt. *"That was a chest wig, by the way. That wasn't my real hair. See if you watch it again, it's all the way up there. That big matt (bares chest) that's not me, this is me. This is mine. It was not a whole matt, I do not shave my neck and my back, okay. I just wanted to make that clear. I just needed to make sure I was covered."*

I'm not making this up.

The capper is Moss's dream, as Steven McHattie does one of the most disturbing and unforgettable scenes in the entire series. This scene was based on an actual dream by Lex Gigeroff, who describes it with his usual unholy glee as a comic scene where a beautiful woman offers a man a chance to play with her or with the garden, and after being torn, he goes for the garden.

The field of heads defies description, every aspect of it, from McHattie's sweat stained, dirt smeared, loin clothed covered body, to his slow guttural enunciation, and the field itself is just weird. This startling vision of human heads buried in the earth stretching off in all directions to the horizon defies conception.

Finally, the crew are galvanized when Lyekka steals Zev's protein. Having stood by while three astronauts are eaten, they panic over a bowl of goo. But this moment of apparent tension dissolves away when the new Xev is born, falling from the orifice of Lyekka's plant, covered with goo, in yet another bizarre but sexual image. And this is how we get the new Xev, a woman born from a dream like Venus born from sea foam.

In short, the episode is structured as a series of dreams, each one connecting to the next, not through formal logic, but through chains of random association just as dreams do. There's no sense of progress, but things happen, no sense of drama but people die. There's confusion but no worry. Rational thought has no place anywhere in this episode. But it works, because it mimics the way dreams work, and fills our vision with an endless stream of disturbing and haunting images.

The performances in this episode are outstanding. Everyone hits their notes more or less perfectly, from Downey's fluttering but earnest confusion to McManus's deadpan indifference. The astronauts, including writer Hirschfield, Roman Podhora and Stephen McHattie are dead on, they come across initially as the picture of deadpan NASA competence, drifting almost imperceptibly over the line.

In particular, Stephen McHattie's performance is stunning, showing a sure hand for comedy and a capacity for weirdness almost unsuspected in such a normally deadpan actor. The only disappointment is Xenia Seeberg, whose brief appearance is barely more than a cameo.

But the episode really belongs to Louise Wischermann. Her Lyekka is literally all things to all men, friendly, seductive, affectionate and completely unforced. She seduces every scene she is in.

"It was tricky," Cordell Wynne, the creative producer for the episode comments. *"We wanted to make her sexy, but sexless at the same time. An idealized form, very sensual, but with a Barbie doll quality. At one point, we were going to have these large prosthetic boobs, to emphasize the 'Playboy centerfold' look, but we didn't go with it."*

Wischermann remembers that her original costume was a sort of latex body stocking that took six hours to put on, it was intended to make her look naked, but sexless. The difficulty with that costume wound up being the reason why they decided to keep changing her characters costumes with each appearance.

She's a predator, a plant, but you can't help but be won over by her. It's no wonder, and completely believable that Stan falls completely in love with her and it seems somehow natural that she'd love Stan right back It's an impressive performance and a spectacular debut for the character.

"After Doreen had backed out of continuing her Wist character," Wolfram Tichy said, *"it was clear that a new persona was required. This was mostly Lex Gigeroff's creation, which he came up with once he had met Louise in Berlin. I actually hired her only when this persona was developed."*

The shame of it is that the character of Lyekka is more or less underused through the rest of the season, appearing in only five episodes. In **White Trash**, for instance, she's reduced to a cameo at the end to dispose of Pa Golene. In **Patches in the Sky** she reappears briefly in one of Stan's initial dreams. In **791** and **Twilight** she's basically there to get the crew out of trouble after she's eaten her fill. Only in **End of the Universe** does she get a more substantial role. We want to see more of her, we want her to do more, but in the succeeding episodes, we get only tantalizing moments.

There are reasons for this. For one thing, Lyekka's a powerful character. In **791** it's pretty much admitted that she could go three rounds with Kai.

Like Kai, you'd actually have to write around her. Otherwise, she just shows up, solves the problem and then where's your episode? The writers already have to wrestle with this problem with Kai, so I suspect they'd rather just ignore a new headache.

The other part of this, I think, is that Lyekka is probably really hard to get a handle on. Carnivorous friendly plant woman.... hmm.... carnivorous friendly plant woman?

How do you write a character like that?

In their rules for the LEXX universe, the beans wrote that *"there shall be no godlike super-intelligent aliens... Unless they're willing to come and write for us."*

In a sense, that applies to aliens as well. Lyekka's personality seems frighteningly basic: She likes Stan and she likes to eat, but apart from that, it's really difficult to conceive her psychology or personality, if indeed she has any that we could recognize.

When the writers had to deal with Kai over the course of the series, they really found Kai difficult. Not only was he superhuman, but he had practically no motivation.

In any situation, he simply wouldn't react. Kai's essentially an alien, or alienated intelligence. I suspect that having painted themselves into a corner with Kai, they were reluctant to do the same with Lyekka.

This is a bit disappointing, because it would be fun to see her around when she's just hanging out, or dealing with other plant needs besides eating. Also disappointing is that we never get a chance to see any more of her surreal dream vignettes. In a series with the penchant for surrealism like LEXX, this is almost tragic.

* * * *

Lyekka's original title was **Hi Wist** and it goes all the way back to the June, 1996, outline. But probably it dates back even earlier, to **Eating Pattern**, where Doreen Jacobi's character Wist, was created, and both actress and character were well liked, particularly by Michael McManus.

"Everyone liked Doreen," Lex Gigeroff says, *"so yeah, we were thinking of bringing her back, almost from the beginning."*

The plan to have Jacobi back actually precedes Eva Habermann's dropping out of the second season. **Hi Wist** was originally planned in June, 1996, as the nineteenth episode of twenty.

Then late it moved up as the seventh episode of thirteen in the second season, according to the mid-1997 promotional flyer, before migrating to third episode in the December 1997 outline.

It's significant that between the June 1996 and 1997 outlines, they were prepared to drop a third of the episodes, but hung onto **Hi Wist**, and steadily moved it up the list.

The plans at the time were that Doreen Jacobi would sort of reprise her character. However, Wist II would not be a satellite worm creature from **Eating Pattern**, but merely a plant woman who'd read the image of Wist from Stan's dreams, and created herself in that image. She would prove she was benign by restoring Zev to life.

After Habermann dropped out, **Hi Wist** was moved up to third episode, following immediately upon **Lament for a Love Slave/Somebody Dies/Terminal**, and was revised somewhat to allow for the creation of a new Zev. From here, Wist was to become a semi-regular on the series.

But, in one of those odd happenstances that seem to plague LEXX, Jacobi wasn't able or available to do the role. She'd fallen into the part almost by accident when another actress broke a leg, and now she was falling out of the part. According to some unconfirmed reports, her agent wasn't fond of Michael McManus.

The role would go to Louise Wischermann, the character of Wist was buried forever, and a new character, Lyekka would be created for it. Wischermann, a Brazilian/German actress brought a warmth to the part and had a chemistry with Downey that Jacobi's more alien character lacked.

The treatment of **Hi Wist** from June, 1996, is pretty sketchy. The basic concept of what Wist is, and her recreation of Zev is there.

But there's no sign of Potataho or the astronauts, or the planet destroying force. This new Wist is more uncertain and vulnerable; she's closer to the frightened girl Wist that Kai saw in the monitor in **Eating Pattern**, rather than the confident pattern worm.

The astronauts, Potataho and the planet eating force do appear in the treatment of **Hi Wist** from December, 1997. But this is much straighter and far less surreal than the finished product. The basic story is there, but the fantasy sequences, the relentless surreality of images and situations is not.

Instead of dragging her victims into fantasies of fulfillment, this Wist feeds somewhat differently:

"Soon bones are found picked clean of flesh. The survivors suspiciously observe that this only happens when Wist is not around. Their suspicions are confirmed when they actually see Wist break up into thousands of flying, seed-like, flesh-hungry, shimmering components that attack and consume the third astronaut. The components then reform into a relaxed and good-natured Wist, who explains 'Sorry, that's just what I do.'"

The concept of the Wist personality has shifted back to the predator, from the frightened, vulnerable girl.

In the December 1997 outline, the dream sequences are still absent, Wist is revealed to have been growing in LEXX for some time.

One of the Potataho astronauts is a woman, which becomes significant.

Wist devours by breaking into thousand s of flying seed like components. She politely says that this is what she does, and prepares to sleep, asking Stan to water her regularly. 790 realises that Wist can convert matter, and asks her to reconstitute Zev. Wist agrees to try, recreating the form of the female astronaut, with the soul or mind of Zev.

Another interesting difference in the June 1996 treatment is that originally, Kai and Stan witness the destruction of Potataho and the formation of the Divine Order symbol. The treatment notes they're 'baffled and concerned.'

In the treatment for the previous episode, Someone Dies/Terminal the Mantrid drones devour the Medsat while Stan and Kai are distracted arguing about whether to blow it up. The original series treatments clearly have the heroes much more aware, much earlier on, that something is going on.

So where does the Surrealism come from?

"It was all in the script," creative producer, Cordell Wynne, told me. *"Everything was in the script, the field of heads, everything. We only brought it out."*

I suspect he's being modest.

This was a consistent thing talking to LEXX people; they're all such self-effacing bastards. No one would ever take credit directly for anything, you'd have to go and talk to other people to find out what their contribution was, and then go back and confront them with it, and then finally, they'd acknowledge that maybe they did have some minor role.

In point of fact, a number of people point to Cordell Wynne as being the creative force who pulled **Lyekka** together. Paul Donovan in one interview, for instance, notes that he thought it was a complete mess initially, but that it came together.

"Cordell was one of the original partners of Salter, all the way back to Defcon 4." Bill Fleming said. *"He's a brilliant visual artist. He would have been a brilliant person to have as a designer. A lot of work went into trying to create the visual effect of the character. It's so hard not to look like Ed Wood. It's too difficult. Mantrid is much more tangible, guy with a glass jar for a body,*

everyone can visualize that easily. But Lyekka, well, it can be visualized, but everyone's vision is different."

Mark Asquith, a documentary producer who was around at the time, observed, *"It wasn't just the writers. You'd see producers throwing stuff in. We were there for part of Lyekka, Cordell was producing it, watching the post-production, Cordell threw a lot of stuff into it. Television is such a community art, it isn't just Paul, it's a huge group of people. Obviously, Paul is at the helm of it. It's a giant community."*

"I also think, one of the other wacky things about LEXX, was for me, that sense of freedom," Asquith went on. *"What they do, structurally, they seem to tell a lot of different kinds of stories structurally. They took a lot of chances. Its wonderfully subversive, here they are taking Apollo astronauts, this big exploration thing, the whole thing is subverted and its turns out to be about potatoes. It's exhilarating. You see that one image of Steven McHattie watering the heads... That's not normal television."*

There were, by the way, only twelve heads in front of a greenscreen. They were just cut and repasted over and over again until they stretched to the horizon with the magic of CGI, as Asquith shows in his documentary.

This episode, together with **Nook,** featured the only location shooting of the second season, if you discount the hellhole of Electropolis upper floor in 791. The field of heads sequence with Louise Wischermann and Stephen McHattie was shot out at Paul Donovan's farm outside Nova Scotia. You can tell they're in natural sunlight.

"Only a few people who got to go out there," Kimberly Boyd, 3rd Assistant Director told me. *"They came back with sunburns, everyone was so envious. They got to see the light of day. We were still shooting in the studio that day."*

"Lyekka works, that was where the idea was to shoot models and embellish them with composited CGI material," Alex Busby notes.

Lyekka was marked by a merger of real and unreal scenes. The field of heads was the obvious one of course. But the flight of the Eagle one spaceship also featured a real model with a CGI background and effects.

The Eagle One was the creation of Dave Albiston, whose model work also showed up in Mantrid, Terminal and 791. Of his works, this ship is my favorite. Costing $3200 it's an amazing piece of work, invoking yet alien to the ships of the modern space program. It's something that NASA might have built in an alternate universe.

Finally, credit must be given to the cast. Of the guest cast, we've already met Hirschfield and Wischermann. Roman Podhora (Astronaut Boosh) had previously appeared in Paul Donovan's **Tomcat: Dangerous Desires**.

Steven McHattie, playing Captain E.J. Moss, is a distinguished Canadian actor, who stars in the critically acclaimed **series Cold Squad,** about a police task force which uses new technology to solve old crimes. In addition to lengthy movie credits, he'd worked with Paul Donovan as the title character in **Life With Billie,** had played a villain in **Caribe** (scripted by Donovan) and had appeared in Salter Street's **Emily of New Moon.** He would return to LEXX in the fourth season as the reincarnation of his character on Earth.

CREDITS

Creators: Director - Stephan Wagner; Writers - Lex Gigeroff and Paul Donovan; Production Designers - David Hackl and Ingolf Hetscher; Creative Producer - Cordell Wynne

Main Cast: Brian Downey (Captain Stanley Tweedle); Michael McManus (Kai, Last of the Brunnen G); Xenia Seeberg (Xev Bellringer, Rejected Wife/Love Slave/Cluster Lizard); Jeffrey Hirschfield (Voice of 790); Tom Gallant (Voice of LEXX).

Guest Cast: Louise Wischermann (Lyekka); Stephen McHattie (Captain EJ Moss); Roman Podhora (Science Officer L.L. Boosh); Jeffrey Hirschfield (Flight Officer P.T. Bando)

LEXX 2.04, Luvliner

Story

The crew of the LEXX pick up a transmission from a floating brothel called the Luvliner. Enthusiastically, they decide to visit, since Stan is desperate for sex, and Xev wants anyone... except Stan. Arriving at the Luvliner, they discover it's a lot sleazier than they expected, and their host, Shlemmi s creepy. Nevertheless, they decide to make do.

Xev finds a muscle boy, but is frustrated when all he wants to do is relate soulfully to her. Meanwhile, Stan finds himself disappointed to be assigned a plain older woman, but they begin to talk. The robot head, 790 is horrified to discover that he's the object of sexual desire for Shlemmi, who uses an electronic costume to have sex with it.

But Shlemmi has a deeper agenda; he's sick and tired of the Luvliner. He summons a mercenary named Aulk, to help him capture Xev and Stanley and take over the LEXX. On board the LEXX, Stan is tied to the control podium and forced to blow up the Luvliner. Ault then throws Kai's cryopod into space, intending to use the LEXX to destroy it. Xev fights Ault, as the two struggle, Kai returns.

Review & Commentary

"A lot of people didn't like Luvliner unfortunately. But I really believe that episode was a lot better on the page. There were a lot of problems; there was a lot of stuff. I'm not one to put responsibility off on others, but I think that there was something that was lost. The tone, I think a lot of people took offence. They didn't like the tone. They found it got really dark and ugly. I knew that

was in there, I was fine with that, but I think it was a delicate balance that episode needed so it didn't get too dark and ugly. It became too dark. Some of the fault was in the writing; the balance of tone was not achieved...." Jeff Hirschfield.

It's easy to crap on these people. They're their own worst critics. Both Jeff Hirschfield and Lex Gigeroff at different times told me they just couldn't watch LEXX, the gulf between what they wanted to do and what they did is literally too painful.

Luvliner was actually one of three episode scripts that Hirschfield wrote during 1996 and 1997 while they were waiting for approval for the second season. The other two were an episode length version of **Love Grows** and an ultimately unused version of **Brigadoom. Luvliner** itself was an evolution of an earlier script called **Loveline**, which played out somewhat differently.

As such, **Lafftrack** and **Luvliner** seem to represent a kind of "raw" version of LEXX, untamed by Showtime, unsoftened by German sensitivities. It's raunchy, it's crude, it's basic and very primal and nasty. This is about as far from **Star Trek** as you could get, our heroes are completely selfish, searching for nothing more than to get laid. It's wonderfully sleazy, apart from Stan and Xev's gutter motivations; everything else has a nasty sheen, including sets and extras you wouldn't want to visit without large doses of penicillin.

One of the pleasures of the episode is watching the awkwardly named Jeff Pustil, play the equally awkwardly named Shlemmi Akakak, the trashy, traitorous brothel manager. Pustil was actually an old hand with Paul Donovan, almost from the beginning, appearing in **South Pacific 1942, Siege, Defcon IV** and **George's Island**. In LEXX he would return again and again in the third and fourth seasons. He seems to specialize in playing traitorous little toadies, which I have to assume, has nothing to do with his real persona, or Paul Donovan wouldn't keep having him back. Jeff manages to hit precisely the write notes, obnoxious and bullying when in charge, obsequious when intimidated. Hirschfield gives the character a kind of gutter poetry.

Babes, boys, beasts, thinner or fatter/

Hunks, chunks, monks, twins dipped in batter/

the wiggle, the jiggle, the ooo-la-la,/

people to spank you and sheep to go 'Baaa.'

Too often in LEXX, dialogue is merely functional. It rarely sings or sparkles. Shlemmi's trash poetry is one of those rare exceptions.

Yes! Yes!! Goodbye, dog pound!

Goodbye smell of urine and drunken whores

and creepy old men with hair on their backs

and their hands down their pants.

See ya skin lesions, open sores,

stained sheets, soiled underwear everywhere

and overall rude behavior! Die! Die!

"I loved Shlemmi," Jeff Pustil says, *"he was fun, he was mean, he had his own agenda. It was an opportunity to play a character and not have to worry about redeeming qualities. He was a Ron Jeremy of low rent brothels. He had rhythm, it was just like a certain kind of poetry. For the most part with Shlemmi, a lot of stuff in the script was there, it didn't need to be worked, all this gaudy poetry."*

Arguably though, Luvliner goes too far. There's a vicious quality to the episode. For one thing, I can't recall another episode through the entire series where Xev is beaten up so brutally. When you think about it, LEXX is a fairly nonviolent adventure series.

Unlike a lot of American film and television, where gun battles and fistfights are the punctuation and grammar of adventure, LEXX has almost always been comparatively restrained. Violence is suggested, or it's briefly seen and then cut away frequently.

Both Canadian and German productions have always tended to be less violent than American ones. Partly, I think this is a function of technical ability. American film and television grew out of

Burlesque and Wild West shows, rodeo and slapstick. Stuntmen and explosives technicians were there from the beginning, and movies and television in Hollywood have decades of tradition and experience.

But Canadian and German societies media are simply tamer, the censorship regimes or issues of public acceptability have always been different. The Germans have never had a problem with erotica or depictions of full or partial female nudity, but shy away from explicit violence.

"It was a German thing that there would be no more of that after the movies," Hirschfield recalls. *"There'd be no severed limbs, no decapitations, no anything like that. They really came down hard on the violence. Especially certain kinds of violence. Basically, anything that desecrates a human body. Even though of course, it's not desecration, its madness. So that had to change, and the script changed accordingly."*

That was one of the ideas that the series writers wanted to play with, the fact that Kai was unstoppable. Cut off his head, he'd just put it back on and keep coming. He could be dismembered and continually reform himself. In three of the first four movies, Kai is literally dismantled. In fact, in original versions of **Lafftrack** and **Luvliner**, episodes written during the hiatus between seasons, Kai loses his head in each.

Originally, **Luvliner** was to have had Kai's head being cut off. In the original script, Kai's body is cast off towards the sun while his severed head remains on the bridge making smart alec comments.

"In the first draft, what I was so angry to lose....," Hirschfield recalled, *"in the cryopod, the guy's got Kai's head. They're kicking it around, they're spinning it around. And Shlemmi got into that. At one point, he's got Kai's head in one hand and 790 in this hand and he's as happy as a kid in a candy store."*

This rawer, nastier LEXX was considerably toned down. **Lafftrack** preserved its decapitations because they were so essential to the episode. **Luvliner** lost its decapitation, but preserved a gratuitous cruelty and violence that seems out of place with the rest of the series.

Not everything worked well; Shlemmi's 'robot sex' outfit is simply silly. It's straight out of Toxic Avenger/Troma cheese.

"Shlemmi's sex costume?" Pustil agrees, *"It was hard to put on too, it wasn't really comfortable. It had all these sharp parts, these wires and electrodes. There were too many things that weren't comfortable. It could have been a lot simpler."*

"The guy is basically screwing a robot head," he tries to explain. *"As an actor you have to commit to that or it's not going to work. That seduction scene, I wasn't that excited about it until I got there. Then I got into it. You have to take it through the characters thought processes and what's going through his head. He's so sexually starved even though he's in a brothel. This was something he can totally control. It's hard to get too analytical, because if you are, you just push right through. You have to accept it's another world."*

Sexual perversions are tricky things, occasionally its alluring, often it's disturbing, sometimes it's funny, but all too often the reaction is one of incomprehension. The urge is outside of our framework, we have difficulty relating to it. Hit the wrong note, take the wrong step, and it's about as fun or funny as a drunken uncle wearing a lampshade on his head at a party.

Despite Pustil's best efforts, when Shlemmi comes out like that, you can hear suspension of disbelief, always a fragile thing, snapping like a senior citizen's bones under a monster truck. There's no amount of sleaze beat poetry that's going to save him. As the episode goes on, we get used to it, but we're never ever quite okay with it. It sticks there like a pebble in the shoe.

More successful is Diego Chambers, Aulk, another of Jeff Hirschfield's villains who take such glee in being bad. Chambers is a charming screen presence, conveying exactly the right amount of sleazy Eurotrash menace. He's got the look and he's got the easy confidence the role demands. He plays off well against Pustil's edgy impotent viciousness. They're like a kind of evil Abbott and Costello. The two got along well offstage.

"We were on the flight out to Halifax together," Pustil recalls. *"We met at the airport; he's from Toronto as well. We got along really well. We had a good time shooting; we had a good time waiting to shoot, hanging out on the set. We had a lot of laughs."*

Overall, Luvliner isn't a bad episode. I think Hirschfield is right, it misses greatness, in the end Shlemmi's robot sex outfit is too silly and other elements are just a little too dark.

That said, it basically works. It's defiantly not about anything but our basest impulses. There's no moral lesson to learn from this and the characters don't come away as better people. It's an interesting window into some of the original conceptions of the series before they'd really gotten too deeply into story arcs and open ended plotting. Bottom line, a decent piece of work.

* * * *

There are a few minor notes. The director for this episode was Stefan Ronowicz, a big bear of a man with a Polish/British accent, was one of Paul Donovan's old teachers at the London Film School. His background was primarily as an Editor for documentaries, but out of sentiment, Paul apparently invited him to try his hand. Donovan often sought out people he liked or found interesting. This apparently was one of his first directing jobs.

Perhaps because of Ronowicz inexperience, there were a lot of re-shoots by Donovan and Willie Stevenson for this episode. Overall, the second season had a high level of re-shoots, possibly because of new or inexperienced directors unfamiliar with the television medium.

Alternately, line producer Norman Denver commented, *"Sometimes it looks fine, but it's Paul's show, and if he wants to reshoot, who is going to tell him no."*

The Luvliner itself was a physical model built by Dave Albiston. *"The Luvliner itself,"* he says, *"was an 8000 dollar model. There's a lot of hours in that thing. It had to be built, it had to be shot, then it had to be destroyed basically - weathered down. Because the Luvliner was a broken down scam basically."*

This was the first episode of the second season shot in Canada. Dennis Murphy remembers it as a kind of challenge, a test of fire for the Canadian production crew.

"We were proving ourselves," Murphy said, *"the Halifax production crew, I mean. We had these Germans, we had these people from Toronto, all of these really experienced production people, and they were looking over our shoulder as we were building the sets and props. This was the episode where we showed that we were up to it, that we could do the job."*

"It's an interesting thing about Luvliner," Murphy added mischievously, *"we used a lot of sex toys, dildos and things for dressing the walls and sets... After the shoot, all those props just seemed to go missing..."*

Submitted for your entertainment, as Rod Serling would say... For the record, I wasn't able to verify this, but given how bizarre LEXX could become, behind the scenes, I'm not prepared to dismiss it out of hand.

If you watch closely, you'll see Jeremy Ackerman. Ackerman had a minor role in **I Worship His Shadow** as a transport major.

If that's too obscure, try this: There's a small throwaway joke, blink twice and you'll miss it. One of the Luvliner patrons is dressed in what looks very much like a Captain Kirk uniform from **Star Trek**. The hooker he's talking to is saying *"I won't do that..."*

It's either a joke on Trek or a joke on Trekkies, take your pick.

****

CREDITS

Creators: *Writers - Lex Gigeroff & Paul Donovan; Director - Stefan Ronowicz; Production Designers - David Hackl and Ingolf Hetscher; Creative Producer - Willie Stevenson*

Main Cast: *Brian Downey (Captain Stanley Tweedle); Michael McManus (Kai, Last of the Brunnen G); Xenia Seeberg (Xev*

Bellringer, Rejected Wife/Love Slave/Cluster Lizard); Jeffrey Hirschfield (Voice of 790); Tom Gallant (Voice of LEXX).

Guest Cast: *Jeff Pustil (Shlemmi Akakak); Diego Chambers (Aulk); Ellen-Ray Hennessey (Rissha); Steve Sisk (Flintock); Jeremy Ackerman (Proo); Noah Denby (Vartan); Paul Day (Consort); Andrew Smith (Man); Rick Collins (Fat Man); Tom Tasse (CG); Dave Maddeaux (Male customer); Angela Vermier (Female voice)*

Lost LEXX, Brunnen-H

Story

The LEXX is attacked by Brunnen-G fighters similar to those from Kai's home planet that was destroyed at the beginning of the first picture of the miniseries. The fighters are piloted by "Valkyrie"-type women who sing a variation of the Brunnen-G song ("Way-yo-way…").

Our heroes - Stan, Zev, Kai and 790 - are divided as to how to respond to this attack. The fighters certainly cannot destroy the LEXX. Kai is unsure what to do because they seem like his people. Stan is also uncertain, because they are very attractive babes. Zev sympathizes because they are a bit like her.

The women manage to board the LEXX and more or less take over. Kai does not resist them. They turn out to be the last remnants of a race called the Brunnen-H, distant cousins of the Brunnen-G. They are very aggressive and don't like men, although they are willing to be a little flexible about this when it comes to Kai, because he is not a functioning man in the traditional sense and is kind of a relative.

Zev is soon won over to become one of them and turns against the fellas in the crew. Kai's head is removed and he is made a spectator as 790's head is placed on his body and put into gladiatorial combat with Stan. Stan would be easily defeated except that 790 has only rough control over Kai's body.

At the end, Zev splits with the Brunnen-H and remains loyal to her crew. She helps defeat the Brunnen-H who eventually escape into space.

Although unknown to our crew the Brunnen-H do not get far, as the entire squadron of Brunnen-H fighters are consumed by a swarm that briefly form the shape of His Shadows' symbol.

(special thanks to Lex Gigeroff)

Commentary

Damn, but I wish they'd made this one. It seems like such a fun episode, more likeable than some of the episodes they actually did.

But Brunnen H, originally scheduled as the fifth episode starting with the June 1996 outlines, was the first of the planned episodes of the second season to fall off the map, and it vanished without a trace. The only echo of it anywhere in the series lay in **Brizon**, when he pilots a stinger ship much like Kai's, and Kai observes this.

Why was it dropped? Who knows?

The idea of a race of space going Amazonians seems to be perfect for LEXX, and its roots go all the way past delicious pulp science fiction like **Cat Women on the Moon** and **Queen of Outer Space** into Norse and Greek mythology. Xev's divided loyalties, Kai's ambiguous response and Stan's hapless situation all seem like classic LEXX, and of course, a duel to the death between Stan and a Kai/790 is just over the top. Certainly I can't imagine anyone in the LEXX cast and crew having any profound objection to an attack of beautiful dominatrixes.

It seems quite odd that they didn't make this one. After all, this was essentially a 'ship in the bottle' episode with most of the action taking place on the LEXX itself, on existing sets.

There's a substantial guest cast here, but then again, **Wake the Dead, White Trash** and **Twilight** all had four significant speaking parts, and **White Trash** and **Twilight** had a veritable army of extras, so it seems well within the production budget, and early enough in the series planning that it didn't seem out of the question. Especially since it was scheduled early in the season before any possible budget crunch.

Even the special effects seemed modest enough. The CGI design and development for the Stingers had already been done in **I Worship His Shadow,** so it seems feasible to recycle and tweak that scene have the Stingers go swarming over the LEXX.

Perhaps Michael McManus simply didn't want to wear a 790 head? But then again, they could have just put a stunt man in his costume and no one would have known the difference.

The bigger problem here was that the German co-producers were absolutely opposed to any more gratuitous head chopping and dismemberment.

They'd gotten away with it in Lafftrack where it had been a real threat the characters faced, it had been excised from Luvliner where Hirschfield had played it for laughs, but here it was sort of half-gratuitous - Kai was being mutilated/ decapitated not because the Brunnen H intended to murder him, but rather, for their entertainment. Maybe that upset the Germans. After all, no one thinks about killing a fly, but plucking its wings and legs off is kind of sick.

This was an episode that was well within the boundaries of possibility. If the **Salesman** seems too ambitious to be feasible on a limited budget, this one seemed entirely doable. Shame that it wasn't.

"Well, it wouldn't necessarily have been inexpensive by any means...," Lex Gigeroff reflects. He furrows his eyebrow in concentration. *"I don't think there was one specific reason why we dropped that story thread ... we never really got a solid plot together on it I suppose..."*

LEXX 2.05, Lafftrack

Story

Flashback to a scene of the last two survivors in a fighter jet dogfight across a tiny world, arguing about a poetry channel. The scene ends in ruins, with both dying.

Present day: The crew of the LEXX arrive at Television World theme park, lured by the television advertisement. They go down, Xev wants to have fun and goes in boldly, while Stan is a lot more nervous, but is eventually lured in. The two find themselves in a series of television scenarios staffed by humanoid robots playing the various parts.

Stan walks into a medical drama, and then three's company, but his nervousness and uncertainty undoes him and he performs poorly. His ratings keep dropping, and he's sent to lower end television shows, eventually ending up on a children's show with clowns, before being sent to specialty channel.

Kai sensing danger goes in search of Stanley Tweedle, eventually rescuing him just in time. Specialty channel involves decapitation, after which your living head is placed in a television set to become part of the audience for the robotic shows. It's the responses of the decapitated audience that form the ratings by which people live or die. 790 keeps wailing for Xev in every show he's placed in, and so he too winds up a head in a television set.

Xev initially has fun as the star of a variety show, but her insecurity undermines her, and she's sent to lower and lower stations. Eventually, she ends up on an exercise show where she refuses to play.

Meanwhile, Stanley ends up going back through his previous shows, but with a new and aggressive attitude. Eventually, he manages to rescue his friends. They take one last look at the banks of severed heads in television sets, now gone dark, before leaving.

After they leave, the mysterious swarm devours the Television W

Review & Commentary

There's some good stuff in **Lafftrack.** Visually, a lot of it is simply amazing. The dogfight that opens the episode is breathtaking from the start, half video game, half star wars, all parody; it's exciting and funny at once.

The shots of the LEXX looming over the planetoid, or in the background after Stan and Xev land are breathtaking. We're given a tiny television world so small that you can see the curvature of the horizon just standing on it, where all the buildings and backgrounds are forced perspective, but so brutally forced that they're visibly distorted, giving us a strange George Herriman, Krazy Kat style landscape that's both familiar and disturbing. LEXX once again comes through giving us visual imagery so strange and arresting that it really does almost move out of science fiction and into surrealism.

Lafftrack's strength, and its weakness, is this skewed perspective, this sense that everything is recognizable, but also that it's subtly wrong. Even inside the **Lafftrack** world, where they're on the show, it remains skewed. The robots who fill out the television programs look like people and at first glance act like people, but after a while, they start to seem wrong, their movements a little too stiff, subtle hisses and whirrs, their words automatically preprogrammed. The overall effect is this cumulative sense of awkwardness and wrongness.

The plot, of course, is the generic LEXX plot. Our heroes come to a world, they split up, one by one they get in trouble, and one by one they help to rescue each other.

Much of the humor comes through the interactions of the cast with the television programs and the robots, often as they fight with them. Stan's kicking the head off a child is shocking, even if it's just a robot. Kai's called '*Mister Whereistanleytweedle*' by the robots who are programmed to automatically take the first response as a name. 790 is hopelessly crude.

Xev plays it up, like a cat in heat, but she also gets to show off different sides to her character. The episode has the feel of being replete with in jokes; possibly it gets funnier the more you know about television shows and particularly about television production. Still, the subject matter is broad enough that most people should pick up a lot of the gags.

There are some interesting wrinkles. Xev never seems to have a clue that she's ever in danger, not even when she's about to get her head cut off. Instead, what we get at one point is a kind of emotional melt down, which gives us a window into her personality.

In her first 'show,' a musical cabaret, she's a total sex bomb, raunchy and explicit; she needs to be the star, needs adulation and worship. But in the second show, once she is the star, when she's finally got 'people' listening to her, she reverts back to this desperately unhappy person; she's never left the fat unloved girl behind.

It's a revealing moment for the character, because in almost every episode, Xev is overtly sexual, she's at pains to constantly remind us of the fact that she's got a love slave body and that she's half Cluster Lizard. It's necessary, of course, for the characters to explain their salient features each episode, so Kai always has to mention he's dead and Xev has to work in somewhere that she's half cluster lizard and half love slave.

But this constant repetition works for the Xev character. Cumulatively, it comes across as if she's trying to reassure herself, because, deep down, she still feels like an unloved little girl who grew up in a box. Her over the top qualities and bragging are defense mechanisms for buried insecurities.

Stan's journey, in contrast, is almost the opposite. Where Xev is lead in through her lust for adventure, Stan is drawn in by appealing to his loneliness and insecurity. In fact, the appeal is almost exactly the same as Tim Curry's appeal in **Supernova**. In both scenes, Stan knows he shouldn't go in, he's already seen Xev charge in to god knows what, but in both cases, appeals to his vulnerability overcome his fear and caution. This is different from the come-ons in **Luvliner, Love Grows** and **Stan's Trial** where there's no apparent downside and he goes rushing in. In these cases, he knows better, but does it anyway.

Why? Because deep down, like Xev, Stan's a lonely unhappy person, and he'll risk his soul for love. This foreshadows the situations in the third season episodes **Gametown** and **Beach,** where he finally does lose his soul in a quest for love.

In his 'Lafftrack TV shows,' he initially starts off all right, but his insecurity continually leads him further and further down, and he's helpless to prevent it. But when he finally hits rock bottom, suddenly he rebounds. Now that he knows the rules and what's going on he becomes more confident. When Xev and Kai are depending on him, Stan comes through.

Still, the underlying suggestion for both Stan and Xev is that they're both isolated, miserable, empty people, and it's this emptiness that the TV world preys upon, to trap them in. The message seems to be that a hollow medium victimizes hollow people.

Structurally, the episode is an in-joke on television. At various points the writers have admitted they've grown up on and been influenced by 70's television. They're the junk food generation, and nowhere is that clearer than here, where we see in quick succession, parodies of **Three's Company, Welcome Back Kotter, General Hospital**, the **Tonight Show**, a variety show, a game show, an exercise program and even a kids show. The bottom of the barrel is

Specialty Show, which is a sort of grim 'reality' show, kind of a dark inversion of Survivor before that series was created.

Although the end result in this episode is decapitation, in an earlier outline from June, 1996, Stan was being booked to 'play the short role in a murder mystery' while Zev was about to be 'syndicated' - physically turned into radio waves for sale through the Galaxy. The subject was television, ideas were being pitched.

In handwritten notes to the June, 1996, outline, some additional TV ideas are jotted down. Zev might wind up on a **Mary Tyler Moore** show where no one notices her scantily clad figure, Stan winds up on a version of the **Cosby Show**, and Kai ends up as Jack Benny-like 'dead-pan comic.' One interesting idea which fell by the wayside in the notes is that the robots were 'learning machines', and when Stan calls the LEXX closer, the robots all act like they're in a Japanese anime or sci fi movie, allowing Stan to escape by heroically 'sacrificing' himself and his partners by going to the LEXX.

In a way, it's a mass media take on **Dante's Inferno**, imitating the structure, as our characters enter and descend through the circles of television hell, each new format being more awful and mind numbing than the last, until they finally reach the specialty show where they're decapitated and converted into a mindless, powerless, bodiless audience.

Or perhaps I'm reading too much into it. Gigeroff may simply be depicting career rise and then decline, as performers catch a moment and then steadily lose their pull. The final level, decapitated heads in boxes is reminiscent of **Hollywood Squares**, a game show that actors appeared on after their careers died, trading on the last vestiges of their recognition.

Or maybe he's making a comment about the progressive dumbing down of television or its audiences.

One things for sure, it's not a happy message. Xev, who's having a ball at first, temporarily moves up, but soon plummets. Stan enjoys his **Three's Company** riff but finds himself unable to keep up.

Shifted to a **General Hospital** drama, he goes off script trying to crawl into bed with a patient. Playing the game results in a fatal slide. Television is like a vampire, inevitably sucking all the energy out of the player.

Like water swirling down a drain, we have the sense that everything and everyone sooner or later leads to specialty show. It's clear that this has been the fate of just about everyone who's entered TV World.

This is a dead world, going through the motions. The artificiality and repetition of the TV world situations emphasizing how dead it is. Even the robots are nearing the end of their functioning life spans, it's not quite apparent at first, but their movements are jerky, repetitive, a little bit off. They're wearing out and breaking down, as is everything on TV world. When the sets go dark it's weirdly intimidating.

Although it's supposed to be light and funny, the underlying text is really much darker the brightness and color is simply paint and makeup on a corpse. The darkness underlying **Lafftrack** tends to undercut the humor, but it makes the episode more memorable. There's a creepy edge to it that sticks in your mind.

One of the final images are these endless banks of severed but somehow living heads, each one trapped in their box, passive observers. There's a grim quality underlying the whole episode. The final scenes of Stan and Kai staring mutely at the endless rows of severed heads waiting to be entertained is a jarring moment of pathos. It's one of those weird surrealist inversions, the audience members have been swallowed into the television sets. The final function of the televisions is not to show, but to watch.

Perhaps the biggest weakness of **Lafftrack** is the banality of its message. Television is stupid and stupefying? Television gets progressively dumber? Television is empty formula that you could run a chimpanzee through? Hey, they have run chimpanzees through it, and we've watched it.

There's a disturbing suspicion, as we watch this, that the real target may not be television itself, but the people who watch it, which might just leave a sour taste in the mouth of the viewer. After all, no one likes to be insulted.

This is one of the most layered episodes, not just in the progression of the characters through scenarios, but the depictions of the scenarios themselves. At first, our heroes' progress through the TV shows is played for laughs. But beneath that, the TV shows themselves are empty and robotic; the script alternates between lightness and increasingly existential dread. Initially, I found it difficult, but over time, I think I've come to see it as one of the most interesting episodes of the second series.

* * * *

This is Lex Gigeroff's episode with the vengeance. Not only does he have solo writing credit, but he also acts in it, playing no less than five roles, and on top of that, his brother, Andre Haines, has a part.

This is actually one of only two episodes that Lex has sole writing credit. The balance of his roughly fifty writing credits on LEXX are shared with combinations of the other writers for the series. Of course, this probably under-represents his involvement. During the fourth season, for instance, he was pretty much the writer on the scene at the sets every day. "*I was everyone's bitch,*" he told me once.

But the fact that his work is almost all collaborative makes it hard to get a handle on his writing style. Hirschfield is easier; he's got several solo credits that allow us to assess both his strengths and weaknesses. Gigeroff's sample is smaller.

In person, and I think, in writing Gigeroff is highly structured. Hirschfield is anarchic, he loves throwing rude stuff at you from nowhere. Lex, by contrast, likes to build his effects carefully. Consider this joke he once took a lot of glee in repeating for me:

"Okay," he goes, his eyes sparkling, he's grinning. "Kai walks into the situation comedy, and they try to get him to play the TV game, and he goes 'the dead are not funny.'"

"So then Kai goes into the medical show, and the same thing happens again, and he goes, 'the dead are not dramatic.'"

"So then Kai goes onto the Children's show, and there are balloons all over the place, and he goes, 'the dead are not...' and he stops, and Kai says....,"

And here comes the punch line...

"You know, I used to like balloons as a child."'"

Gigeroff is sitting there, waiting for me to burst out laughing. Meanwhile, for a change, I'm the one thinking about easing towards the inviting, but oh so distant, exit.

Another time, he told me this elaborate story about how he'd gotten Rutger Hauer all excited over this great new ending he'd come up with for **Eating Pattern**, letting it out bit by bit, to Hauer's mounting enthusiasm, until he finally revealed it was the end of **Blade Runner**.

But there you go, that's how his humor works. He builds it like a house of cards, each step leading to the next, becoming larger and more elaborate, until he's got this towering edifice ready to deliver the punchline. Or perhaps a better way of describing it would be leading you by a rope down a pleasant garden path until you turn that last corner and come face to face with the slaughterhouse. It can be quite effective.

On a larger level, **Lafftrack** plays this way, with events progressing from one level to the next, building on each other for a cumulative effect. Each of the characters proceeds through a kind of step by step descent or ascension to specialty show, until Stan finally breaks free. But when he does, he too proceeds step by step, moving on up until he finds what he needs to win the game. The moments when Stan or Kai break the patterns are the payoffs.

Of course, this is just an observation. It hardly defines the man. Lex also distinguished himself as a 'scramble' writer on episodes like **Girltown** or **Viva Lexx Vegas**.

He was a little bit crushed, by the way, when he discovered that the legions of female Kai fans, instead of getting the balloon joke, took it seriously as a window into Kai's youthful character.

Lex the actor is on display here as well. His five roles are Mr. Beedle, the landlord in the situation comedy, the TV World announcer, the specialty show executioner, the talk show host and Farty the clown. Between acting and writing, this is almost a one man show.

As an actor, Lex has a chameleon-like quality. My first time through, I actually didn't recognize him from role to role. It didn't seem like the same person. This is a consistent trait. His 'bound man' at the beginning of **I Worship His Shadow** is unrecognizable, as is his Doctor Rainbow or President Hufferton in later seasons. Hell, his look has changed dramatically from one interview to another. As an actor, he seems to have a gift for burrowing inside a character until you lose sight of the man altogether.

According to Lex, he hadn't originally intended to play five roles. The story is that the actor who was going to do it dropped out at the last minute, and Lex was the only one who knew the complex script well enough to wing it. This is plausible, but frankly, I don't particularly care one way or the other. He does a credible job in the roles.

This, by the way, was the episode where the set fell on top of him. It was the kid's show scenes, some carpenters hadn't quite nailed down a flat, he stepped on fabric or something, and it came down on top of him. No harm done though, it was just a frame. Mostly fabric.

* * * *

This was actually Xenia Seeberg's first episode. Although she appeared on television first in **Lyekka** and **Luvliner,** those episodes had been shot in Halifax, after photography was completed in Germany. Of the five episodes partially shot in Germany, the first two, **Mantrid** and **Terminal**, had featured Eva Habermann. This was the next, and **Stan's Trial** and **Nook** followed.

In magazine interviews, she reported being very nervous about the shoot. But none of that nervousness is apparent onscreen. Instead, Seeberg takes to the role and never looks back. Mark Asquith, who was doing a documentary after their return to Halifax, saw a strong, confident actress.

"She was honest, she was smart and funny, but came across vulnerable. She wanted to be smart, wanted to have comedy, was willing to parody her image. She had a great sense of awareness of what she could do, I can pull this off, I can't pull this off. I saw the rushes of her in the classroom, there's something very much... she's like a 1930's German cabaret star, she brings a sensual quality, but a humor in the sensuality, broadness. It's more theatrical in a weird way, she always felt theatrical to me. Her acting feels a lot bigger to me than the previous Zev."

Certainly Seeberg is in her element when she does the Variety Show scene. There's definitely a cabaret feel to it. The Variety Show also reveals her character, Xev's secret flaw, the deep well of insecurity. Other elements are on display, a restless thrill seeking, a passive sullenness. Seeberg displayed the full emotional range of her character in this episode, which is remarkable, when you realize that this was literally her first real chance to inhabit the role.

* * * *

And of course, this is the episode that introduces Lex's brother, Andre Haines to LEXX. In a way, I feel badly about mentioning it here, since Andre is a talented and generous person in his own right. Andre would actually go on to help write the songs and sing for **Brigadoom** and guest star in **Girltown.**

In **Lafftrack,** Haines played the fleeing Librian fighter pilot, in the last dogfight between the sole survivors of Lister and Libris. His enemy was Mark Owen who would also appear in subsequent episodes. Haines auditioned and went through readings for the role; his presence here is either coincidence. I don't know it sort of feels like one of Paul Donovan's odd affectionate gestures.

* * * *

Although it occupies a comparatively tiny part of the show, most of the people I talked to about Lafftrack from Salter Street wanted to talk about the dogfight sequence. I'm not sure why. Personally, I liked the visuals of the tiny TV world better; it just seemed a funkier concept. But there was an almost obsessive quality when people talked about the dogfight.

"The two fighters are compressed, fattened versions of Russian Mig and American Saber, pushed them into almost comic shapes," Mark Laing, the designer reveals. *"A lot of design work went into them, and into the model of the planetoid and communications structure. We were talking about the way the street should look, I remember, and Paul said 'I just want them to look like that,' referring to the view out of his office window on Barrington Street. Basically, TV world is based on old Chicago style architecture, late 19th/early 20th century."*

Willie Stevenson, the creative producer for the episode offers this confessional, *"What happened ultimately, was sometimes we'd produce a result which we felt was a failure, but people thought was a campy interesting new look.... the beginning of Lafftrack. The dogfight chase on the tiny planet... that was intended to be serious. A Paul idea we desperately tried to execute in a short time. In the end, it looked like cheap TV and we went with that, we tried practical effects with the budget we were on. The intention was not to make it look campy to make it look real, but the approach was to use real models without motion control, if you do that, you just don't get a real look. In the end, we went with the cheap TV look and people liked it, they thought it was groovy and surreal. I think that was the case with LEXX, on all fronts on all levels. It was like that a lot of the time with LEXX. It's interesting... but a lot of people like the campy elements. From what I get about the fans, fans like that strangeness, they don't know that it's not intentional."*

Frankly, I have to wonder about how serious it was intended to look. This is a fighter dogfight to the death over a poetry channel. If that doesn't give you pause, then consider that during the fight, the ships chase each other in a circle around a town square. Or consider Laing's comment that the ships were actually stubby, deformed, comical versions of American and Russian fighter jets. Despite Stevenson's sincere comments, I think that realism was out trying to score with a hooker when this was being written.

"I did the fighter jets in Lafftrack, and I also shot that sequence," Albiston noted. *"The crash was a little hokey. They didn't seem to want to use motion control, they might have been afraid of it. So we put spaceships on sticks and wound up whipping them around. If they'd used motion control they wouldn't have had to melt so many models. The guy that shot the stuff, Ian Bibby, said the same thing. The scale wasn't huge, we were making small models, we didn't have a lot of money or a lot of time, four or five days. We'd work around the clock to get them done."*

With respect to the TV World itself, Albiston reveals: *"The city was built by Laura and her brother, it was built on a motorized wheel, we used a superscope lens. We used a snorkel cam basically, to get it down at street level, and then the camera didn't move, so we had the camera on a 360 degree prism. I thought it looked like Thunderbirds myself."*

I got the Thunderbirds reference. I have no idea what the hell the rest of that was, but I'm quoting it just in case someone does.

CREDITS

Creators: *Writer - Lex Gigeroff; Director - Paul Donovan; Production Designers - Mark Laing, Marc Preisner and Gerry Kunz; Creative Producer -Willie Stevenson*

Main Cast: *Brian Downey (Captain Stanley Tweedle); Michael McManus (Kai, Last of the Brunnen G); Xenia Seeberg (Xev Bellringer, Rejected Wife/ Love Slave/ Cluster Lizard); Jeffrey Hirschfield (Voice of 790); Tom Gallant (Voice of LEXX).*

Guest Cast: *Lex Gigeroff (Announcer CG/Talk Show Host,
/Executioner, /Farty the Clown /Mr. Beatle the Landlord);
Barbara Schmied (Slinka, long hair/Patient/Breast
Actress/Guard); Sandra Keller (Yo Yo, short hair/Nurse/Scooge
Guard/Game Show Contestant); Rosemary Friedrich (The Wife);
Nikolas Artajo (Kid); Thorsten Feller (Liggum); Gabi Fleming
(Dead female body); Thomas Arnicke (Student/Cowboy
dude/Talk Show Guest/Game Show Host); Alexander Muller
(Student/Cowboy dude/Game Show Contestant); Mirko Szabo
(Student/Cowboy dude); Sebastian Kokot (Student/Cowboy dude);
Oliver Stolz(Student/Cowboy dude); Andre Haines (Space Pilot
Chased, Liberian); Mark Owen (Space Pilot Chaser, Listerian)*

LEXX 2.06, Stan's Trial

Story

Once again, Stan is lured to a space going brothel, the Seles Pleasure Transport. But he has some history with this one. Back when he was an Assistant Deputy Courier Second Class for the resistance, he'd stopped off there and been made very welcome.

Unfortunately, the delay caused by stopping off had resulted in him getting captured, and his capture had resulted in the Divine Order obtaining the defensive codes that they used to destroy almost Reform Planets, causing him to go down in history forever as the Arch-Traitor.

Stan's luck holds, because the Seles Pleasure Transport has been taken over by the Reform Planets, who have used it to set a trap to capture Stan. Taken into custody, Stan is put on trial. Xev wakes up Kai, who has no motivation to rescue Stan. Kai's sense of fairness dictates that the trial play out, although he agrees to defend Stan.

It does not go well, however, and Stan is convicted and sentenced to death, albeit Kai argues for a painless death. Stan accepts his guilt. Xev is distraught, if Stan dies, then they will be unable to pilot the LEXX and she will be trapped. Kai assures her that she will live on.

However, it turns out that the Chief Prosecutor, Jihanna is a corrupt sadist. She murders one of the prostitutes for her own pleasure. Upset that Stan is sentenced to a painless death; she decides to murder him in the most painful way possible, using flesh eating worms.

Kai stops her, and finding that justice has been discredited, they leave. Stan is free, but his guilt remains with him.

Review & Commentary

For Lex Gigeroff, the best moment in **Stan's Trial** wasn't in the episode, or the production, but in a photo opportunity. "We had this giant statue of a nude eel woman for the brothel set," he said. "Anyway, Gerhard Schroeder, the Chancellor of the German Democratic Republic came to visit our set, and as it happened, unfortunately for poor Gerhard he posed for photographs he did it right in front of the statue. The photographers went wild, because he was standing directly underneath a giant bronze pudenda."

It was similar for David Hackl, production designer. It wasn't so much anything in the episode itself, but rather, *"I often laugh about some of the things we talked about in the Art department, I remember in second season, sitting there in a meeting for Stan's Trial saying 'Okay, that's the set, pretty much organized. Now, as far as special effects goes, who's going to blow the maggots in a tube up Brian's nose?' Someone in the art department said, 'Oh, I'll do that.' A stranger sitting in the art department would go, what the hell are they talking about."*

Unfortunately, little of that sense of fun actually made it into the episode. **Stan's Trial** suffers from several critical misfires, and unfortunately, there aren't any strengths. **Stan's Trial** stands as one of the weaker episodes of the second series.

The usual culprits of time and budget aren't to blame this time. This was one of Donovan's interregnum scripts, written in the eighteen month period between the movies and the series. There was, theoretically, more than enough time to write it. It was also the fourth of the original five episodes shot in the first block of filming in Germany, so the second series wasn't yet approaching a major budget or logistics crunch. So, what went wrong?

At first, the subject matter, a trial set in a brothel, seems perfectly suited to LEXX's style of outrageous excess. Unfortunately, the episode never takes off visually. There are only a few instances of baroque excess, a statue on the main set, the CGI exterior of the Seles Pleasure Transport.

But for the most part, the set design is sparse to the point of being perfunctory. Instead of a Mad Hatters Tea Party or something out of Jean Genet or Marquis de Sade, the trial might as well be held in a hotel conference room meeting for all the impact the setting has.

Where are all the feather boas? The garish colors? The black velvet paintings? Where are the random bits of lingerie floating around everywhere? Where's the overstuffed furniture not really designed for sitting in? The tack, the tat, the lurid peep show stuff, where's all the bad taste on overdrive, the decadence and sensuality? Who handed the production design over to the flying nun?

For that matter, where are the barely there costumes? The trashy hooker looks? The decadent fright house wigs? Outrageous bosoms? Make up applied with a trowel? We only see a few of the prostitutes of Seles Pleasure Transport, and they're slender girls without make up and dressed relatively demurely. Where are the decadent customers and clients of every stripe? Seles Pleasure Transport inhabitants should resemble the cast of a Roman bacchanalia.

Of course, we might assume that since the Reform Planets squad took over, they evicted all the customers, cleaned up the place and forced the girls to tone down their act. That's possible, but if that's the case, it's never explained in the script. All there is, is a passing mention of a group of dedicated Reformers waiting at Seles on the long chance that Tweedle might return. Any suggestion that Seles might have been the subject of a puritanical pogrom is wanting. If it was intended that this be so, then the script is badly underwritten.

Alternately, if that was the plan, it might have been fun to have followed through on the idea of a puritanical pogrom, prostitutes forced to dress as nuns, etc., erotic art and fixtures delicately covered in appropriate places... But nothing like that appears.

I'm forced to conclude that the empty corridors and sets are simply evidence of a lack of thought or thinking, either on the part of the creators and designers or on the part of the German set construction crew. This poverty of visual imagination showed up in other episodes shot in Germany that year, particularly in **Terminal** and **Nook.**

There is one spark of interest in the costume production. The clerical robes of Prosecutor Jihanna and her retinue, the uniforms and armor of the Reform soldiers, and even the giant Holo-Judge who presides over the trial are all reminiscent of **I Worship His Shadow.** Perhaps it was simply a matter of not reaching very far, but on the other hand, there may have been a suggestion there that the Reform Planets heretics were really no better than the forces of the Divine Shadow.

The script sags. There's no other word for it. It sags badly, sodden and lumpy. This is a courtroom drama, and courtroom dramas have sizzle and bite. There's terse exchanges, fast dialogue, verbal sparring. There's a long cinematic and television history of courtroom drama and intrigue, and this script seems to ignore all of it. Rather, it's slow and mannered, lacking snap. Jihanna makes assertions, Kai points out that she hasn't proven anything, Jihanna makes more assertions. Dull, and worse, tediously repetitive.

In fact, the prevalence of flashbacks made me wonder if this was intended to be a clip show. But it's far too early in the production year for that. Still, all but one of the flashbacks are recycled footage from the first season.... essentially the scenes detailing Stan's escape from the Megashadow's attack and his capture by Feppo and Smoor. (the one 'new' flashback scene is Stan, wearing a helmet to conceal his hairstyle, negotiating with the voice of Seles). They add a production value and sense of spectacle and immediacy that the episode desperately needs, but their insertion is awkward and slows down the courtroom intrigue.

And yet, the issue of Stan's guilt and moral culpability for his actions was a major theme for Donovan. He would return to it again in **Patches in the Sky**, and again in the **Beach**. Stan's guilt for past actions would be referred to in **I Worship His Shadow, Gigashadow, Wake the Dead** and **Brigadoom**. It forms the through line for the entire **Fire and Water** story arc, and it seems to be an intrinsic part of Stan's character.

"Stan's consistently the character haunted by his past," Mark Asquith, the producer responsible for the second and third season documentaries. *"Stan does the right thing as often as the wrong thing. What's interesting is that he often does the right thing for the wrong reason, and vice versa. Stan was really the only character that had a really compelling true arc of lost or unobtainable love for one character. For Stan its Lyekka, and it's consistent all the way through, it gives him a certain depth. It's quite poignant for Stan. He blew it, he has to live with that."*

And in fact, ultimately, that is what this episode is about. Stan blew it, people died. He has to live with that. Stan's guilt is not the guilt of committing offences, not Jihanna's guilt of malice and murder. Rather, it's the guilt of weakness and cowardice, or perhaps simply the guilt of simply being human.

One of the better moments of the episode is at the end, when Stan comes to term with his responsibility for the deaths of a hundred Reform planets. Of course, acceptance doesn't make it better, and it doesn't really change who Stan is. But it's a worthwhile moment.

There are small pleasures in this episode. The exterior shots of the Seles Pleasure Transport were a CGI artifact outsourced by Salter Street to a company called Blink. While it's doubtless in the script, they did a stunning job. The pleasure transport, which resembles a neon wirework of a dismembered female torso with a docking bay in the crotch is both beautiful and show stoppingly audacious.

It seems calculated to make Andrea Dworkin keel over dead in her tracks. And with cause. As a conception of a space brothel, you can see it, chrome and highlights, neon, television screens, and shameless marketing of a female form. On the other hand, it's a female torso, shorn of head, arms and legs, it's a Black Dahlia level of misogynistic imagery. I'm speechless, astonished, and a bit horrified.

Points go to Xenia Seeberg's performance. Her Xev, reacting to the trial, is genuinely affecting. Her instinctive denial of Stan's guilt and her fear for herself as she realizes she's stranded on Seles after Stan's conviction seem heartfelt and genuine. Seeberg didn't always get great scenes, of the three central characters Xev was often handled perfunctorily, so it's nice to see her character displaying genuine and natural human emotions.

For almost completely the opposite reason I liked Nina Franoszek's cartoonish performance as Grand Prosecutor Jihanna. Her acting is broad, cartoonish, loopy, her character is shrill. Jihanna seems to be one of Hirschfield's type of villains, one of those who just revel in their villainy, and seems out of place on the episode. Literally alone in the entire episode, Franoszek seems to be the only one to realize that the only way to play this is excess and more excess. This is after all, a trial in a brothel, there's a certain thing that goes with that.

Interestingly, this episode appears almost intact in the June, 1996, season outline, even down to the extensive use of 'flashback footage.' The only thing missing in the 1996 outline is the Seles Pleasure Transport itself, which shows up in the December, 1997 outline. Stan is captured by cute and available-seeming women who turn out to be Mossad-type agents.

Here, Franoszek's Jihanna is described as 'an extremely overbearing Marcia Clark (the prosecutor for the OJ Simpson trial) type with none of the, er, charm' and handwritten notes observe that 'Marcia is really pissed because she is the only woman ever to be turned down by Stan, they met when she was a clerk for the Reform Planets and he was an Assistant Deputy Back Up Courier, and as a result of that reputation has not been able to get a date ever again.' That's a peculiar bit of backstory that seems to have been altogether, and perhaps regrettably, abandoned.

Little of the warped tasteless sensibility that went into statue of the Bronze Eel woman, or the exterior shots of the Seles Pleasure Transport, makes it into the interior sets. The production never ever goes over the top, and they needed to. They needed to badly.

The bottom line is that if I want to watch sincere ponderous characters sincerely pontificating ponderously, in ponderously empty hallways... Then I'll just go and watch **Star Trek: The Next Generation**, thank you very much.

CREDITS

Creators: Writers - Lex Gigeroff and Paul Donovan; Director - Srinivas Krishna; Creative Producer - Stephan Wagner; Production Designers - Gerry Kunz and Ingolf Hetscher

Main Cast: Brian Downey (Captain Stanley Tweedle); Michael McManus (Kai, Last of the Brunnen G); Xenia Seeberg (Xev Bellringer, Rejected Wife/Love Slave/Cluster Lizard); Jeffrey Hirschfield (Voice of 790); Tom Gallant (Voice of LEXX).

Guest Cast: Nina Franoszek (Grand Prosecutor Jihanna); Benjamin Sadler (Prosecutor Nool); Susanna Metzner (Lissha, Jihanna's victim); Peter James Scollin (Guard 1); Harvey Friedman (Guard 3); Michael Halbeck (Smoor, flashback); John Dunsworth (Asteroid Commander, flashback)

LEXX 2.07, Love Grows

Story

In space, the crew of a Stripper Ship is carrying a cargo of biohazard waste at the end of a long tether. The crew, consisting of a bored Captain, his juvenile first mate, Rexum, aren't very interested in their jobs to the displeasure of the remaining crewperson, the priggish Lorca, and are going through the motions. The captain is watching a video about a porno planet. An accident occurs and the ship is disabled, the crew contaminated.

On the LEXX, the familiar love triangle is going on - Stan wants Xev; Xev doesn't want Stan, but wants Kai; and Kai has no desire. The LEXX picks up the porno planet broadcast, and Stan orders the LEXX to home in on it, believing it to be real.

The LEXX finds the disabled Stripper Ship and swallows it. The Stripper crew escape digestion and end up meeting our heroes, just as Xev was finally about to break down and give herself to Stan. Stan is disappointed to find that the porno planet is just a video. Xev immediately forgets Stan and puts the moves on the heroic Captain, and it looks like she's going to get laid. Meanwhile, Stan tries to make the unattractive female crewperson, Lorca, comfortable.

As this is going on, the bio-toxins of the Stripper Ship spread from LEXX's stomach, causing the crew to change sex. Even the LEXX is affected. Stan and the male crew members are all traumatized by the loss of their masculinity. Lorca and Xev respond with pleasure and heightened aggression. Lorca attempts to molest the feminized Stan, but is knocked out by Xev, who drags Stan off with her caveman style. Kai observes proceedings with indifference, having no motivation to interfere.

Kai informs the crew that the toxins inducing the sex change will kill them within 60 hours. But this turns out to be a false deadline, as the LEXX's immune system kicks in, restoring everyone. The Stripper ship crew flee into the LEXX where they meet a hillbilly named Pa Golene... screaming ensues.

They are forgotten as the LEXX crew discuss the ramifications of the incident. The LEXX intercepts another porno broadcast, but Stan decides to ignore it. It turns out this one was for real, as the image cuts to a pair of women desperately broadcasting their need for men.

Review & Commentary

Art is subjective

The trouble with **Love Grows** is that it's a French bedroom farce, but it just doesn't have the energy and lightness to be a farce. Instead of people capering about madly, doors slamming, shouting and romance, and all the airy confection that the French are so good at in movies like **La Cage aux Follies** by contrast, **Love Grows** seems leaden and dark.

The right notes of frivolity and outrageousness are never quite hit. Instead, bizarre things happen but are treated too seriously. The actor's relationships don't have the sweetness we need for something like this. Instead we've got Xev cutting her heart out for Kai, or Lorca's barely concealed, and justified, nausea for her crew. We start out bitter and weary with no one being genuinely likeable.

What should have been fun moments are suffused with meanness. When Xev comes on to the male crew members in the galley, she does it in front of Stanley, who we all know has lusted after her from the beginning. There's a cruelty there, unconscious or deliberate, which simply doesn't sit well with the audience.

It's throwback to the original conception of Zev seen in the original **Love Grows** and **Back to the Cluster** treatment, a self-absorbed often callous woman full of contempt for Stan and desire for anyone else. Still, it's a nasty moment. We're more likely to echo Lorca's comment, "disgusting" rather than find it appealing or erotic.

Xev, as literally the only person who copes with her sex change, becomes a monster. As a man, Xev is swaggering, macho, overconfident, perhaps a male version of her love slave persona, but it isn't played lightly. She brings a kind of mass or weight to the performance, which is convincing. But she's a step from being an out and out rapist, selfish and violent from the start. Again, where she should be fun, she's almost not.

Interestingly, in published interviews, Xenia refers to this role as one of her favorites. One where she could let loose and ham it up. You can tell she's having fun with it as she reproduces every swaggering creep who's ever hit on her in a bar. She's also got many of the genuinely funny lines.

The male cast simply descends into panicked hysteria and never quite leaves that state. Reduced to nothing more than running away in some sort of notion of feminine panic, they cease being interesting to the audience. The camera acknowledges this because it largely stops following them.

Page Fletcher starts off reasonably well with a rendition of a he-man starship captain, even if he's just the captain of a garbage scow named after exotic dancers. But once the sex change hits, it's as if he has no idea what to do with his role. Fletcher by the way, has a minor cult status all his own. He starred in **The Hitcher** a late night, cult anthology series from 1983. He's also starred as the titular cyborg in **Robocop: Prime Directive** in 1990.

Janet Wright does better with the character of Lorca. Brian Downey remembers being very uncomfortable with the fact that she was put through the shower scene. Wright was a well-established comedienne and actress, who later found a measure of fame playing Brent Butt's mother on the cult Canadian sitcom, **Corner Gas** from 2004 to 2009. She passed away in 2016.

The bedroom antics between Lorca, Xev and Stan should be funny but once again, it's just grim and violent. Stan is pathetic; Xev is violent, only Lorca even tries to hit the right notes. Where there should have been a chase, the triangle is settled with a punch out, with Xev tossing the protesting Stanley over her shoulder and taking him off to bed.

Sorry. To the extent that the audience has built sympathy with anyone in this, it's with Lorca and possibly Stan, but definitely not Xev. Instead of **La Cage**... we get **Alley Oop**, with caveman Xev clubbing her rival and dragging fem-Stan off to her cave. Any way you look at it, the sexual politics here are repulsive rather than funny. This is too rapey to be comfortable.

There are odd decisions circulating around the masculine/feminine dichotomy. The personalities are changed in cliché ways; the feminized characters become confused, submissive and retiring. The masculinized characters become aggressive. For one thing, the only sign of the gender change, apart from the acting, seems to be in digitally heightened or lowered voices. Apart from that, despite references to 'boy parts' and 'girl parts' there's little evidence of secondary sexual characteristics changing. Nobody grows boobs or fatter buttocks or shapelier waists.

Some forearm and facial hair disappears, particularly in the Captain's scene in bed with Xev but that's so badly edited the impact is lost, because it keeps disappearing and reappearing.

Xev's body remains 'Xev-like' rather than becoming more masculine, although this may have been an impossible task. Even clothing remains the same, which stands to reason, the crew of the Stripper ship wore Unisex and Xev and Stan's costumes don't look portable.

It's likely that many of these things were explored and abandoned because they looked really stupid. I think the image of Stanley Tweedle in falsies is something we could all do without. It seems probably that they were simply unable to find visual motifs that looked good. But the overall effect is that the gender switch seems minimized in visual terms, which blows off half the charge you might have gotten from a situation like this.

To be fair, the episode does have its moments. The long opening scenes with the Stripper crew are engaging. It's bored, space travelling, garbage hauling crew are very reminiscent of those John Carpenter's **Dark Star**. Interestingly, both Carpenter's Dark Star and the stripper ship have an observation dome where crew members retreat to get away from each other.

Their struggle through the bowels of the LEXX works both visually and dramatically. It gives a real sense of immense scale, of being in the guts of a gigantic creature. The synopsis from December, 1997, went further with this, with a wild raft ride and some moth flying, this was cut for cost and time, but it's hardly necessary. The image of the crew as three tiny specks crawling up the LEXX's stomach is enough.

And of course, for once, the LEXX gets some decent lines, rather than simply saying *"Yes, Stan."*

There's a surreal moment when Kai, staring hard, gets down on his knees on top of 790, his face hovering intently and for a moment we are not sure what the hell he's doing. Has the dead man been affected? Will he too get into the spirit of things by kissing 790? No, he's just finding a fleck of blood. It's fun, but sadly, a scattering of interesting moments hardly makes an acceptable substitute for a good story or performance.

The whole episode is decidedly plot free. People come to the LEXX, wackiness ensues, problem emerges, problem goes away, people go away. The thing about the gender switch virus being ultimately lethal is just there to give Kai something to talk about, a dramatic red herring, nothing actually comes out of it.

The problem, once raised is disposed of by a Deus ex Machina. Hirschfield, having no way for the crew to solve their problem just has the LEXX's immune system clear it up. All right, maybe that's vaguely plausible, but at the same time, it makes everything that's happened before, irrelevant to the solution. The characters could have done anything, or nothing, and the episode would still have ended with the same solution. That's just sloppy,

In just the same way, nothing is resolved with the crew of the stripper ship, either between themselves or with the LEXX crew. Like the 'mortality' problem, they too are simply disposed of by an even wilder Deus ex Machina. In a way, the disposal of the Stripper ship crew is even more radical than the LEXX's solution. We know the LEXX has been there all along and we know it's been affected by the virus. An immune response is farfetched but it's not out of the blue.

The sudden appearance in the final scenes of a redneck hillbilly who presumably slaughters the Stripper ship crew is so out of left field its whiplash time. In the December, 97, season outline, **Love Grows** was intended to follow after **White Trash**, with Pa Golene being established as running loose in the ship. Here, he's so completely out of the blue that you're convinced the writers just have no idea what they're doing.

Despite the confused logic relating to virginity and its loss, the whole incident seems to have no effect on the crew. They never seem to wonder where the Strippers are. They never think to search for them. Do they just assume that Lyekka ate them? Or that they fell off something and died?

In the next episode, **White Trash**, when Stan wonders if there could be anyone else on board the LEXX, he ought to know that there are. As far as he knows, the Stripper ship crew should still be alive. It's not as if they could go anywhere.

It's as if the episode was so bad that there's an unconscious attempt to evict it from the history in the series. It's like a kind of virus or toxin that LEXX is attempting to expel.

For my money, this is probably the worst episode of the second season. Other episodes might fail, but this one misfires. It's difficult to find something positive to say about it.

It reeks. Before I watched **Midsummer's Nightmare**, this episode took my prize for worst LEXX ever.

* * * *

Some of the episodes go back a long way. Back when the first season of movies was in post-production, the Supreme Beans shot DVD extras where they talk about the scripts they're working on. Lex Gigeroff is doing **Lafftrack**, Jeff Hirschfield is working on **Luvliner**, and Paul Donovan is writing the **Return of His Shadow**, which will become **Mantrid.**

Love Grows goes back further than any of them. Originally, **Love Grows** was intended to be one of the original feature movies, following **after I Worship His Shadow** and before **Back to the Cluster**. The original **Love Grows** made it all the way to script form before being abandoned.

How early was it? It was so early in the production history, that Kai was alive. In the script, he's a sort of warrior monk. It was only later on they decided to make him undead.

The original story also turned out quite differently. No gender bending takes place, instead, the crew of the Stripper ship, exposed to the chemicals that they're hauling, begin to mutate into all sorts of bizarre monstrosities and chase the crew around. It's very over the top. The original **Love Grows** is examined in the first volume, **LEXX Unauthorized, Backstage at the Dark Zone**.

Watching it carefully, there are clear signs that some of the script was written much earlier, the capricious cruelty of Xev to Stan, or the particularly petulant scene between Xev and Kai, for instance, makes more sense immediately following **I Worship His Shadow**, when she's still a cauldron of hormones, than it does now, when she's much more under control.

The best scenes are those closest to the original script. The scenes on the Stripper ship work, with a bored, working class crew hauling their burden through space, for instance. The devouring of the ship by the LEXX, the crew's escape, Stan's search for the porno planet, and even the initial gallery scenes all work reasonably well.

But clearly a Universal Studios horror monster-fest was going to be way too expensive to carry off, so clearly they opted for a different kind of transformation.

The episode only really starts to fall apart in a toxic way when the whole sex-change plot starts to reveal itself. At that point, it becomes perfunctory, incoherent and even obnoxious. The changed sex roles are cliché and shallow. The necessary light touch, always uncertain in this episode, vanishes entirely. The characters almost literally forget to act, and in any case, seem to have nothing to do.

Love Grows doesn't really survive the transition from movie to episode; the shift from monsters amuck to a gender bending comedy just doesn't work. Perhaps it might have or could have but it never finds the right balance, never quite works. It needed to be so much lighter and sillier.

There's not a lot to say about the production side. The Stripper Ship interiors are the only significant new set and are used only briefly. The closing scene with the desperate 'real girls needing men' is pretty perfunctory. The production relies mainly on its guest stars, its performances and its premise.

For once, the Stripper is not a Dave Albiston model, but is entirely CGI, produced by Cage Digital. Cage Digital was a Halifax based company, unrelated to Salter Street, which had started up during this time. During the second season, Salter was doing so much CGI that it couldn't handle it all in house.

"Paul had talked to a local animation house that had just formed," Alex Busby notes. *"Cage was formed out of a school that was teaching here. McKenzie College. The graduates were then going into the owner's new company called Cage Digital. It was a rough start, what he was saying his company could do, they couldn't always manage. The animators were very young, so they were learning on the job."*

Their first work had been on **Lyekka**, and they would also wind up doing CGI for the Mantrid drone arms. But for my money, their work on **Love Grows** was their best for LEXX. The Stripper combines a gritty realism which it really doesn't deserve, given that it's so obviously based on a long haul truck, with **Bugs Bunny** style antics when it goes through the barrier, stretches its tether and suffers the rebound.

Interestingly, I actually met one of the CGI artists who'd worked on the scene when I was at Electropolis in the fourth season. His name was Steven Driscoll, and he was appearing as an extra, an ATF Agent in Moss. He'd been minding his own business going out for donuts when one of Salter's crew spotted him, decided he fit the ATF costume, and dragged him back to the studio to be an extra. It was a fittingly Lexxish encounter.

CREDITS

Creators: Writer - Jeff Hirschfield; Director -David McLeod; Production Designer - David Hackl; Creative Producer - Norman Denver

Main Cast: Brian Downey (Captain Stanley Tweedle); Michael McManus (Kai, Last of the Brunnen G); Xenia Seeberg, (Xev Bellringer (Rejected Wife/ Love Slave/ Cluster Lizard); Jeffrey Hirschfield (Voice of 790); Tom Gallant (Voice of LEXX).

Guest Cast: Page Fletcher (Captain); Janet Wright (Lorca); Sam White (Rexum); CJ Fidler (Porno Girl); Alison McMullin (Porno Girl); Sherry White (Porno Girl); Greg Cormier (Porno Guy); Terry Nicholas (Real Girl Needing Man); Lisa Wang (Real Girl Needing Man); Maury Chaykin (Pa Golene);

LEXX 2.08, White Trash

Story

A uniformed refugee from the Divine Order is creeping through the bowels of the LEXX, obviously terrified. The source of his terror turns out to be Pa and the Golene family. He screams.

Elsewhere on the LEXX, Stan wonders if possibly there are other people on the ship. His question is answered when Pa Golene, and his children, Junior, Cissy and Norb show up in the feeding chamber. The Golene family were sent to the Cluster as prisoners of the Divine Order, but managed to escape and have been hiding on the LEXX the entire time.

At first, friendly, Pa Golene becomes increasingly menacing, deciding that he will be the new Captain. After blowing up a planet, they set a course for Vermal. Meanwhile, Xev latches onto Junior, who although somewhat repulsive, is the only half decent man she's seen in a while. Junior, for his part, only wants to return home, to party on their homeworld, Vermal.

Cissy for her part becomes enamored with Stan, and the two end up in bed. Cissy relates the story of a spaceman who came to Vermal, and was killed by Pa. Pa Golene catches them and decides that they have to get married. But later, when Cissy argues with Pa, she confronts him with the murder of her mother, who had an affair with the spaceman, and he pushes her off the bridge of the LEXX, killing her.

Meanwhile, the youngest child, Norb, has revived Kai, who shows up on the bridge. Pa Golene flees from Kai. Xev and Junior go down to Vermal, where Junior is killed by a rival clan. Kai and

Norb also go down to Vermal, where Kai helps Norb repair the spaceman's ship and the two seem to bond.

Pa Golene returns to the bridge of the LEXX finding Stan alone, and discovers that his son, Junior, has been killed down on the planet, by his rival, Pappy Glulene. After Norb, on the LEXX's screen, announces that he's really the son of the Spaceman and not Pa, Pa forces Stan to blow up the planet. Xev and Kai escape in a moth and Norb escapes in his true father's ship.

Norb flies off into space to have adventures. Xev and Kai return to the LEXX

Review & Commentary

White Trash is an odd thing. It shouldn't work, but somehow, when you watch it, there is quite a bit to like. From cool visuals of strange planets, mysterious cameos, over the top performances culminating in Norb's dramatic escape

The consensus among LEXX's creators is that **White Trash** is a failure. Neither Donovan, nor Gigeroff nor anyone else I spoke to seemed to really like or support it.

"It was an experimental episode," Donovan said once, *"that didn't work out."*

I've never gotten a satisfactory answer from anyone as to what the experiment was, which could have been part of the problem.

"It was a weak episode," Chris Bould says of the first episode he directed. *"but I didn't know that beast that was LEXX then. So you come in as a director, you're given a script. I was just there to do a good job and hope I'd get another show. I must have done quite well, since I wound up directing more episodes than any other person."*

But as to why it doesn't quite gel, there isn't really a consensus.

"I think we went too broad," says Lex Gigeroff. *"You know how it is, when everyone is trying too hard, going deliberately big. That just doesn't work; humor can't be forced like that."*

"The acting was over the top," a crew member notes in agreement..

On the other hand...

"We didn't go far enough," production designer Mark Laing argues. *"These were supposed to be hillbillies, but they all had perfect teeth. We should have had dental prosthetics. And that little mark on their faces, that should have been a huge mole out to here (gestures) with hair on it. We just didn't push it as far as it could go."*

The stereotypes of trailer trash hillbillies may have put some off. At least a few fans from the American Deep South were offended because they thought they were being made fun of. And perhaps they were, LEXX has never been shy about going after American stereotypes.

But then again, the Golene's and Glulene's of Vermal appear to have been based, or at least inspired by Canadian hillbillies. Back in the late eighties and early nineties a series of raids on a backwoods Nova Scotia family created national headlines. The Goler clan, mostly illiterate, mostly unemployed, seasonal laborers and truck farmers living partially on social assistance, had been an isolated extended family in the recesses of the Annapolis valley, but soon they were the subject of newspaper stories alleging lurid tales of inter-generational incest, violence, mass child abuse and even darker hints. The stories shocked a complacent Canadian society, which had always taken its relative affluence for granted.

It's not clear that the Golers were the direct inspiration for Pa and his brood. But they were so prominent in the newspapers in the area for a time that I think it's impossible to argue that they weren't in the back of the creator's minds.

"Of course we talked about the Golers," Cordell Wynne admits. *"They were right there in Nova Scotia, this was a Nova Scotia crew, everyone read the*

newspapers. It was how we explained the idea to the crew, how we thought about it."

I don't believe there was a one to one correlation. There's no correspondence with any one member of the clan, or any incident reported in the papers. Rather, it's more along the lines of someone going, *'Let's do a hillbilly episode'* and someone else going, *'Hillbillies? You mean, like the Golers?'* For the production at least, the Golers were a sort of mental shorthand.

The other big problem for many people, apart from its obvious trailer park stereotypes in space kind of thing, is that the LEXX crew are almost bystanders in their own show.

Instead, the show is about the final fall of the Golene Clan. If you watch and listen, the writers artfully slip the family's backstory in, a tale of illicit romance, of murder, of a possessive insane domineering father. It's a story that isn't simply told, but woven, each retelling, by adding a newer darker layer. The family story is rendered again and again, first by Pa, then by Sissy and then by Norb, each telling adding a new perspective, revealing a few more secrets. Each reference adds a little more. I find this a really interesting, layered approach to backstory, there's a Tennessee Williams quality to it.

That in itself sets the show apart, since often in episodic television, the guest characters that the main cast encounters are almost ahistorical. They're only significant when they step into the episode and cease to be important once they're gone. Their lives, their previous adventures, their goals are only tangentially. Here, there is a whole different life on display, and literally, it takes over.

The episode stops being LEXX and becomes the saga of the Golene. And of course, the fact that the story is actually around the guest cast, Pa and his brood, also complicates this cognitive dissonance, because we're continually watching the wrong characters, Stan, Xev and Kai. We're not sure who we should be focusing on, or rooting for.

I spoke to one of the crew about this, just to test the idea out, (Because when I pitched it to Lex Gigeroff, he just stared at me blankly.)

"Well," they said, *"I think that's probably a weakness of the writing. A more polished professional writer would have focused the script better rather than allow it to drift. The 'A' story should always be about the main cast."*

With all due respect, I kind of like it this way. Not every story has to be written according to some formula set in Los Angeles and which was stale thirty years ago. I see **White Trash** as an experiment in storytelling, and I don't necessarily see that something a little unfamiliar is automatically bad. I'm not even prepared to say that **White Trash** fails as an experiment in storytelling, only that it's different.

White Trash is one of the earliest LEXX episodes. A reasonable version of it appears in a June, 1996, series outline. In that version, the Golene family consists of Pa, a Mistress/ Concubine, two grown sons and a little boy. The Christian Murray part is a 'man in a stunning gold suit' who winds up in LEXX's food processor, Stan notices bits of gold suit and a gold ring in his meal. Pa is still possessive of his daughter, especially because he's suspicious that Stan is interested in her mind, rather than her body. The two grown sons kidnap Zev, but 790 talks the little boy into helping them rescue her, which results in LEXX blasting an asteroid belt into rubble to force the moth out of hiding....

By the December, 1997, outline, the story has taken its current form. The mistress/concubine and one of the grown sons has been abandoned, as much for budget as story reasons, and the Little Boy has grown his own subplot as the son of a space pilot.

Key scenes and ideas are consistent in both versions, and in the screen version. For instance, Stan encounters the Golene clan in the galley of the LEXX. Cissy has a thing for Stan, much to Pa's annoyance. Zev, willingly or unwillingly goes off with the older son. And Pa is a glorious psychopath who wants to assume Captaincy of the LEXX.

The writers seemed to like the notion of the Golene saga. According to a series outline from June, 1996, Pa Golene and possibly his daughter, Cissy, survive **White Trash** and Pa reappears in two lost episodes, *Sniff the Bliss* and the **original Brigadoom**. According to the later series outline from December, 1997, Pa Golene survives **White Trash** and reappears in **Love Grows** (which was to take place after this episode) and then again in the original version of **Brigadoom**. There may have been some notion of keeping Pa handy as a comic relief plot device/character, sort of a low brow equivalent to Lyekka/Wist.

This seems somewhat surprising considering Maury Chaykin took the role. Chaykin is one of the most successful Canadian actors, appearing in almost every Canadian television and film production and in a great many Hollywood productions. I'd be surprised that Chaykin had the time, or that the producers had the budget, for a semi-regular role on LEXX. But then again, perhaps a more regularly available actor was in mind for the role.

Chaykin's performance is both the weakness and the strength of the episode. Pa's is the story that is at the core of **White Trash**, and when you look at it as "*The Tragedy of Pa Golene*" then it falls into place, and Stan, Xev and Kai literally become supporting players.

Chaykin's Pa is a larger than life character, inherently dangerous, full of quicksilver unpredictability, a man capable of anything. The guy is also a human cartoon, literally a crayon drawing of every stereotyped redneck myth there is. But Chaykin also takes the character across the emotional range; Pa is literally different in every scene, jubilant, lustful, full of murderous rage, playful in flight, petulant and often at the oddest times. Think of his final conversation with Norb, the fondness for the boy when he says "*Aw, I knew that...*"

Chaykin moves the character smoothly from one dramatic mood shift to the next, always affecting the unconscious menace of a true psychopath. In some ways, Chaykin's portrait reminds me a little of Dennis Hopper's Frank in **Blue Velvet**.

Chaykin is normally a much more serious and restrained actor. In fact, some members of the crew thought he took himself too seriously and considered himself an ""*Actor*"" (But then again, Kim Boyd, who worked on the show as 3rd Assistant Director said, *"Maury is an interesting person, he's had some pretty major Hollywood films as a character actor, and he doesn't boast about it."*)

Chaykin had worked for Donovan in a couple of previous movies. He was in **George's Island** for instance. He also appeared in **DefCon 4** where he played, wait for it, a redneck cannibal with a sexual appetite for teenage girls (typecasting?). Here, however, he's almost completely unrestrained.

The quicksilver nature of Chaykin's performance is balanced by Susan Dalton as Cissy. Again, think back to the almost detached way she originally relates her mother's death, you almost have to think about it, perform an intellectual double take to realize her father murdered her mother.

When she 'seduces' Stan, it's not romantic but it is irrepressibly joyful, it is sex as a wonderful carefree thing without commitment or baggage, it's a deliriously charming and dirty scene. In fact, almost every scene where she's with Stan is a delight. They have wonderful chemistry together.

She's wonderful to watch in scenes with Chaykin, because her character is literally managing Pa. Watch how in an initial background scene, she literally watches over her brother. She watches Pa continually edging close to conversations, glancing at his expressions, responding to his quicksilver changes of mood, constantly defusing and managing his tempers, trying to head off the violence that's always under the surface. She's a sane person trapped with a maniac, always needing to stay a step ahead of him to keep herself and others alive.

But there are a couple of moments when Pa's attention is on something or someone else, and if you watch carefully, her smile fades and her look is one of pure contempt. And when she stands up to Pa, it's an amazing scene.

Interestingly, one of Paul Donovan's (creator of LEXX) earlier films was **Life With Billy** (Starring Steven McHattie who guest stars in episode 2.3, **Lyekka**) the story of an abusive, murderous, wife-beating, small-town bully and his abused wife. Based on a true story, and a book of the same name it's an interesting and sometimes quite disturbing look at domestic violence and dysfunction. With **White Trash**, in Pa and Cissy, Donovan returns to the theme, treated now in a cartoonish but effective way.

The final standout performance is Brandon McCarvell's Norb. Comparisons are irresistible between Norb and the **Star Wars: The Phantom Menace's** young Anakin Skywalker. They're both painfully precocious kids with father issues, rather astonishing technical ability who wind up piloting fighters and wear these oversized pilots helmets. But of the two, Norb is the darker and more interesting. Anakin Skywalker is basically a dumbed down Tom Sawyer who seems to walk about in a cloud of cheerful obliviousness. Norb is sharp, he watches things, he has brooding secrets and his own agenda, and yet, he has his boyish elements and bursts of enthusiasm. He just seems more real to me.

Norb's last minute escape from certain death to freedom is a highlight of the episode. Partly, this is because it's well timed and well done. His little ship racing down the length of the LEXX is visually stunning. But it also works because the Beans mean business. The creators have never hesitated to kill or maim what appeared to be main characters; they've wiped out whole civilizations and planet after planet. So, if the audience is wondering if they'd hesitate to off a ten year old boy.... They shouldn't wonder too long. In LEXX, particularly, there's a real chance that Norb isn't going to make it, and when he does, it's that much more thrilling.

This episode also features some fascinating little cameo appearances. Michael McManus, in addition to playing Kai, also dons a cowboy hat and blond wig and becomes the lasso swinging Vermal who ropes junior. He can be seen in several scenes.

I've never had a good explanation for just what the hell Michael McManus was doing there.

"He just wanted to try something different," shrugs Jeff Hirschfield, *"he was bored I guess."*

That makes sense, the role of a dead man probably left McManus wanting to play a bit now and then.

In light of the numerous reincarnations of characters in the third and fourth season, including two separate reincarnations of a 'living Kai', and in light of Prince's comments in **The Game** that Kai's living essence, separated from his physical form is drifting around the universe, being born and reborn, it's tempting to see this *'Cowboy Kai'* as the first of the living Kai's, and a subtle foreshadowing of the metaphysical subplots of the later seasons.

Michael McManus in particular, seems prone to over thinking these sorts of things, so I wouldn't put it past him to consciously play the cowboy as a live version of his dead character, or to lay on a metaphysical conceit.

Tempting, but not necessarily accurate - there's no evidence that the writers or anyone else at this time were thinking along these lines. On the other hand, this wasn't something I asked anyone about. My inclination is that it probably wasn't an explicit conscious thing. But I think that there may have been an unconscious element. And I tend to believe that events like this one started the ball rolling in certain directions, casting the same faces, may have inspired certain thinking.

Still, the fact remains that it is there. A literary evaluation of the series as a whole, without reference to the backstage stuff, might well make a reasonable case for foreshadowing. And who knows, there might have been some subconscious or subliminal stuff at work.

Cowboy Kai isn't even the first reappearing cast member. Writers Lex Gigeroff and Jeff Hirschfield, and actors - Holger Kunkel in Germany, John Dunsworth from Halifax, and Patricia Zentilli from

Toronto, all played at least two different characters. Halifax particularly was a small acting community; you were likely to see the same faces again and again.

It's not like the writers weren't noticing. So that's suggestive. Further to that, the idea of reincarnation, or of people living again, was implicit in the first season's theme of a circular universe, and time cycling again and again. Throw in Paul Donovan's fondness for working with people he's enjoyed working with before, and the reincarnation tropes of the third and fourth season seem like an almost inevitable development.

Besides, Maury Chaykin, in addition to his role as Pa Golene, also has a cameo second role, as Pappy Glulene, Pa's nemesis. No good explanation for that either.

Christian Murray appears early on as the 'Gold Lame Man' although his costume appears to be that of a fleet officer from the Divine Order.

The 'gold lame' credit appears to derive from the original concept of the character in the earlier drafts and outlines - remember that the remains are fed into the LEXX's system, and Stan finds gold threads. There seems to have been a last minute costume change that didn't make it to the credits.

"When I got there, the costume was different and they never changed the credit. That was my big scene, I was eaten by Maury Chaykin," he laughs. Christian also appeared in **Twilight**, wearing a robot head as 792, and he's written for Salter Street series including **This Hour Has 22 Minutes** and **Daily Thoughts For Modern Living**.

Jon Kristopher Loverin, who plays another redneck, Gloodel, would return to LEXX in small roles. He shows up as a handler in the third season episodes **Fire and Water** and **May**. He also appeared as a prison executioner in fourth season opener **Little Blue Planet**.

Finally, there were a couple of funky surreal images that helped to make the episode. There's an amazing, and totally unscientific rendition of the planet Vermal, looking like a green rotting fruit. And there's an equally amazing view of a ringed planet with a hole through it, so it's shaped like a donut, that Stan accidentally blows up.

The donut planet may not be quite so unscientific. I'm told it's a Weizsacker Object, named after a German theoretical physicist or mathematician who posited that under some circumstances, you could actually have a stable toroid (donut) shaped cosmic body. When first told of this, I thought it was an obvious joke, 'Weizsacker = wise acre,' but apparently both the physicist and his theories were real.

I'm pretty sure that the guys who came up with the donut planet had never heard of a Weizsacker Object. They just wanted to do it because it looked cool. That's fair.

Frankly, I suspect that the creators didn't really have anything special in mind here. They didn't want to think about it, they just wanted to do something wild and off the wall. They got their wish.

Behind the scenes, it seems like everyone had a good time working on this one. Brian Downey once told me it was his favorite show of the second season. Everyone seemed to have a blast.

"That was the redneck inbreeding episode," Kim Boyd exclaimed. *"Oh my god! There was a line in that just went on and on! 'Party on Vermal!' It floated on the set for days and days and days! 'Party on Vermal!' that was the planet. That phrase just would not die! The Germans loved that, they loved the sound of it!"*

Party on Vermal, maybe it's not any more complicated than that.

CREDITS

Creators: *Writers - Lex Gigeroff, Paul Donovan and Jeff Hirschfield; Director - Chris Bould; Production Designer - David Hackl; Creative Producer - Cordell Wynne;*

Main Cast: Brian Downey *(Captain Stanley Tweedle); Michael McManus (Kai, Last of the Brunnen G); Xenia Seeberg (Xev Bellringer, Rejected Wife/Love Slave/Cluster Lizard); Jeffrey Hirschfield (Voice of 790); Tom Gallant (Voice of LEXX).*

Guest Cast: *Maury Chaykin (Pa Golene/Pappy Glulene); Susan Dalton (Sissy Golene); Dave Carmichael (Junior Golene); Brandon McCarvell (Kid/Norb); Jon Loverin (Gloodel); Karl Lewis Johnson (Glootus); Christian Murray (Gold Lame Man); Michael McManus (Cowboy Vermal)*

Lost LEXX, Sniff the Bliss

Story

The LEXX lands on the militantly politically correct Planet Carob. *(Handwritten note - The crew really really need some rest to stay on this one. LEXX must be getting low on some needed resource....)*

Our heroes are welcomed into the main commune, but must follow the strict rules which include learning about crystals, developing recipes for vegetarian chili and renouncing the patriarchy. Visits to the Museum of the Oppressive Male are mandatory. *(Handwritten note - All signs must be obeyed and all things to do with any bodily function have euphemisms to describe them. A bathroom for instance, is a 'daily use body waste disposal site.')*

Stan becomes enamored with one of the female leaders on the planet. Under her influence and because he wants to please her, he is converted to the cause, becoming the ultimate zealot. He turns on Kai and Zev because they aren't buying it.

However his new 'consenting yet still independent partner in sharing' refuses to sleep with him until he reaches the 'Seventh Level of Enlightenment' which involves a lot of gender neutral education and tree planting.

Things go awry when Stan is caught flirting with a teenage student. In fact, she is the one who turns him in. The penalty for such a heinous crime is death: A horrible ordeal where the offender is turned into compost. Kai and Zev are already in prison, punished for missing their turn doing the dishes.

But this new age planet has a dirty little secret... Fat people are kept in squalid camps, deemed failures of the regime. They are assumed to be gluttons who consume more than their share and aren't able to contribute as much to the common good.

With the help of Pa Golene, Zev and Kai escape prison and rescue Stan. With Kai and Zev's help, the fat people succeed in taking over the planet. The former rulers are all forced to eat meat dipped donuts and watch nude mud wrestling. Our heroes wave goodbye to the fat people and take off in the LEXX. The new rulers of the planet are in for a grand future...

....except that moments after the LEXX disappears, the PLANET EATING FORCE rolls through and eats the entire planet. (Special thanks to Brian Downey)

Commentary

Sniff the Bliss, Dorkadia and **Lafftrack** all seem to fit in with each other as very specific and very vicious social satires. Although only **Lafftrack** ultimately made it into existence, the three episodes give us an insight into the sort of thinking that was originally going on during the early development of the show. Essentially, take some aspect of Earth life, blow it up to outrageous proportions, and then whale the tar out of it.

A lot of this stuff seems heavy handed. Feminists, nerds and couch potatoes? Oh yeah, we're going after the controversial targets there. Ultimately, **Sniff the Bliss** doesn't seem to have gotten much past the June 28, 1996, series outlines. Which is probably just as well.... Meat dipped donuts? Yuck.

One point of interest is the appearance of Pa Golene, called 'Daddy' in the early drafts and outlines. In the June 28, 1996, outline, the Golene saga appeared here, in **White Trash** and in the early **Brigadoom**.

In the December, 1997, outline, this episode was dropped, but Pa was moved to the early Love Grows and his son would appear in The Little Boy/Norb. For whatever peculiar reason, the Golene family was planned to appear early on and repeatedly.

In fact, they were more established than Wist, who was only going to reappear in one episode in the 1996 outlines. Who would have thought? They must have just liked the idea of a violent, homicidal, bisexual hillbilly chieftain in outer space.

LEXX 2.09, '791'

Story

The crew of the LEXX are dozing when a distress signal comes in. The signal is ignored until Lyekka wakes from her pod, needing to eat. She proposes to investigate the distress signal, to see if there's anyone she can eat. This makes Xev uncomfortable, and Kai raises the issue of keeping a homicidal predator on board, but Lyekka states she's not easy to kill.

Xev, Kai and Lyekka go down to the planet where the distress signal is from, with Kai suggesting they leave Lyekka down there. Once on the planet, Lyekka goes off on her own. The others discover it is a crashed prison ship with survivors. While Xev and Kai try and rescue the survivors, 790 finds the headless body of a cyborg guard and begins working at reanimating it, so it can have a body to make love to Xev. While the others are occupied, Lyekka starts eating the survivors.

790 manages to activate the cyborg and join with the body, but things don't go well. The cyborg's body takes control and turns out to be a sexual psychopath. It lures Stanley down to the planet and then terrorizes him. Stanley tries and fails to eject the cyborg out an airlock.

The only survivor, a warrior named Desh, turns on Xev and Kai, trapping them and escaping in a moth. But she's eaten by Lyekka, who then rescues Xev and Kai. Kai then saves Stanley from cyborg rape by taking off 790's head. The four return to the LEXX. The crashed ship blows up.

Review & Commentary

791 is an almost perfect LEXX episode, even the harshest, most self-critical members of the LEXX crew look back on it with a certain amount of pride. It's wicked and witty, rude, profane, shamelessly mixing genres, sexy and it all pulls together. The inspiration is obvious, of course: Alien.

But it's a cynically fun take on Alien. When 790 receives the distress call, he simply ignores it, reasoning that no good can come of it. It's startling but unassailable logic.

Then there's the journey down to the hostile planet, the strange journey through a labyrinthine alien space ship, encounter strange bodies of the former crew and even make a passage down an oddly vaginal tunnel. Kai, when he encounters what he thinks might be 'some sort of alien pod,' sticks his face right in it. It's a scene that originally occurred in **Gigashadow** when Kai stuck his face into what turned out to be a Cluster Lizard pod, but it works again. None of us watching can help but riff on that same scene in Alien

But **Alien** is only the starting point. From that point on the episode begins to mutate in all sorts of strange ways, suddenly **Alien** becomes **Frankenstein,** morphs into **Cruising**, and for one delirious scene its **Saturday Night Live**. The script bears Hirschfield's anarchic style.

"It was always the idea," Jeff Hirschfield notes, *"it was even Paul's idea actually, that 791 would turn on Stan. But I'm the guy who gets to write it out specifically. And so making him dance, the filthy filthy lines, 'sizzle my pizzle' 'I can smell your funk' and all that sort of thing is mine. The decision was to make it rude, but maybe I'm the rudest. (Laughs) That might be it."*

Despite the anarchy of the plot twists, each of the characters behaves rationally, at least for them. Bad writing is when the characters actions are dictated by the needs of the script, rather than being believable responses of a particular personality to a particular situation. Here, everyone does what's expected of them.

Xev goes down to rescue people, she's established herself as a person willing to try and care about people. 790 is completely indifferent of course, Stan would rather stay where it's safe or go someplace pleasant and Kai simply doesn't care.

Lyekka goes down to eat. Her motivation is very simple, she needs to feed, there isn't anything deeper than that. She's so elemental she's almost sweet. For once, Kai and Xev question the wisdom of keeping a predator on the ship, or the morality of her eating people they're trying to rescue.

When 790 finds a headless body, we know exactly what he wants to do with it. Stan is lured down by the assurance of safety and the promise of beautiful girls. Even the sociopathic cyborg 791 and the innocent seeming but murderous Desh fulfill their roles.

Everyone, except perhaps Kai, has a separate agenda, be it altruistic or selfish with no regard for anyone else, and the chaos emerges quite naturally as a result of these crossed purposes.

Having said that, the story only opens the door for such bizarre touches as Stan's disco dance scene, or a relentlessly aggressive homosexual robot with gimlet eyes and fanged mouth going *"I can smell your funk, Stanley!"*

The costumes and casting were almost perfect. Amy Kerr projects sweet innocence, jaw dropping sensuousness and lethal sociopathy in turn. Her costume is absolutely stunning.

"Costume people just think of actors as meat to be wrapped," Mark Laing, the Production Designer, recalls, *"so we didn't have any warning when Jill Aislin called the Director and myself in to take a look at Amy in her costume. She was just the sweetest girl, but when we walked in there and saw her in these astonishing little wisps of latex, our mouths just dropped, our tongues rolled right out. It was astounding. I wish we'd have been able to spend more time on it, Amy's coming out of her pod had the potential to go down in history as a defining moment of fetish television. As it is...."*

Brian Carter's outfit was ultra-masculine; the tall muscular black actor was outfitted in eight inch platform boots and bronzed football padding with stereo accessories. The effect was to make him a walking muscle car, the epitome of every racist homophobic nightmare.

In short, the episode succeeds on almost every level, both in terms of character, in a chaotic but logical story, to a succession of surreal and bizarre scenes, to its overall look and texture. It's funny, it's funky and it's rude to the core.

Almost as interesting as the episode itself was the circumstances of its shooting, which has almost an epic quality of hardship to it.

"We went into the guts of Electropolis where no human was ever intended to bring a film crew," Mark Laing recalls, his voice lowering. *"It was hard on the crew, we went up, we went down, we went up. It was a tough one to pull all together."*

Electropolis was originally a power plant, before it was renovated and turned into a big sound stage/film complex. But before that happened, the plant stood empty yea so many years, which meant that after a while, what with rats and pigeons and various forms of decay, it got to be pretty unpleasant in there. The power plant was eventually renovated into a film production stage with one of the biggest green screens in the world, and became a home for LEXX and yea there was much rejoicing.

But the upper floor wasn't renovated. Nope, the upper floor was left alone, with its accumulation of thirty years of bat droppings, pigeon droppings, rat feces, with its populations of rats, bats, pigeons, dung beetles, earwigs, cutworms, new species of mold and vermin practically spontaneously generating, building their own little toxic ecosystems and minding its own business.

"It was my idea to shoot up there because it looked interesting." Willie Stevenson says. *"But we're talking about a pigeon shit infested long disused power plant. We had the place worked over by a safety guy, railings put up and everything, but it was still pretty tough..."*

When they were up there, everyone but the actors wore masks, and there were strict instructions not to rub our eyes or touch your face with your hands. I'm not sure what would have happened if they had, but it probably wouldn't have been pretty.

The place didn't even have plumbing or power going to it. So all the equipment, the lights, the cameras, hundreds of pounds of stuff had to be lugged up those stairs by a handpicked team of sweating, cursing, groaning Himalayan Sherpas at time and a half. And let's not forget the power cables that had to be run downstairs to make it all work.

Since they were using 'found space,' they didn't have the advantages of a set where the layout is designed to accommodate camera and lights. Instead, they had to work camera, lighting, sound and equipment in and around the geography of a space which had never been intended for it.

At other times, people had complained about the heat in Electropolis. One would imagine that it was or would become be extra hot up there, factor in lack of ventilation, lack of air conditioning and all those hot studio lights that they need to shoot the thing... Let's just say, if people looked a little sweaty during this episode, there's a reason for it. Oddly, according to Brian, heat wasn't a big issue.

Are we getting a picture here? Smothering dry, the air thick with dust and vermin, every surface coated with the residue of acidic droppings, hundreds of pounds of delicate equipment having to be carried up by hand, everything heavier, slower, more laborious and awful. Think of it: Sixteen hours a day, day after day.

So basically, we're talking 'location shoot in hell' with the only upside being that maybe they didn't have to travel so far to find a decent bathroom.

No one was having a good time here. Guest star Brian Carter, who played the 791 cyborg had to wear a 790 helmet, a claustrophobic experience at the best of times. But in this case, the helmet had to be fitted with electronics, screens and cables to display the facial features. Back in **I Worship His Shadow** smaller actors had worn 790 heads, but their face screens hadn't been animated. In some shots here you can see that the 790 head has actually been pulled apart and bolted together to fit onto Carters head. It must have been unbelievably uncomfortable, heavy, awkward and claustrophobic.

"And dangerous," Sven Bergman offered. *"His face was right up against all those wires and electronics. If something went wrong..."*

I never had the chance to interview Carter, but I did talk to Christian Murray, who'd worn a functioning robot head in Twilight, playing 792. Here's how he described the experience,

"The helmet for 792. It was pretty bad, actually. I had no visual perspective, so I didn't know if I was walking into a rut. The electronics were rigged in there. They worked hard to get that, I had the cord coming out the back of my head, so I could only be face on with the camera. I couldn't have my back to the camera at certain times. I could only see about a foot in front of my feet. That was my world for five days."

Murray was comparatively lucky in that the script, or perhaps circumstances called for his robot to be slow moving, and he was working inside the studio where it was flat and safe. Carter, on the other hand, was forced to navigate around the treacherous wilds of Electropolis' upper floor, going up and down stairs, sneaking out from behind corners and moving around crowded rooms, that's a whole other challenge.

The script and storyboards called for almost catlike movement and gymnastic contortions from 791. In one when the Cyborg closes in on Stan's it's hiding up on the ceiling on a huge pipe, and gracefully swings onto the catwalk before him. There was no way that was going to happen.

Another scene that didn't make it into the finished version was, early on when 790 is struggling to remotely operate the cyborg body, at one point after picking up 790's head, the torso of the body swivels completely around and starts jamming the robot head, face first, against the cyborg butt cheeks. Obviously, they decided it would just take a little too much time. Of course, considering that Brian Carter could barely or simply couldn't see at all out of that mask and was wearing eight inch platforms, they wisely decided to forego calisthenics which might get him killed and left Carter stomping clumsily like a Boris Karloff monster.

Amy Kerr, who played the murderous Desh, didn't have it much better. *"I spent a lot of the shooting days literally crouched in a box, covered with freezing ultrasound jelly, waiting to poke my head out of the pod. That odd tremor in my leg after I crawl out of the pod is real, or it was originally. I'd been in the box so long crouched in an awkward position that I got a mild muscle cramp. The Director, when he saw it, liked it so much that we kept it, and so I had to do it for every take."*

It's a good decision. That gentle tremor gives the crouching Desh an almost inhuman quality, she's like those newborn colts or antelopes who minutes after being born are ready to get up and start running. Desh, literally moments after freedom, is ready to start killing again.

Amy's appearance as Desh in **791** was recycled as a flashback in the third season episode, **The Beach**, and footage of her also appeared in **Rated: LEXX**, the broadcast version.

In the fourth season, she reappeared as an extra in five separate episodes, playing one of a group of schoolgirls who keep showing up in backgrounds. *"There was almost no difference in how I was treated from being a guest star to being an extra. Everyone was very nice and treated me the same. The only thing was that as an extra, I didn't get a dressing room."*

I found her to be a charming young woman, interestingly; her voice is quite high pitched. She told me it was digitally lowered in the episode.

John Dunsworth, returning again as Berk, the guy who spits on Kai, also spent his time crouching in a box. *"That was one of my favorites,"* he remembers. *"I really got into that part. Sometimes you do a role and it's a tiny thing and you're over and you're on your way. But sometimes you get into them. I really got into that, and we did it in one take. I wanted to do it three more ways. I was so involved with this story about this guy who desperately wanted to get free and clear, but he just had so much venom in him. Climbing down into that thing and coming out covered with goop, I think it must have connected with something in my soul."*

Dunsworth had appeared in **I Worship His Shadow** and Gigashadow and would reappear next in **Brigadoom**. Mike Pellerin, the other head in a pod would also reappear in an upcoming episode of LEXX.

The egg pods themselves were designed by Mark Laing, who spent a lot of time and effort on them; they were almost a labor of love.

The crashed spaceship was another model built by Dave Albiston, its Bridge and its Cargo section are separate modules connected by a long tether/corridor. The overall result is that we're looking at the corpse of some long necked dinosaur as much as we're looking at a derelict space ship. It's a subtle tip of the hat to the organic curving ship of Alien, and to the biomechanical sensibility of LEXX.

Interestingly, the Stripper ship from Love Grows also consists of separate modules separated by a tether. Coincidence? One ship is a model, the other is CGI. It may simply have been a cool look, or perhaps both ships were intended to come from the same civilization.

Behind the scenes, one of the most interesting choices was the director, Jorg Buttgereit. Who is this guy? And how do you pronounce that name? Well, I can't help you on the second count.

But as to who he is?

Why he's just Germany's most warped film maker.

Jorg hit fame, or at least notoriety, with a nifty little piece of work called **Nekromantic,** about a coroner's wagon attendant and his girlfriend who are into sex with corpses. He brings his work home with him. They have fun. She leaves, taking the stiff with her. The boyfriend mopes around kills a prostitute and then does something extremely graphic. **Nekromantic II** is an unrelated sequel about a man dating a necrophiliac, which personally, I'd consider a major lapse of judgement. There's an amazingly funny deadpan moment when he's bustling around her apartment, and finds a set of leftover male sexual organs in the fridge. He also did **Schramm** and **Der Toddking**, in case you're wondering, Todd is German for Death.

Buttgereit's films are actually banned in a great many countries. They're weird little numbers, half art house productions, half gore flicks, with an odd sense of humor running through them that most people don't pick up on, simply because the subject matter is so bizarre and grotesque. Half hip humorist, half gross out territory, and all low budget art house films, he's established a unique reputation. Certainly, I doubt if there's anything else like them out there. Unfortunately, his experience with LEXX didn't turn out very well.

Brian Downey thinks Jorg got a bit of a raw deal, *"The shoot was so physically brutal, with the heat, the droppings, the need to drag every piece of equipment up there, and working with a raw location rather than a set built for the purpose, that he couldn't help but experience problems."*

Brian may have a point, because the experience really does come across as a remote location shoot, with all of the hardships attendant. That's a brutal row for any young director to cope with.

On the other hand, Paul Donovan, who's the man who decides, felt that Jorg's style as a director just didn't cope with the demands of a television production. In his art house films, he's got the luxury to take a walk around the block and think his next shot over. On the other hand shooting an episode calls for a brutal pace, sixteen hour days, eight days or so to get the episode in the can. Buttgereit's more relaxed approach just didn't mesh with the pace of television production.

I think they've probably both got a point. Buttgereit came from the stop and start world of art house cinema, where you don't have money but you've got nothing but time. I know people who've worked on their low budget art house feature for five years. So he was probably somewhat unprepared for the more rigorous and immediate demands of a television shooting schedule. Maybe he could have coped better under less trying circumstances, but 791 sounds like a bad shoot to try and cut your teeth on.

The result was extensive re-shoots. But of course re-shoots became a running joke through the second season, and were not confined here. Partly, this may have been a result of a number of new directors. Often scenes had to be re-shot or the coverage was inadequate, resulting in the budget and production schedule slowly going off the rails.

Still, the results in this case speak for themselves.

"791, in the end, was quite a good show. It looked good," Willie Stevenson, concludes. *"What made it? Work. Simple as that."*

CREDITS

Creators: *Writers - Jeff Hirschfield and Paul Donovan; Director - Jorg Buttgereit; Production Designer - David Hackl and Mark Laing; Creative Producer - Willie Stevenson*

Main Cast: *Brian Downey (Captain Stanley Tweedle); Michael McManus (Kai, Last of the Brunnen G); Xenia Seeberg (Xev Bellringer, Rejected Wife/Love Slave/Cluster Lizard); Jeffrey Hirschfield (Voice of 790); Tom Gallant (Voice of LEXX).*

Guest Cast: *Louise Wischermann (Lyekka); Brian Carter (Cyborg/791); Amy Kerr (Desh); John Dunsworth (Berk); Mike Pellerin (Were);*

LEXX 2.10, Wake the Dead

Story

The LEXX comes across a drifting derelict spaceship bearing a resemblance to a Volkswagen Van. Stan wants to ignore it. Xev insists on checking it out, and ends up rescuing four teenagers, Tad and Canana, the good girl and boy, Enox the troublemaker, Laleen the slutty one, Gibble the fat nerd and who have been in cryosleep for 287 years. She brings them back to the LEXX and revives them.

Stan and Xev try and play host to the displaced teens, but there's a generation gap. Their slang and their attitudes are hard to grasp. They seem impressed by the LEXX, but kind of obnoxious. When shown Kai, they want to wake him up, something that Stan rejects. Later, they party.

After everyone goes to sleep, two of the teens, Enox and Gibble return to Kai's cryochamber, where they try and wake him up, ordering him to go crazy and kill everyone inventively. Stan shows up and chases them off.

But the damage is done, and Kai wakes up, looking yellow eyed and scary. He then proceeds to hunt down the teens one by one, murdering Gibble and Tad in inventive ways. Laleen makes out with Stan, but goes to take a shower and is killed there. Stan and Xev try and save Canana and Enox, but they are killed.

Finally, Stan and Xev are trapped on the bridge with Kai, as he tries to decide which one to kill first, and how. Just before he does it, he freezes and collapses, his protoblood having run out.

Review & Commentary

Wake the Dead is a fan favorite for two reasons, first because of Kai's outrageous rampage, and second, because the episode parodies slasher movies so effectively.

A bunch of partying teenagers on their way to a recreation planet where a previous bunch of partying teenagers were all horribly hacked to pieces takes a wrong turn in their spaceship and the next thing you know, they're on the LEXX.

Already a lot of the slasher movie clichés are established. We've got the virgin girl, the bad girl, the good boy, the fat kid and the wild boy. They're off on their own for a party. There's the obligatory reference to the previous massacre. Even getting lost on the way is a standard trope. Of course, we've got the false scares, the flirting and partying. There are the obligatory 'sensitive teens talking about life' moments.

Where the episode really comes to life is when Kai becomes the unstoppable psycho killer. It's such a completely left field idea, but it's so logical and solves so many problems. Why go through the trouble of trying to import an unstoppable killing machine to slaughter the teenagers when you already have one on Board? And if it's Kai doing the killing, then we don't have to worry about how the murderer copes with the Brunnen G. The only problem is how to stop him, and that solution is built in as well.

Michael McManus recalled in a magazine interview with Paul Spragg, "**Wake the Dead** *was the second one Chris Bould directed, and we had to fight so, so much, both of us, knocking down all the people who were very nervous about that story, very nervous about Kai letting his hair down, about the extremity of it.*

Even the makeup girl was saying to the executive producer 'You can't do this. The girls won't love Kai any more, because this show is terrible! He can't look ugly and he can't put his hair down.' We're going, 'What are you talking about? Rock 'n' rollers for years have been dining out on exactly those fucked up kind of things.' That show gets more romantic response than anything else

I've ever done! People really like it and find it really sexy. It was a pleasure to shoot, great to do and a lot of fun."

The really interesting thing about that story is that a lowly 'make up girl' was able to go up to the Executive Producer, Paul Donovan himself, and bitch out. In Hollywood, or Toronto or anyplace else, storm clouds would gather, the wrath of God would descend, and the little production person would be a smear on the sidewalk. That this could happen at all, is a little glimpse into the world of Salter Street, and into Paul Donovan.

But actually, it does work, the whole yellow eyed thing, the hair in disarray, the way he staggers around like a Goth Sasquatch. This was director Chris Bould's second episode, his first was the flawed **White Trash**. But here, Bould and McManus hit their stride with wild invention and manic enthusiasm"

"I said, 'Let's take Michael's hair down and bring him out of the toilet!'" Bould exclaims, *"I guess subconsciously, there was a bit of **Trainspotting** (Scottish movie about fun loving heroin addicts) in me. They said 'You can't do that, he's got a bunhead.' No, if we're going to go major psycho, this is a great opportunity. It was great fun. I built a little see saw so we could lift him up through the toilets. Just about every bit of that episode was done in camera. We actually flew Michael through the air. That wasn't CGI, that was Michael. He just went sky high. They said, 'Oh we need a wire man, a stunt man.' We just said 'Bugger off.' I said, 'Smack your wrist! Smack your wrist, like getting your protoblood!' Then he just takes off, goes sky high! There were mandates from Paul Donovan, 'You can't look into the camera, you can't go handheld.' Michael, when he comes down in the shower to Patricia, I put him on a skateboard, pulled him along, he looked right into the camera. Les Krizsan was going, 'We'll all get fired' I said, no it's a perfect opportunity, that's exactly what should happen."*

McManus plays a great psycho killer; he really does seem to be having the time of his life doing it. Interestingly, McManus's performance as Psycho-Kai seems to come closer to his real life personality than Kai does. Not, of course, that he hacks up teenagers in his spare time, but rather, the almost twitchy energy he brings to the role, the sense of attention scattering in all directions, the glib intensity all seems to be part of McManus's natural personality. Of course, all actors use themselves as the raw material for a performance, but still, McManus's normal Kai is much more restrained and still.

Both Xenia Seeberg and Brian Downey stretch their characters in this episode. Xev and Stan become almost parental figures. Xev, for instance, is only a little older than the teenagers, but she's almost a mother figure. She turns down chances for sex, even sending Tad away. When Canana attacks, Xev doesn't tear her apart but talks to her and has a moment of emotional intimacy.

Stanley, this time out, seems braver and more resolute, more of a captain. Perhaps it's because he's not being seriously challenged by the teens. Indeed, he occasionally comes across as the cranky old man. But overall, he seems more level headed and serious. He shows genuine anger, not a typical emotion for him. He also shows considerable courage when he tries to save Canana and remains on the LEXX to confront Kai, or when he offers himself first to Kai. Stan's not a brave man, but he can be brave.

But the stretches for Stan and Xev aren't quite the same as Kai. Kai, after all, snaps completely. The portraits of both are more natural extensions of their personalities. Stan, at heart is still a lecher and still frightened and insecure. Xev's libido and thirst for excitement remain. But both characters come to situations where they have to subdue their impulses.

The new elements work well. The spaceship, built by Dave Albiston, is based on an old Volkswagen van, but inside it's a riot of color. The teenagers themselves, even the 'good ones' are awash in tattoos and neon bright color. The underlying aesthetic of brutal functionalism remains, but it's overlaid with vibrant colors and shapes.

"That scene in the space van," Patricia Zentilli remembers. *"That was amazing. That scene, when we're in the van and Gibble wakes up, it was initially a really short scene. But Chris said, 'What a beautiful set! We have to do more in this!' So he made the scene longer."*

There's an understated suggestion that they're mining old material here. The Volkswagen van spaceship is more reminiscent of the 70's and 80's than it is to any futurist vision. It's a sly visual nod to the period and look of the genre. Even the 'teen' members are a strange mix of seventies and eighties and futurism, what you might get if you took the standard clichés of that day and projected into the future, throwing in modern tattoo, piercing and graffiti fetishes, which simultaneously makes them both anachronistic and futuristic. In fact even the teens themselves have been frozen in time for 286 years. They're literally fossils.

Part of the appeal of LEXX is that they're willing to have their characters do these things. Quite often, on shows like **Star Trek**, characters aren't allowed anything that might resemble a taint of imperfection.

For instance, in Paramount, all the **Star Trek** books were reviewed internally to make sure that they conform to the series characters and continuity. One of the persons in charge of this, apparently, had been a really big Ryker fan, and dead set against anything that besmirched her hero. So the poor bastard wasn't allowed to swear, to have one night stands, to go on a drunk, and even if he goes undercover to pretend to be a bad guy, they're not allowed to actually attribute anything bad to him. Basically, this gives us a character whose idea of cutting loose is to listen to mediocre jazz in the holo suite. If he had access to a holo suite, Stanley Tweedle wouldn't be listening to jazz.

LEXX is a show where Kai can go mental and slaughter the entire guest cast. So what? He's slaughtered thousands of innocent people as a Divine Assassin. It's a show where the crew lives with the fact that Lyekka eats humans. Stanley occasionally blows up a planet. Xev is allowed, not only to be a zombie, but to eat someone's brain. Poor Ryker will never be allowed to eat a brain.

Of course, it's not that they really want to do these things. But the fact that they can adds an element of unpredictability to the characters, it gives them a bit of extra range that keeps us watching. And there's an odd blasé aspect to it all. Kai doesn't really care, he's dead and he was malfunctioning, live with it. Xev seems a little embarrassed to have eaten someone's brain, like it's less of a moral issue than a kind of social faux pas, like farting in an elevator. Stan often seems absolutely horrified by these things, watching a guy get squashed like a bug or realizing his moth has crushed a person, and he does have nightmares about this kind of stuff, but apart from that, it doesn't change his basic character and he spares us all the pissing and moaning.

Let's face it, if Jean Luc Picard accidentally killed someone, it would be a 'big emotional moment' weighted with moral freight. Xev eats the occasional brain. Stanley accidentally kills six people before breakfast. They may be horrified, but then they have breakfast and gets on with their day.

I guess the moral of the story is that LEXX isn't good for us. But it's fun.

This wasn't one of the episodes originally planned for the series. In fact, by this time, the production schedule and budget was already beginning to force economies on the series. Episodes which had required extensive set construction were under pressure. What was needed was something which could take place on board the existing sets of the LEXX, with minimal new building.

It seems to have been one of the 'ship in a bottle' episodes created as the production schedule slowly drifted off the rails. It was done in a creative white heat; Jeff Hirschfield remembers that it was written in a week and a half from concept to first draft.

At a question and answer session, Paul Donovan talked about the genesis of that episode: *"Jeff was the main writer on that one. He wrote a couple of versions, I was really mean to him about them. But that was okay, because he likes that sort of thing. Finally, he got mad and went off and disappeared for several days. After a while, I called him up and asked him what he was up to. I said, 'I'm on to something.' One day, he showed up with it, and it was great we shot it almost unchanged. The guest star worked. Lauren Abrahams, who played Lomea had never acted before, she was in high school. She was fabulous. The other guest stars were hugely experienced, it was a good show."*

We pointed out that he seemed to be talking about **Twilight,** an episode starring Lauren Abrahams, Louis del Grande and Mary Walsh. Perhaps he was confused. Donovan just laughed. *"Yes, but it was the same thing happening on both with Jeff."*

** ** **

This was the first appearance in LEXX of the lovely Patricia Zentilli, who was kind enough to bless us with a shower scene as Laleen. Laleen, by the way, is from a planet called Bingo 44, which is a Maritime Provinces in-joke, though if you're a little old lady who goes to Catholic Church functions, you'll pick it up.

Chris Bould is credited with her discovery. *"I cast locally. In this particular show, I cast Patricia Zentilli. Wonderful actor, incredible funny bones. Very professional. She was terrific. I've had opportunities to work with her a few times since on LEXX."*

Almost by accident, Patricia turned into one of the major recurring characters on LEXX. She reappeared in **Brigadoom.** She featured in three episodes, and appeared in flashbacks or as a ghost in two more episodes, of the third season. She guest starred in nine episodes in the fourth season. That's a record that matches Ellen Dubin's or Louise Wischermann's, or even Eva Habermann's. Patricia is unique in that among the major actresses to grace the series, she never tried out for Zev. In fact, she's simply a unique and very lovely person.

"When I was fourteen I used to ride a unicycle to school. My parents emigrated from South America, Mom's side is from Poland and Dad's side is from Italy, I grew up in Halifax. I was the class clown. I wanted to be a clown. I went to study clowning in Switzerland when I was 16, then I went travelling, Africa for a year with Canada World Youth. Then I decided to go to Dalhousie University and studied acting for three years. I studied in the states at a place called Shakespeare and Company. It was good, meeting all these people; it got rid of my inferiority complex. I moved to Toronto, and kept getting work in Halifax. I did a lot of plays at Neptune, a lot of theater."

So how did she wind up on LEXX? It was a total fluke...

"I was down in Halifax doing a Leonard Cohen review, and there was an airline strike. So, I thought I'd look and see if there was something to audition for. I went to see the casting person, she said "there's LEXX, but they want sexy babes...."

OUCH!!!! That must have hurt.

"I went home; she called back and said 'The next episode is about teenagers. Could you play a teenager?"

Which makes me wonder, were the casting people blind? That's a cruel thing to say, but for god's sake, just look at her!

"I went and did wake the dead. It was a blast. I was a bit nervous. I had no idea about LEXX, I watched a few tapes. I had no idea who Kai was or why we were in space. It was my first big role in a TV show. I learned a lot and I got spoiled because Chris was amazing. He lets us discover things, make choices, and he gets really excited, which is fun."

"Except I had to be in the shower. It wasn't so bad. I was nervous. In the end, you saw my bum, but barely anything else. And it was kind of comedic. The tattoo? I had to go down to the tattoo parlor in Halifax, he'd draw it on with a permanent marker and the makeup woman had to touch it up every day. It took him about an hour to draw it on there."

CREDITS

Creators: *Writer - Jeffrey Hirschfield; Director - Chris Bould; Production Designers - Mark Laing and David Hackl; Creative Producer - Cordell Wynne;*

Main Cast: *Brian Downey (Captain Stanley Tweedle); Michael McManus (Kai, Last of the Brunnen G); Xenia Seeberg (Xev Bellringer, Rejected Wife/Love Slave/Cluster Lizard); Jeffrey Hirschfield (Voice of 790); Tom Gallant (Voice of LEXX).*

Guest Cast: *Andrew Bigelow (Tad, good boy); Andrew Bush (Enox, bad boy); Nicki Barnett (Canana, good girl); Bruce Fillmore (Gibble, fat boy); Patricia Zentilli (Laleen, bad girl)*

LEXX 2.11, Nook

Story

The LEXX approaches a planet covered completely by water, except for one small island. They decide to visit, and encounter a crude agricultural society made up exclusively of men. They form a semi-monastic order of brothers. Not only are there no women, they've never seen a woman, and have no idea what one is.

The crew decides to stay for a while. Xev finds all these men enticing, and most of them are equally fascinated. The two principal exceptions are Brother Traygor, who is more interested in Stan, and Brother Randor, who dislikes the visitors altogether, but tolerates them. Randor reveals to Kai that this settlement was founded long ago by great men who sought purity, and created a low tech male utopia, raising new men as clones. The society guards knowledge carefully, copying classic texts - but to avoid poisonous knowledge, copying brothers cannot read, and reading brothers cannot copy.

Brother Traygor is a copying brother who has broken his society's rules by secretly learning to read. He yearns for Stan, and after deliberation, Stan goes to meet him in an assignation. But when Stan arrives, Traygor has been murdered. Brother Randor blames the visitors and demands they be expelled, but the other Brothers of Nook are so innocent they don't even understand the idea of murder, and allow the crew to stay.

The Nookians are preparing a festival - the 'Night of No Rules' where they wear disguises and party. Xev goes as a cat, and takes off with three brothers to lose her virginity. Stan tries to sneak in, but is excluded. Kai follows Brother Randor, who confesses to having killed Brother Traygor. Brother Randor is convinced that his paradise has been tainted by the outsiders, particularly by a woman, and has activated the Island's self-destruct.

Unable to stop it, Kai flees with Xev and Stan. Watching them leave, Brother Randor delivers a sermon, as destruction overtakes the unsuspecting Nookians.

Review & Commentary

The original title of this episode, which first shows up in the December, 1997, outline was **The Unexamined Life**. It's a quote from an old philosopher which appears in the episode itself, "*the unexamined life is not worth living.*" He's dead now, and I can't remember his name, make of that what you will.

Actually, I fibbed: It's from Plato's '**Apology,**' attributed to Socrates, during his trial for corrupting the youth of Athens, by getting them to question their elders.

Sandwiched between **Wake the Dead** and **Norb**, this episode represents a change of pace. In contrast to the frantic activity, to the action and slapstick of the surrounding episodes, **Nook** is slow paced, almost sedate. The style is completely different, the camera dwells on scenes rather than moving briskly from one to the next, the characters make speeches, their dialogue rings with ideas.

In brief, the LEXX comes to this world which is entirely ocean, but for a single small island. On the island is an exclusively male colony, the Nookians, their leader, Brother Randor, tells the crew that they've lived there for generations without women, in a simple pastoral existence. Xev, seeing wall to wall men decides to stay a while. Stan's not thrilled, especially when one of the Nookians, Brother Traygor falls in love with him... Meanwhile, the '*Night of No Rules*' also known as the '*Night of Brotherly Love*' is coming up quickly.

More than a few viewers have compared this episode to the Sean Connery film **The Name of the Rose**, or the novel of the same name. There similarities are there. Both are murder mysteries set in a medieval monastic society, both are concerned with the import of secret knowledge. Having said that though, Nook goes further in terms of its identification of knowledge with sexuality and with identity. In some ways, the secret library in **The Name of the Rose** is a MacGuffin, here the importance and consequences of secret knowledge are turning points.

Nook also, or perhaps alternatively, seems to draw upon the Biblical story of Eden, a paradise untainted by knowledge or sexuality, into which worldliness comes. If so, then Donovan's got some harsh criticism for God, as represented by Brother Randor.

This is by far the gayest episode of LEXX, in its depiction of an exclusively male society. But is 'gay' a meaningful term here? The concepts of homosexuality and heterosexuality is a relatively modern concept, groups like the Romans, ancient Greeks, medieval Arabs or native Americans don't seem to have had such careful distinctions. Indeed, all-male colonies, the monasteries, were a staple of medieval Christianity.

Nevertheless, it's clear that Brother Traygor is genuinely gay, not just innocent of women. Unlike the other Brothers, he's not interested in Xev at all, but in Stan. He is also the one most clearly driven to challenge the restrictions of his society, a challenge that precedes our crew's arrival on his planet.

Oddly enough episode also has some of Xenia's most genuinely erotic moments in the series. In the massage sequence, her arousal and the growing arousal of the men around her is intensely sensuous. For once, Xev's lust isn't played for cheap laughs, but as genuine desire. Her flirtations with the men of Nook are both honest and charming.

Even the scene of her losing her virginity is genuinely fun, where it might have been anything but. The loss of virginity is off screen, of course, but the scenes leading up to it, where she flirts while dressed as a cat are engaging. She seems happy, excited and playful. She's like a little girl at a birthday party, just enjoying herself. Compare this with the sleazy encounter with the stripper ship Captain in **Love Grows**, or the antics in **Luvliner**. This episode presents the most positive and mature views of sexuality seen literally throughout the series.

Interestingly, she comes away from sex without any trace of guilt. There's often a puritanical attitude towards sex in film and television, even when sex is shown, it must be 'sex for the right reasons' I.e. - true love. Alternately, it has to be shown as a mistake, sex makes the girl a victim, she must suffer consequences which might range from remorse or regret, social censure, disease or pregnancy. But in this case, yes, she lost her virginity. She did it with three men, none of whom were the man she loves, but she has no misgivings at all. Xev comes out of her experience thoughtful, but without any regrets whatsoever. She did it, now she knows what it is; she's happy and absolutely unapologetic.

The model for the society of Nook is a medieval pastoral monasticism. A unity that excludes violence by excluding thought. In this society, knowledge is the most dangerous coin, necessary but managed like radioactive isotopes with careful rules to protect people from exposure, some Brothers copy books but are unable to read, brothers who can read do not copy books to avoid exposure to their ideas. Knowledge in Nook's society is seen as poisonous, a threat to their unchanging existence, something Randor himself admits when he confesses his sickness. In Randor's view, the only way to live life is unexamined, knowledge and awareness is anathema.

There's biblical allusions here, Brother Randor doesn't seem to distinguish sexuality from knowledge. His Nookians live in a kind of Edenic state, without knowledge of evil. They're so innocent that when they look at a murder victim, all they can do is speculate that perhaps he was pecked by some kind of bird with a long sharp beak. Randor fears the strangers, and particularly Xev, because he sees them as bringers of knowledge to the community, knowledge not safely contained and controlled.

More than that, Randor seems to fear the idea of female sexuality in and of itself. Women, he tells us, were the source of sexual conflict from which the founders of Nook fled. It's even worse because not only is Xev a woman, but she embraces sexuality and sexual pleasure. Although she's never had any, she's thoroughly in favor of it. Whereas the Nookian culture is thoroughly repressive, allowing only one night for sex, and that night the shortest of the year.

To Brother Randor the concepts of knowledge, gender and sexual freedom all seem to be rolling around in his head, mixing and merging into some amorphous 'bad thing.' Outwardly, Randor's almost always restrained and calm, but beneath the surface, the boy's just a cauldron of repressed psychoses. And this is the self appointed guardian of Nook's utopia, its most earnest advocate.

But how stable is Nook's society really? We have Brother Traygor, a copying brother, violating the rules by learning to read. We have Brother Randor, the nominal leader of the society running amok with secret knowledge. And we have the 'Night of No Rules', a celebration night where the Nookians can escape the relentless pressures and monotony of their existence. Brother Randor's endless unchanging utopia seems shot through with cracks and flaws, not the least of which is himself.

Although Brother Randor blames Nook's destruction on the irreversible changes, the female taint, brought by Xev, this seems to be a bad rap. In truth, Xev was going to leave sooner or later and then Nook was going to settle back to its old routine. But of course, an absolutist like Randor can't even tolerate the memory of Xev – the fact that she was ever there is an irretrievable taint.

The truth is that Brother Traygor, a copying brother who has learned to read, who yearns for Stanley and is prepared to break his own societies rules to pursue that love represented far more of a threat to Nook's society. He's in a state of quiet rebellion against the complacency of his society, having broken a cardinal rule he's prepared to break more. Traygor claims the unexamined life, a life without knowledge, without feeling, is not worth living, and yet for him, Nook is a society which eschews knowledge. He's living proof that Nook is no utopia, and willing to say this.

The real threat is brother Randor himself. Although he idealizes Nook, he himself doesn't follow its traditions. The leader of Nook's society is its worst subversive. He delves endlessly into forbidden knowledge and confesses as much. He uses it to disable Kai, to understand what Xev is, to judge the strangers as threats, to murder Traygor and attempt to frame the strangers and to ultimately murder his own people and destroy his world.

Randor believes destroying Nook in order to save it, a perverse concept. He can't bear the tainting of his idealized vision of his society. If it can't be perfect, then it's got to go. But at the same time, Traygor is living proof that the idealized vision of Brother Randor simply doesn't exist. Everyone would be happy. The society he's out to save exists only in his head.

It's significant that it's Traygor and not some random brother or Xev obsessed brother who Randor murders. Randor's grounded enough at least to recognize and eliminate him. It signifies to us that Randor's at least partially aware of the lies he lives under. The real danger that Xev represents is not to Nook society, but to Brother Randor's illusions.

> *"Since the landing, we do not concern ourselves with the past. The past is the same as the future will be, and always shall it be so."*

That's an odd remark, reminiscent of the overall fixation with cycles of time seen through the series. One of the conceits of the first season was the concept of future past, that time moved inevitably in a circle, playing out the same way over and over again, and that if you could see far enough into the past, you could see your own future.

Throughout the second season there are other references to existence being cyclic in nature, such as Kai's poetry about *"the wheel"* in **Twilight** or the players in **Brigadoom** and even the robots in **Lafftrack,** endlessly playing out their parts. Cyclic, or perpetual existence is also a feature of the societies of **Fire and Water**, not only are people perennially dying and being reborn, but the two worlds themselves are locked in an endless cycle from which there seems no escape.

In **Fire and Water/Heaven and Hell,** the concept was of an eternal and unchanging system of reincarnation where the past was the future. This might suggest that on some level, Nook is a microcosm of the themes of the entire series.

Certainly, the society in Nook seems to be a forerunner of the low tech 'heavens' of the next season. Nook is a planet of water, an endless ocean, with but a single (artificial) Island, on which has been established an 'idyllic,' low tech, paradise. Nook's men are free of any past, any awareness, self-knowledge, or any kind of knowledge, an orderly perfect society, unchanging and eternal, its future the same as its past, its members born without sexual reproduction. It even has its own version of reincarnation; its members are the endless clones of prior 'great men.'

Endless stability is not seen as a good thing. Rouma in **Twilight** is full of zombies; the robots in **Lafftrack** are literally breaking down as we watch and Stan's judgement of the players and of the Brunnen G in **Brigadoom** is not flattering. At the end of **Heaven and Hell**, Prince can only welcome the end of everything he's ever known. Nook seems stable, despite the cracks in its makeup, but overall, the message seems to be that the changeless cycles only spiral into decay.

Of course, I'm only speculating here, as to Nook's thematic relevance to the series as a whole. But interestingly, this seems to be one of the more important episodes for Donovan. When venturing into cyberspace he's named himself 'Brother Randor' after the character in Nook (which might make sense if, as I've speculated, Randor represents God in a variation of an Eden story). He's also referred to a few times it in different public interviews. It's tempting to see Donovan's solo scripts, particularly one with such a strong intellectual pretensions, as revealing of some of his themes and guiding ideas.

LEXX is frequently under written, and sometimes this is fairly irritating. For once this is a good thing. If this was a more conventional science fiction episode, there would have to be an 'official moral' at the end: Some point where a narrator or leading character would give a little speech for the audiences benefit just so we understood what the whole thing was about.

Not in this case. The only thing close to an 'official moral' comes from Brother Randor, who should be considered a disreputable source, since he's singlehandedly taken it upon himself to murder his whole world.

In this case, LEXX remains relentlessly silent as to its official moral or dominant theme. Indeed, it goes out of its way to repudiate the traditional morals with Xev's uninhibited meaningless group sex and Stan and Traygor's nascent gay romance. Instead of delivering an 'official' meaning, we're left with the story and the need to puzzle it out for ourselves, to take draw our own conclusions.

Which isn't necessarily a bad thing.

****

As an afterthought, we should acknowledge that Nook has been criticized for being seen as catering to a homophobic cliché - that in film and television, gays are transgressive and therefore gay characters are killed as a sort of implicit moral judgement. There's certainly a noticeable history of this sort of thing.

Does it apply here? Well, Nook is arguably a 'gay' male only society, and it is indeed wiped out. But then practically no world survives an encounter with the LEXX, either getting blown up by the crew, or devoured by Mantrid's drones. So the destruction of Nook is pretty standard.

One might question whether Nook is genuinely a 'gay' society, given the interest and focus on Xev shown by the men. But regardless, Brother Traygor is definitely gay, and he definitely dies.

His sexuality isn't portrayed as wrongful, he's by far the most sympathetic and developed character, and Stanley is open to his offer. But he does die. My view is that the story mechanics and issues are focused on other issues. But if one wants to insist on a homophobic subtext... the matter can be debated.

* * * *

Here's an odd and possibly useless bit of production trivia that's just too weird to leave out. The chickens seen in this episode had their feet wired to the ground. According to Mark Laing, *"Chickens are the worst actors on earth. You point a camera at a chicken, and sure enough, she'll go everywhere but where you want her to. You'll notice we didn't have a 'no animals were harmed in the making of this episode' disclaimer."*

My practice in doing this book has been to try to corroborate as much as possible. People always have different perspectives, memories can play false, sometimes it's just fun to pull the writer's leg. On this one, I haven't been able to verify it, but what the hell. It's strange enough to be true, and compared to a lot of stuff going on behind the scenes, it's not strange at all.

"We did shooting in Berlin," Bill Fleming, the Director of the episode and second season producer, said. *"Part of that was the German co-production; actually, it was financially tied in that we had to work at Babelsberg. Second season, we thought we'd get a better handle on prep if we started in Germany, and then followed up in Canada. That's what we did. Shot parts of* **Lafftrack, Terminal, Mantrid, Nook, Stan's Trial***... Pretty much the bulk of those."*

Back in Halifax, Electropolis studios was still getting up to steam, and the LEXX Bridge was being built, sets were being relocated from the waterfront, so the scheduling was probably inevitable. Eventually, scenes on the LEXX Bridge and sets and in the moth for all of these episodes were shot in Halifax.

The outdoor scenes of the Nookians at their garden were shot later that summer at Paul Donovan's farm outside Halifax, at the same time as the field of heads from Lyekka.

"Even initially," Fleming recalls, *"I'd been pretty excited by the locations we'd encounter in Berlin. Especially in and around the east side, where there was a lot of destruction and devastation. From the war, from the communists, East German rule, it was all massive and crumbling. We didn't think about it much in terms of LEXX, it was just interesting locations. These are pretty wild. It wasn't until we got in there. It was around when I was starting to think a lot about what Nook was going to look like, this monastic, medieval community."*

The visual esthetic of Nook is a step down from the brutal functionalism of other episodes. Instead of heavy rusting machinery, we've gone even more low tech.

"Essentially," says Mark Laing, *"I wanted to go for a technology based on leather bladders, bellows, advanced wood technology. It was as far as you could go with wood and leather technology."*

"I was going for a monastic community," Laing recalls, *"the theme was, Scandinavian Stave Church architecture extended into a whole monastic community. I have drawings we never did see of that monastery. It was partly Anglo-Saxon, Norwegian stave church, early monastic. Nook, I'm very proud of the design work for Nook. I hate to sound like sour grapes. It's not sour grapes, it's just the way things work, I sent the drawings and I don't know what happened to them, but a lot of it just didn't make it onto the screen."*

There are some impressive visuals, particularly of the cavernous dining hall, or the Brother Randor's laboratory where new Brothers are cultured. Some of the CGI, the outdoor scenes, the massage scene and the 'night of no rules' sticks in mind.

But there are some twee bits. The costumes are particularly clunky, crude and ill fitting, justifiable perhaps, because they're the products of a crude society. But they don't have a 'lived in' comfortable look; they seem stiff, as if they'd just been put on the day before. It just doesn't sell.

In the scene where Stan flees Traygor's murdered body and shuttered windows open to watch him go, the set is most reminiscent of a **Pippi Longstocking** production. All too often though, the rustic pastoral sets often simply look cheap and shoddy. There's a fine line between a convincingly detailed low tech society and what looks like an ambitious high school production. Too often what appears on the screen in Nook falls on the wrong side of that line. This is despite the fact that they spent a fair bit of money at it.

"Our construction costs in Canada were way lower than construction costs in Germany," Fleming observed. *"It was a factor of relative value. At Babelsberg, it was going to cost us three times what it cost in Canada. Wages were higher, taxes were higher. On top of that, studio costs were high and the studio was billing its construction costs in a corporate way. So they'd add 70% or something.*

"When we built in Canada, the carpenters were employees of LEXX, but in Babelsberg the carpenters were employees of Babelsberg. Parts of Babelsberg were amazing, parts were primitive. It's a wacky place. The parts we were in were sound stages built in the early 30's. When the East Germans ran it, it had 2500 full time employees. By the time we got there, it was down to a couple of hundred. They were trying to make it pay for itself. It was incredibly pricey to build sets there."

"For some reason, I can't remember," Fleming said, *"we were shooting Stan's Trial and Terminal in the biggest studio in Babelsberg, which was insane. You look at those episodes, they're very tight and confined, there's nothing huge in those sets. Yet we're creating the exteriors, the courtyard in Nook in the smallest studio."*

"It was purely because of the way that the shows had scheduled to shoot and how we had to finish off. We couldn't set the show up in the big studio cause we were shooting another show there. Bad planning. I must have been partly responsible in retrospect. Oh my god, we had to shoot this courtyard, in front of the gate, in this tiny studio. In the slightly bigger studio we used for the interior. It was ironically bizarre when we realized that. I'd love to get back to widen up the thing. It would have taken a huge amount of money to build."

But for Bill Fleming, the experience became a turning point that would have important repercussions for the third year.

"We were staying in Potsdam," he recalls, *"on the edge of the former palace area. Literally, our hotel looked onto the grounds of the palaces. It was just a*

huge vast acreage, from the time of Frederick the Great and the Prussian kings. Right across from the hotel, there were a series of cloistered archways and small castles. Much like a monastic community. I thought, 'Wouldn't it be great if we could shoot here?'"

"I'd speak with our German production manager about going out there, and he'd go 'We can't.' I started getting a dialogue. They were very conservative, very studio bound. It was kind of ironic Here we were next to all these incredible locations, and then we'd go into the studio and spend vast amounts of money and create sets which exist. I could have gone and done two days of exteriors outdoors and it would have looked immeasurably better."

"We had this incredible location we could have used! It was such a perfect Nookian kind of place. Old stone buildings, obviously monastic and churchlike. Small chapels, large churches, walkways into gardens. Ponds of water looking across at these cloistered roofed over walkways that wandered all over the place, they were so still that sometimes it was like a mirror. We could have gotten the camera in there shooting across the water, seen people reflected.... We could have done wonderful things."

"Here I am, on my afternoons off, walking through it and then going into the studio and realizing we're not only cursed by logistics, we're actually shooting in the smallest, most cramped studio, where everything costs so much and nothing looks half as good."

Out of that frustration came the idea, and more than that, the drive, to try location shooting. Perhaps if Babelsberg had gone better, or the surroundings less dramatic, it wouldn't have had such an impact and he wouldn't have pushed the idea. But Bill Fleming, that year, wasn't just a Director, he was a co-producer, and so inevitably, he had a huge influence on the ideas shaping the series.

For LEXX it was a controversial and risky idea. Up until this time, LEXX had been almost entirely a studio shoot. In the first season, there had been only one significant outdoor location shoot, a flashback sequence from Gigashadow where a man had been chased up against a chain link fence. Paul Donovan's history as a film maker, from his London Film School training, to his early films, **South Pacific, 1942** and **DefCon 4**, had been heavily set driven.

"The idea of using second unit stuff," Fleming recalled, *"and tying it in... We were initially afraid to go out. We had created a very studio look. We weren't sure about mixing that with outside shooting, real daylight, that was risky. If we could craft the show a little to take advantage of locations, if we could figure out what could be done to augment or add to stuff..."*

LEXX was a series heavy on CGI effects, which were normally done against greenscreens in studio. The idea of taking a series outdoors onto location seemed to conflict with that. CGI depended on control of all the elements, which meant studio locations. Putting a greenscreen outdoors...? What about wind? Shifting daylight? Rogue shadows?

But then again, Paul Donovan's outdoor shoot at his farm for scenes from **Lyekka** and **Nook** used greenscreen effectively, and proved that location footage could be merged seamlessly with an episode.

"When we finished the second season, I really pushed for shooting locations. Our production manager over there was very much against it. Citing location costs, location shooting was very very expensive. If you can shoot independent low budget feature films, though, it's got to be viable..."

Regardless of Nook's thematic relationship to the third season, the experience of shooting and producing the episode introduced the idea of location shooting, which became a key part of both the concept and the development of the Fire and Water serial.

CREDITS

Creators: *Writer - Paul Donovan; Director - Bill Fleming; Production Designers - Gerry Kunz and Mark Laing; Creative Producer - Jorg Buttgereit*

Main Cast: *Brian Downey (Captain Stanley Tweedle); Michael McManus (Kai, Last of the Brunnen G); Xenia Seeberg (Xev*

Bellringer, Rejected Wife/ Love Slave/ Cluster Lizard); Jeffrey Hirschfield (Voice of 790); Tom Gallant (Voice of LEXX).

Guest Cast: *Matthew Burton (Brother Randor); Matthias Klimsa (Brother Traygor); Martin Honer (Older Brother); Tom Strauss (Brother Deal); Philipp De Roche (Brother Stack/ Rat #1); Milton Welsch (Rat #2); Adrian Mattiske (Young Copying Brother);*

LEXX 2.12, Norb

Story

Norb, the boy from White Trash is cruising through space in his rocketship. He encounters a candy-cane space station, but even as he tries to make contact, it turns gray and begins to disintegrate. He flees but the devouring swarm chases him. Unable to lose them, Norb issues a distress call and hits the ejector.

On the bridge of the LEXX, Stan hears the distress call, and for once he decides to ride to the rescue. Norb is picked up by a moth and brought back. The boy is severely withdrawn, which they put down to the trauma of his near death. After he is left alone, Norb calmly detaches his arm, which then flies off on its own.

Later, Norb shows up on the bridge. Stan encounters him removing a cube of brain tissue from 790 and crushing it. Norb then announces that he has a message from Mantrid, and dissolves into drone arms. Kai destroys the drones, but there is at least one more on the loose.

Soon the LEXX is complaining of feeling unwell. The crew discovers that the LEXX is infested with drone arms, which are breaking down the LEXX's tissue to make more drone arms. At this rate, the LEXX will be devoured from within. Kai reconstitutes 790's brain cube, and the crew flee the LEXX. But 790 reveals that the LEXX can purge the drones by reversing his thrusters. This will require Stan to return to give the command, before fleeing outside the LEXX. The scheme works and the drones are destroyed.

Mantrid's head appears on the viewscreen, he announces that he has fused with the insect essence and is a new form of life. He claims he could have destroyed the LEXX at any time, but wanted to play a game with them. He promises to save them to last.

Review & Comments

Norb is a roller coaster episode from start to finish. Forget plot, forget characterization, this is the official action episode, and probably the most action packed of all the second season episodes.

Originally titled **The Little Boy**. It initially showed up as the 19th episode of 20 in the December, 1997 season plan, it was to be the episode where an oblivious LEXX crew would finally realize the danger Mantrid posed. Norb was moved up to 12th episode to add more tension to the Mantrid story arc. Largely a 'ship in the bottle' episode, there are only two guest cast members who are in only a few scenes. The episode is entirely shot on standing sets. Even Norb's space ship has been recycled from **White Trash**. Despite this, the episode stands out for its clockwork pacing.

Norb opens with one of those gorgeous surreal visions that the show throws away so effortlessly. In this case, a candy cane space station that looks like a child's theme park. It's weird and beautiful all at the same time. And when it suddenly begins to decay, the consuming grayness is genuinely shocking. It's so fresh and childlike that it hurts to watch it disintegrate. The death of its candy colored cheerfulness is genuinely disturbing; it's like finding a worm in an apple that you just bit into.

"For Norb, the effects were a mixture of models and CGI," Alex Busby remembers. *"That's when we really did go towards making it more CG. Models were too difficult and too expensive and too demanding of people. That's when we really did go towards making it CG. Plus the comping (compositing real models with CGI in the same image) wasn't really up there enough yet."*

"We'd shot the model rocket which I hated," Alex Busby continues. *"The candyland space station? Paul wanted to make the model, I just said no. I said listen, 'We'll just do it in CG and see how it looks.' We contracted it out to*

Cage Digital, and they actually did a good job. It's got that smooth look which works for CG."

It's hard to imagine the strangely beautiful station appearing anywhere but in CGI. The 'plastic' looking quality that often plagues CGI is just right here. It makes the station look like a gigantic toy. Certainly, its disintegration couldn't have been achieved outside a computer. The accelerated decay, as it first loses color and then form is almost frightening.

But, Willie Stevenson, the special effects producer winces at the dramatic chase scene follows. *"We were saved by the fans,"* he recalls. *"It turned out to be cheesy looking, but people liked it that way. We were lucky in that we'd try to do something really good, and it wouldn't turn out, but we'd wind up with something odd that people liked because it was so funky."*

Willie is too hard on himself, the LEXX people often are. What he doesn't stop to realize is most people in the audience have no idea what a 'fighter jet' sized spaceship fleeing in a life and death chase from millions of homicidal drone arms is supposed to look like. It doesn't happen to us in real life all that often.

Now, if he'd done a car chase and it looked tosh, he'd be entitled to beat himself up. But the truth is that Norb's desperate flight from the drone arms works just fine on its own terms. It's an effective and exciting scene. The advantage of science fiction is that when you're showing people things they've never seen before, you can get away with more.

The Mantrid drones were real, or at least some of them were. I'd originally expected that the drone arms were just costume bits, a hand and sleeve, with a green ninja outfit to mask out the rest of the actor. Not so.

Props department created a half-dozen full sized models, mounted on poles or booms and operated by wires and rods. Props men recalled the drones as heavy and awkward to manipulate, *"You wouldn't want to meet a drone operator in the middle of the night,"* one joked.

Or perhaps not a joke, I handled the drone arms myself a couple of times, they were stiff and heavy, the hands and fingers activated by wires and tough to pull.

Of course, there were only six, so all of the rest of the billions of Mantrid drones seen in the series are either completely CGI, or one or more of those six, cut and pasted to infinity.

The truth is that the scene works. It's genuinely gripping as Norb flees from the drones, dodging and weaving to stay alive. There's a to and fro quality, a move and countermove quality to the chase that gives it tension. That 'move and countermove' style pervades the episode.

There's a neat bit of characterization when Stan hears Norb's plea for rescue, "my air is running out..." and for once, goes out after him. This seems atypical for Stan; he wasn't interested in rescuing anyone in **Wake the Dead** or in **791**. But then again, Norb's plea reflects his own past, when he was himself lost in a derelict ship with his air running out. It's pushed Stan's button here, as it did in Gigashadow.

Stan also has another nice moment later on, when you can tell he's feeling the LEXX's pain, and as his ship breaks down, he's losing a friend. It's a genuine moment, and as Jeff Hirschfield said once, people go for genuine feelings.

The episode is full of nice little visual and character touches. Norb's scenes of disintegration into component drones are weird and shocking. It's a little disturbing to realize that this isn't the Norb we knew, that the boy is already dead. After all, in television and movies, it's verboten to actually kill a child, even off screen.

Xev turns out to be a cowboy in the moth, which only makes sense when you think of it. After all, she's been stuck on the LEXX for some time, and it just seems natural she'd entertain herself by joyriding in the moths. Xev's excitement is one of those times when the Cluster Lizard half of her actually comes through.

Kai is in top form. Too often, Kai isn't challenged. He's effectively invulnerable, unkillable, superhumanly skilled, knowledgeable and he has no motivation. So, a little too often, Kai winds up standing around until it's time to do something. Here, he has to take an active role and do the heroic bit, and it works. Kai as an action man is appropriately heroic but detached; it shows off the character to good effect. He has a genuinely weird conversation with some Mantrid drones, and an even better moment when he uses his brace in turbo mode. But his best scene is where, having dispatched the Mantrid drones, he simply sits and waits for the LEXX to reverse its drives.

Finally, for once, 790 actually gets a good role. 790 is a fairly limited character: Love Xev (or Kai), hate Stan, indifferent to everything and everyone else. He's got some limited utility as an insult machine and an exposition device, but it's the sort of thing that will wear thin quickly, and after two seasons, it was definitely wearing. But here, we get to find out things about 790, he becomes a little more human, literally, he actually has a role, a purpose in the plot.

Now that I think of it, this is one of the main reasons I really like this episode. It really shows off the actors and especially their characters to good effect. Everyone has good scenes, good moments, and for the most part, it's done without materially distorting the characters. Even 790 stays true to form.

Interestingly, Paul Donovan's feelings about this episode seem somewhat diffident. In an interview in **'Writing Science Fiction and Fantasy Television** he told Joe Nazaro, *"I liked the shows that pushed the envelope, like 791 or Brigadoom.... then there were shows like Norb which was a very straight ahead thriller, and those kind of worked. In a way, they were easy to do, but they're not as satisfying as doing something crazy like **Brigadoom**.... The concept wasn't as interesting."*

I tend to disagree. Most action movies, most thrillers, most adventures tend to be very straight ahead things. It's usually one damned thing after another with quiet spots to break things up. Most American action oriented movies or television episodes, or action sequences follow very simple patterns of escalation.

In a sense, they play out like a poker game. The characters hide their cards (moves) and play their hands, escalating the stakes until you've got a kind of winner take all show down where the hero pulls out his hidden ace for the dramatic royal flush or full house or whatever. It's workable, and it does work, but it's often simplistic and kind of crude. The hero wins, usually because he is the hero, and not necessarily because he's smarter or faster.

Norb on the other hand is highly structured.

"It's all a game," Mantrid says, *"I was just playing with you."*

And it is a game. It's an elaborate series of moves and countermoves. One person does something and then the other counters. It's very formal, often in action movies, the hero and villain are moving and acting simultaneously, or near simultaneously, rather than taking turns.

Escalation raises the stakes, but it's ultimately futile. Norb keeps going faster, but each time he does, the drones go faster too and catch up with him. Kai destroys drones, but there are just more and more of them. Victory, or advantage, comes with the lateral moves, rather than direct confrontation or escalation. The players don't go head on at each other's strengths, they try for end runs, sneaking around back, attacking at weak points or striking indirectly. Norb escapes the drones (temporarily) by using his ejector seat. Mantrid evades Kai by dismantling the LEXX. Ultimately, the crew beats Mantrid not by fighting the drones directly, but by reversing the LEXX's drive.

Unlike many action oriented movies or television episodes, Norb plays as a chess game, a series of increasingly complex moves and countermoves, with the advantage going back and forth each time.

Donovan's been doing this for quite some time. His first successful movie, **Siege**, about a group of residents defending their home against homicidal rednecks, played out this way, like a game with a series of moves and counter moves. His next movie, **DefCon 4,** particularly the bulldozer battle between Maury Chaykin's Vinnie and Jeff Pustil's Lacey, contains structured 'to and fro' sequences where advantage goes back and forth as characters move and counter, and victory is won by an unexpected, but logical, lateral move. Similar contests take place in another Donovan film,**Tomcat: Dangerous Desire**. Within LEXX, we saw this again in segments of different episodes. It would be repeated again in the third season in Battle and taken to its ultimate conclusion in the fourth season in Game.

So this may be old hat for Donovan, but I don't think that the rest of us have really seen a lot of this. It's atypical for a lot of film and television. And it's interesting, in many ways, much more interesting than the typical actioner. The pace, I think, is slower, and the formality makes it stiffer. On the other hand, I think that there is more opportunity for the viewer to really engage in the process, to become committed to the action rather than simply overwhelmed or entertained.

It's more satisfying I think. A lot of conventional actioners simply climax by pulling a rabbit out of a hat. Eddie Murphy has one more bullet left, or Arnold Schwarzenegger comes bursting through with the Helicopter at the last minute. It's a rabbit out of the hat, a hidden ace, it's a nice dramatic flourish, but it's a cheat, a false drama based on fooling the audience to heighten anticipation and then pulling the trick. Here, there is no cheat, it simply builds up carefully, one movement leading logically but perhaps not predictably to the next until we are fully captivated, and when it pays off, it's an honest payoff.

It's interesting, the things I like most about LEXX are its penchant for anarchy and surrealism, its capacity to throw truly startling and strange images and situations at us. LEXX consistently breaks with formula, but still manages to succeed. Plot can be optional, characterization dispensed with, there are episodes that shouldn't work under conventional rules, but they work. LEXX's penchant for breaking or bending rules expands the form, it means that there are more options; we aren't stuck continually in the same old rut.

But I really like this episode, and the rigorously structured episodes and sequences like this, because they are so rigorous and structured. This is LEXX playing out like a Swiss watch, and this works too. It's an unusual approach to structure, at least in popular film and television, but it isn't at all bad. I'd like to see more of it.

Norb is admittedly a very limited episode. No new sets, barely any guest stars, everything taking place on ship, on standing sets. Literally, it's a ship in the bottle episode as I've pointed out at the beginning. But within its limits its exquisitely fine tuned. Every note is perfect, every movement, every beat, every twitch seems dead on, each of the actors and each of the characters is developed and handled with respect, its taut as a drum, full of snap. When I introduce people to LEXX, this is one of the episodes I use. Without apology, this is one of my favorites.

CREDITS

Creators: Writer - Paul Donovan; Director - Paul Donovan; Production Designer - David Hackl; Creative Producer - Willie Stevenson

Main Cast: Brian Downey (Captain Stanley Tweedle); Michael McManus (Kai, Last of the Brunnen G); Xenia Seeberg (Xev Bellringer, Rejected Wife/Love Slave/Cluster Lizard); Jeffrey Hirschfield (Voice of 790); Tom Gallant (Voice of LEXX).

Guest Cast: Brandon McCarvell (Norb); Dieter Laser (Mantrid)

Lost LEXX, the Original Heaven and Hell

Heaven

The LEXX passes into a cloud like nebulae. The crew are lost and confused, but here and there in the clouds they can see people. And they also recognize some of the people, remembering them from when they were alive. Many of them are people Kai killed, and they are a pretty consistent do-gooder lot. The LEXX has stumbled across Heaven....

Eventually the crew make their way to the Gate, garishly festooned with harps, cherubs, etc. They encounter a St. Peter type of figure, dripping in Pentecostal piousness. He asks each of them a series of questions, dragging in every St. Peter-At-The-Gates joke that we can muster.

Maybe Pete and Kai can begin a theological debate, Kai is open to lots of religions while Pete is adamant that there is only one true faith, and he's prepared to bust you in the nose to make his point.

The crew are dispatched to Hell, but our heroes manage to escape. It's a rough, tough, shoot out, and in doing so... They accidentally blow up Heaven...

Which sends them.... straight to Hell.

(June, 1996, Series Outline, Special thanks to Brian Downey)

Heaven II (Handwritten Notes)

Heaven is discovered when they enter another fractal core by accident. They enter a tranquil, open, green, happy, massive plain. The LEXX is stuck and cannot break free.

A tiny figure approaches who identifies himself as Peter ('call me Pete'). He tells our crew they can't stay because they haven't been invited. He checks his list and says, 'Yeah, for sure you're not on today's list, so you gotta go.'

They explain they are stuck, they can't find anything wrong with the interior of the ship, and could they check the outside for damage. They get the OK. They meet lots of folks who should be dead. Stan gets spooked. They are given a final warning to leave. They say they're still stuck.

'Okay, the Big Guy is coming and I wouldn't want to be you when he gets here....' They see a huge luminous cloud gathering and heading toward them.

Stan, in a fit of desperation feeds the LEXX a few flying moths, gets the power up to excess and fires the weapon to blast them backwards - And it works! Except that they see heaven crumble before their eyes - God takes a direct hit and keels over which causes a huge volcanic reaction, driving the LEXX across the Universe and into a dark place.

Where they merge with each other, melding into one, appearing to become a single entity. We hear an off screen voice '

"Welcome to the Nothing. All shadows are here.' Or 'Welcome, Dead Ones, to all evil... long may you die!' "

Hell

Immediately after blowing up Heaven, the crew of the LEXX find themselves in hell.

We have not fully developed the concept of Hell, but it will be custom tailored to each of our characters.

This episode will be more of a nail biter, a darker, more serious story with a lower quotient of humor than usual.

After each of them has been suitably cowed, the real forces of hell are unleashed and things get thoroughly nasty....

(June, 1996, Series Outline, Special thanks to Brian Downey)

Commentary

Heaven and Hell were originally intended to be two consecutive episodes (quoted in their entirety), as set out in a June 28, 1996, Story Synopsis/Scripts in Development brochure for the second season, appearing as 12th and 13th out of the twenty prospective episodes. It was dropped from the mid-1997 brochure, and from the December, 1997, season two outline.

The purpose of the mid-1996 brochure wasn't just to map out what they wanted to do with the series, but also to persuade potential stations to pick up the prospective series. To sell the series, you had to have a promotional package, the miniseries of movies made the second series much easier to sell, but that was only part of the promotional package. It also had to include a kind of map or outline for the upcoming series. Accordingly, we should take it with a grain of salt; they were just getting their ideas down on paper to satisfy an immediate need...

Certainly they hadn't gotten very far with it at this point. **Hell** amounts to little more than an 'idea' for an episode, with almost nothing worked out. **Heaven** was little better, not much more than a premise and a few sketches for a storyline, with an accompanying handwritten notation that seems to have been a completely different version of the story idea. The amount of handwritten notes may suggest that this was an idea that they liked and wrestled with. But it's still barely developed.

The lack of attention given also shows in the placement, approximately two thirds of the way through the outline as the 12th and 13th potential episodes.

Even these sketchy premises seem to have little in common with the **Heaven and Hell** storyline that constituted the third season. There is no Prince, for instance. There is no perpetual reincarnation, although they encounter people that they've met before, or that Kai has killed during his millennia as an assassin. There is no particular vision of either heaven and hell as a place divided into discrete cities or realms for different types of saints and sinners.

Having said that, however, there are at least a few glimmers. **Heaven** and **Hell** would be a two part or multi-episode story. LEXX is trapped in part because it's apparently run out of food. The great sin of Stanley Tweedle would be in blowing up Heaven. They would encounter people they'd known in the past...

Ultimately, what the potential episodes **Heaven** and **Hell** show us is that this basic idea was documentably present even as far back as the middle of 1996, before the first season of movies had completed post-production, and quite possibly, it goes back even further.

LEXX 2.13, Twilight

Story

On the planet Rouma, a desperate squabbling family and their robot are struggling to keep robed zombies from breaking through their barrier. As dawn breaks, they succeed, but what will they do when night falls again.

Back on the LEXX, Stan seems semiconscious. Kai diagnoses him with a sickness which cannot be cured on the ship. They rouse him enough to put out a call for help. Back on Rouma, the family hears the distress call, and radios back that their 792 robot has diagnostic capacities that can cure Stan. Basically, they're grasping at any straw to get off the planet before the Zombies come back.

When the LEXX arrives, we learn that the planet Rouma is covered by impenetrable radioactive mists, with only one small island-like mountaintop being habitable. Rouma is the resting place of the bodies of previous His Divine Shadows, and its unique radiations allow the Shadows corpses to reanimate as zombies. There used to be an entire division of Divine Clerics to look after the former Divine Shadows, but they've all fled, leaving the family - Roada, Heedia and teenage Lomea behind.

When Kai arrives on the planet, he appears to become intoxicated, affected by the radiation, and wanders off, reciting poetry. This leaves only Stan and Xev. Lomea is completely fascinated by Xev and uninterested in Kai. Roada and Heedia help cure Stan, and take Xev on a picnic outside the castle walls. But the minute Xev's back is turned; they flee, intending to steal the moths. The family retreats back to the castle, as Stan and Xev try to make it back. Xev is bitten and starts to turn Zombie herself.

Lyekka wakes up on the LEXX and decides to follow the crew down to Rouma. The 792 Robot lets the zombies into the castle, where they devour the moth. The robot, however, is eaten (mostly) by Lyekka, who proceeds to devour Lomea and Heedia in turn. Roada is fed to zombies. The crew return back to the LEXX where Kai reverses the zombification of Xev by sucking the poison out.

Stan decides to destroy Rouma, but before he can order the LEXX to do so, a swarm of Mantrid's drones appear and devour the planet.

Review & Commentary

The original story for this one came from Wolfram Tichy, the German co-producer. It was one of three or four stories/ideas that he contributed for the third season, the others being **Clizzards of Woz, Passion Flower** and **Lexxstasy.**

Two of these never made it to production, a third mutated fairly radically. **Twilight** came closest to Tichy's original story, but even here, Jeff Hirschfield noted that it altered substantially. I was shocked, talking to Tichy, to discover the real inspiration for Twilight, *Salome's Dance of the Seven Veils.*

"Everyone was contributing ideas," Tichy said, *"we would all get together at the (Economy) Shoe Shoppe (a restaurant/ bar in Halifax), and throw ideas around. There were always ideas all around, even cast and crew members kept coming up with suggestions. One of the things we talked about was doing takes on myths and legends. Transferring well known classic stories and myths into LEXX stories. I always liked the idea of genre travesties. That made me develop the idea of playing out a horror movie against the background of a cheap biblical epic. For me, LEXX was such a genre travesty in itself, and thus an ideal vehicle to try out other clashes of such contrasts."*

"So I thought of Salome...Lomea and Herod...Roada, from the biblical story. Later, we had the idea of them being chased by the living dead Divine Shadows. The attack of the zombies had already been in my initial concept, but

it was only after I came up with the notion that the undead could be the former Divine Shadows. Paul liked that enough to give it a go."

Twilight is LEXX's take on **Night of the Living Dead**, although it seemed to me that a closer inspiration may be Osorio's **Tombs of the Blind Dead** series, about killer zombie monks (Unfortunately, Tichy had never heard of Ossorio). It certainly reproduces the classic tropes of **Night of the Living Dead** and its Eurozombie cousins: A group of disparate and unlikeable strangers thrown together, fighting and betraying each other as the zombies overcome the barricades.

"I can't rule out that Lex or Chris patterned the actual appearance of the zombies after Romero's portrayal," Tichy reflects. *"It is quite likely. But my own idea dates back to much older impressions such as Jacques Tourneur's 'I Walked With a Zombie' and a general fascination with the phenomenon of the undead which branded my ideas of horror films well before Romero. Their monkish apparel was derived from His Shadow's garb in the early movies."*

That said, **Twilight** is one of the highlights of the second season. Funny and gross, constantly surprising, it just seems to take off and never lets up.

The center of **Twilight,** of course, are the performances of Louis Del Grande and Mary Walsh. They were apparently just out of control.

"Those guys never said the same line twice in a take," Mark Laing said. *"Nutcases. They just cracked us all up, we shot a hell of a lot of film, they wouldn't play it safe."*

Chris Bould, the Director recalls tearing his hair out over Louis Del Grande, who was an absolutely charming man, but almost impossible to direct.

"I'd met Mary before," Chris Bould said. *"Those two comedians, my history as a director is comedy. They're both brilliant. But when Mary went to one level. Louie would come in at a higher level, and then Mary would go higher. There was a few times on that show, I was biting my knuckles trying not to*

laugh. It was pandemonium; they were going at it all the time. I had to shut up."

"Louis was a comic genius. But he could never do the same thing twice. I'd go 'Louis, we've done this scene six times, please hit your mark.' He'd go 'Wha wha what mark?' I'd go 'Louis, it's a fucking sandbag!!!' Not even a chalk mark on the floor a sandbag! I relied on his improvisation, if you can't anticipate him twice, you have to cut around him or utilize his talents. It was a fun show but incredibly difficult to work with. Those two people, they're massive personalities."

"I played the robot in Twilight: 792," Christian Murray says. *"It was actually quite hysterical that whole week with Louis and Mary. Louis knew the gist of his lines, but he was acting off the top of his head. There were a couple of scenes where Louis was slapping the robot head, he could never remember the lines, he kept whacking my head. It got to a hysterical point, trying to get through the scene."*

Del Grande is a legendary Canadian actor/writer/producer. He was notorious for his role in Cronenberg's **Scanners** as the man whose head is exploded by psychic force. Later, created, wrote, produced and starred in several years of a comedy/drama series called **Seeing Things**, playing a reporter who gets psychic flashes and must use them to unravel the mystery.

Mary Walsh originally co-starred with Brian Downey in **The Adventures of Faustus Bidgood**, later, she co-starred in several seasons of Salter Street's Newfoundland sketch comedy series, **Codco**, and then for several more seasons in Salter's cult hit, **This Hour Has 22 Minutes**, where she achieved cult status for dressing up like Xena Warrior Princess in order to accost celebrities and politicians as Marge: Princess Warrior. She also appeared in Paul Donovan films, such as **Buried on Sunday**.

"It was pretty funny being on set with Mary and Louis," Brian Downey recalled. *"There was just incessant chatter. Louis never said his lines; maybe he'd say lines from script, maybe not. Mary kept him on track. She could keep up with him. You need someone strong and experienced to keep up with an actor who's insane. In breaks, she would go off with him talking about taxes*

all the time, income tax. That seemed to help, he'd stay on earth. She kept him grounded."

Louise Wischermann gets one of her meatiest roles as Lyekka since her original performance. Wischermann is always a pleasure to watch, and it's often a shame that she didn't get more to do in the series. This time, her appearance with Lauren Abrahams, and their conversation is classic, the actresses glee at their lines is palpable.

Lomea: what do you like to eat?

Lyekka: I like to eat many things as long as they are living and breathing.

Lomea: Like me... ?

Lyekka: Yes.... Or an animal.

Lomea: For example, smalll furry animals?

Lyekka: I love small furry animals!

Lomea: Small, furry, wet, wild animals!!

Lyekka: That sounds tasty!!!

Lomea: Oh it is!!!!

This was Lauren Abrahams' first acting role.

"She was someone I found locally," Director Chris Bould recalls. *"When she was on camera, I'd look from behind the camera to her in the flesh. She had this Claudia Colbert, as if from 30's or 40's films. I could not believe, she had this translucency, this amazing gift that belied her years. She had this amazing quality. Stunning absolutely stunning. She was so young, I couldn't say the things the scene implied, I just couldn't say it. But she knew, and she went whole hog with a real twinkle in the eye. She was just sensational."*

"Lauren had never acted before," Donovan confirms. *"She was in high school. She was fabulous." And* in fact, they liked her well enough to bring her back in fourth season.

Michael McManus gets to do something different with his drunken, poetic ramble across the countryside.

"Michael had the great idea to do the poetry," Chris Bould remembers. *"Lex wrote it, I just kept putting it in. All that stuff was Michael and Lex and I collaborating."*

Bould, as always, was an irrepressible force as director. Here's a choice quote, not that it fits anywhere, but it gives a flavor of the man. *"We were having major discussions, Paul, Michael, Lex and myself. There was a fundamental flaw in the script (Kai talking to a zombie and what to do next)... I said 'Just push the fucking zombie off the cliff!' It just seemed like fun. We got away with a lot of stuff."*

Between McManus and Bould, **Twilight** was filled with gags, from Kai inserting a flower into Lyekka, to the zombies using one of their own as a battering ram.

On a physical level, Twilight proved a difficult shoot though. *"It was incredibly hot, 120 degrees in the studio,"* Chris Bould recalls. *"The zombies were covered in heavy wrapping, not to mention their makeup, it was a nightmare."*

"I built a model the size of this table, polystyrene base and plasticine, of crypts and castle," Laing recalls. The tabletop model was seen in a few establishing shots, and its impressive, adding a gothic feel of mass and space to the episode. *"A very large, probably too large set was constructed for that."*

But the episode was particularly costly and time consuming. Extensive sets were constructed for the episode, but there was little time to build them. Literally an entire castle and interiors had to be constructed. The problem was the studio was in use right up until Friday. To get around that, the set had to be constructed in modules through the round the clock over the weekend at Salter Street's carpentry shop down the road and assembled on Monday at Electropolis studios. It was labor intensive and extremely expensive.

"We had to block shoot that show," Bould remembers. *"We couldn't build all the sets. We had to shoot it in one direction. Then turn the camera around and do the rest of the sets. "*

"Twilight in the second year was what got us," Norman Denver said. *"Been to the carpentry shops? We were finishing an episode on that Friday, shooting on Monday, and we had to build a huge set literally overnight, there was a whole castle, struck in sand and gravel. It all had to be built over the weekend, non-stop work, and then brought over and assembled. It was really expensive. That was a watershed. Paul and I sat down and decided we had to look for a different way of doing things. Building new sets every episode was killing us, budget and production wise. It was all in one building, you couldn't build when you were shooting across the hall. All sorts of problems."*

"LEXX's biggest nut that year, the biggest problem was scheduling," Andrea Raffaghello concurs. *"Apart from Berlin and back, in studio, the only move was across the hall. Sometimes there was a mentality was, to a degree, 'It will work!' We looked at things realistically. It took a lot of looking at what we had to do, what we must do to make it work. Sometimes people might look at a situation and go 'We're stuck, it didn't work, what do we do?'"*

It was clear that the costs and scheduling problems inherent in constantly building new sets for each episode would become prohibitive. It was also time consuming, the Electropolis studios were all one building, and the main studio was this single massive space. Even if you were setting up or tearing down in one part of the studio there was still a huge risk that construction and set up would disturb shooting in another part of the studio.

Emphasis shifted towards finding ways to schedule more effectively and re-use or recycle sets, as well as setting more action on board the existing sets. This would eventually have a major impact on the development of the third and fourth seasons.

"We needed to economize" Denver remembers. *"We needed to do more with a lot less, that drove the story, the third season. We concentrated on just two or three really good sets at Electropolis, and of course some minor rooms. That and the location shootings in Germany and Namibia."*

Oddly, **Twilight** would have fit into the **Fire and Water** season. Like **Nook** it was set on an empty planet, surrounded by an ocean or desert (this time of poison mists), with a single, small, habitable bit of land. Unlike Nook, Rouma was no paradise, but a Dantean hell of an afterlife inhabited by the dead. It's tempting to see the seeds of **Water and Fire**, in **Nook** and **Twilight.**

And it's especially ironic that the difficulties of shooting these two episodes would, inspire two of the key production concepts that would shape and define the entire third season.

CREDIT

Creators: *Director - Chris Bould; Writers - Jeff Hirschfield, Paul Donovan, Lex Gigeroff; Production Designer -Mark Laing; Creative Producer -Norman Denver;*

Main Cast: *Brian Downey (Captain Stanley Tweedle); Michael McManus (Kai, Last of the Brunnen G); Xenia Seeberg, (Xev Bellringer, Rejected Wife/Love Slave/Cluster Lizard); Jeffrey Hirschfield (Voice of 790); Tom Gallant (Voice of LEXX).*

Guest Cast: *Louise Wischermann (Lyekka); Louis Del Grande (Roada); Mary Walsh (Heedia); Lauren Abrahams (Lomea); Christian Murray (792); Gordon White (Crying Zombie).*

Lost LEXX, the Salesman

Story

The LEXX picks up a signal from a tiny asteroid, and on it they find a manic, hyper, twitchy salesman ("Gubby Mok"). He lives all alone there, surrounded by useless pieces of junk. But he promises that he has all sorts of weird and wonderful items on sale. Zev is intrigued enough to convince Stan and Kai to head down to the asteroid.

Once down there, Gubby has great interest in the LEXX. Specifically, what does Stan want for it? Stan says that the LEXX is not for sale, and besides, he's the only one who has a key. Gubby tries valiantly to sell Stan on various other ships and gizmos, few of which he actually seems to possess. Gubby is increasingly desperate for a sale.

Meanwhile Kai notices a strange machine over in the corner. It is one of Mantrid's small, drone-like machines, but it is broken, malfunctioning. Kai asks Gubby where he got the machine. "I got a lot of machines, bub, all very reasonably priced", answers Gubby. Kai goes over and picks up the object, and it instantly kicks into disjointed life. The machine sputters the words, "Must find Mantrid" before falling silent. Kai enlists 790 to work on the mysterious drone.

Except there's one problem. Gubby has absconded with Zev (by knocking her out with a Crème de menthe-like sleeping potion) in his little spacecraft and is taking her to the Slave Market Planet. A virgin like Zev would definitely fetch top price on the Market, especially so since Love Slaves are in great demand these days, now that the Cluster does not produce them anymore. This could be

Gubby's one chance to get himself out of the red from his creditors, who make the Tonton Macoute look like Boy Scouts.

Kai, Stan and 790 give chase in the LEXX. Once at the Slave Market, Kai and 790 start looking for Zev. Stan has half a mind to buy himself a love slave, until he is corralled by a kind of press gang and put on the auction block himself. The winning bidder? Our old friend Smoor (from Feppo and Smoor, of **Gigashadow**), who is delighted at the prospect of hearing Stanley's "delightful squeal" all over again.

Zev comes to in a sealed glass cage, where she is about to be auctioned off. The Auction Chamber is populated by any number of lowlifes, including the impossibly fat and disgusting King Butt, who has made it is his life's mission to acquire as many love slaves as he can (because few survive his affections). He has never lost a bid. Gubby nervously looks around, as he wants to cash her in time to save his skin. The bidding begins…but there are surprise bidders: Kai and 790. They try to outbid the King, and are finally successful. But just as they head to the pay window, Gubby's creditors storm in, demanding their money. They do not seem happy with Gubby's claims that he just needs a few more minutes. They'll take Zev, Gubby, and whatever else they want as an immediate down payment.

Kai and 790 eventually free Zev and they head back to the LEXX, except that there's no Stan. Somehow they manage to rescue him from the clutches of Smoor. Gubby's creditors end up with Gubby.

As the LEXX sails off, the same mysterious swarm-like cloud rolls through and devours the Slave Market Planet.

(December, 1997, Series Guide, thanks to Lex Gigeroff)

Commentary

This obviously was the starting point for **Patches in the Sky**, and in many ways seems to be a more interesting episode.

A much briefer, more rudimentary version of this episode appeared in the earlier June, 1996, series outline. In that version, Gubby kidnaps Zev to a slave cloning planet for mass production to escape his mob debts. Our heroes rescue her by switching one of her own clones, lacking the Cluster Lizard gene, for Zev.

Handwritten notes to the June 1996 version explain why Gubby's so desperately in debt. It seems he took a consignment of slave clones to sell and forgot to feed them. They all died, and he didn't make his sale. The mafia which runs the planet wants to lower him very slowly into molten metal.

This gradually evolved into the version reproduced here, from the December, 1997, outline, so it must have been really appealing to them. It was originally slated to be the ninth episode; it was pushed back when **Love Grows** and **791** moved ahead in the schedule.

Ultimately, all that remains of **The Salesman** is the character of Gubby Mok, his 'come on down' broadcast, a certain cluttered sensibility for the Narco Lounger and a bit with the broken Mantrid drone. **The 'Patches in the Sky'** references of the final version weren't actually in the Salesman outlines, they are transplanted from **Clizzards of Woz**.

Despite the fact that this story was kicking around for a year and a half, even the 1997, treatment isn't fully developed. There are plot holes at this point: Where do Kai and 790 get the money to buy Zev? I can imagine 790 tapping into the computerized banking system. Or perhaps they claimed the money from selling Stan, and used that either to purchase Zev or the seed for gambling stakes to raise the money for Zev? And of course, they've barely got an idea of how they were going to get Stan out of hot water. So, there was a fair bit of work needed to make the script useable.

But perhaps the big reason this episode didn't fly costs and logistics. The cast implied here, both speaking parts and extras, especially on the slave market planet, or a slave cloning planet, seems way more than the minimal extra cast of three actors and three extras in **Patches in the Sky**. Where **Patches** didn't go much past the Narco Lounger, and then recycled existing sets and greenscreen, the Salesman's den looks like a much more expensive set to build, and the slave planet would have taken even more sets and more time. Towards the end, the series was clearly stretching its budget to the limits. It's likely that this episode was simply too expensive.

Smoor in **Gigashadow** was originally played by Andy Jones, who'd co-starred with Brian Downey in **Faustus Bidgood**, and had worked with Paul Donovan in **Buried on Sunday** and **Paint Cans**, as well as featuring in the early episodes of the **Codco** TV series. Obviously, they were interested in having him back. If so, he'd have been literally the only character from the first series to return alive as himself.

LEXX 2.14, Patches in the Sky

Story

Stan is dreaming. At first it's a good dream, but it soon turns into a nightmare as Giggerotta the Wicked appears and begins pursuing him. He wakes up terrified. Xev suggests he blow up a planet or something to feel better.

Elsewhere, we meet Gubby Mok, owner of a junk emporium, and possessor of a Narco Lounger - a dream machine that can project a person inside their fantasies. A customer comes, someone Mok knows well and calls Fruitcake. Fruitcake wants to use the Narco Lounger, offering to pay with a broken Mantrid drone. Mok isn't impressed, but Fruitcake eventually persuades him.

Back on the LEXX, Stan is bullying a robot who is the sole inhabitant of a manganese mining planet. He accidentally blows up the planet. Upset, he decides to look for other recreation, and they intercept the pitch for Gubby Mok's Narco Lounger.

Back at Mok's emporium, Fruitcake goes into the Narco Lounger, but before he does, he mentions the patches in the sky. Intrigued, Gubby interrogates his robot, and discovers that there are indeed patches. Entire sections of the universe have disappeared, and the rate of disappearance is increasing. The universe will vanish completely, come to an end in 103 days. Mok decides to get drunk.

The crew of the LEXX shows up and Stan tries to trick his way into the Narco Lounger. Mok isn't fooled, but allows Stan into the machine anyway. While Stan is dreaming, Mok tells Kai about the patches in the sky and the vanishing universe.

Inside the Narco Lounger, once again Stan's dream turns into a nightmare, as he's confronted first by the mining robot he blew up, and then by Giggerotta, who pursues him with his own guilt. Gubby Mok tries to rescue him, but is killed. Xev goes into the dream machine, but things go badly for her as well. Finally, Kai figures out how to rescue them by pulling them into Fruitcake's dream and then pulling them out.

Stan has had enough of dreams and wants to leave. Fruitcake asks to go back into the machine. Kai mentions the patches in the sky. After they leave, Mantrid drones devour Mok's emporium.

Review and Comment

"Paul Donovan doesn't like Patches in the Sky," notes Les Krizsan. *"That was Robson. I thought his performance was pretty good. You never know with Paul, he has his favorites and I look at it and wonder why. I liked Patches, it was a good set, the way we shot it worked. I liked the way the lighting turned out."*

Ask Paul Donovan about **Patches in the Sky**, and he's likely to turn his head and mumble something about 'creative exhaustion.'

In a sense, he's his own worst critic. He is, after all, the guy with the vision. He's a man who carries in his head a version of **Patches in the Sky** that the rest of us never see. He sees the way it should have been, and then he sees the way it turned out.

That's actually a common malady with artists, that gulf between ambition and accomplishment, between the vision in the mind's eye and the picture that actually emerges on the canvas.

Michael McManus wouldn't watch his performances in LEXX until a year or two later, when time gave him the room to put some perspective on the experience.

Lex Gigeroff said *'It's just too painful to watch.'*

Jeff Hirschfield put it most vividly, *"I can't watch it with a clean slate. I watch it and all I see is what didn't work. That's all I see. Even my favorites, I can't do it. All I can see is what didn't happen. What is should have been. All the moments, great moments that went flat! That's the wrong music! That's the wrong cut! Why isn't that in close up! Oh yeah, we lost those lines, that really works. We're cursed, we're doomed. That's all you can look for in your own work."*

Specifically about **Patches in the Sky**, Paul Donovan allows that by that time they were feeling some creative exhaustion. The Supreme Beans, none of them, really seem to like this episode.

So, how does Patches in the Sky really hold up?

Not bad. Better than *Stan's Trial*, for instance. And far better than **Love Grows**. but not great either. It suffers badly in comparison with **Mantrid, Lyekka, Twilight** or **Wake the Dead**.

There's some very cool stuff: The manganese mining planet with the hole gouged out in it is another fine entry in the LEXX's catalogue of strange looking, surreal worlds. The argument between Stan and the mining robot is priceless, with Stan being wonderfully petty and tyrannical, and the beleaguered robot actually winning a degree of sympathy.

For the observant, there are a few cool bits. Laura Cason, who is one of Fruitcake's dream girls, would also appear in **Woz** as one of the love slaves. And of course, there's the throwaway reference to the *'Wolfram T Galaxy'* a nod to German executive producer, Wolfram Tichy.

Gubby Mok, the proprietor of the Narco Lounger is a lot of fun, projecting just the right amount of cynicism and world weariness. Which makes a bit of sense, if you had a machine that could project you into your own deepest fantasies, I suspect you'd eventually wind up a little tired and jaded. Assuming you ever came out of it.

The subplot, part of the **Mantrid** story arc, is nicely played. Gubby's discovery of the coming destruction of the universe works, both visually and as dialogue. Even his response rings true. After all, if you discovered the universe was coming to an end, what would you do? Getting as stoned as you can as fast as you can may not be a constructive response, but it's a very human response. Besides, what can you do?

The Narco Lounger also looks pretty good. The set is nicely cluttered and junky, Gubby's robot/computer has a charming quality, inhuman and birdlike. It maintains that look and feel of rough functional decay which characterizes the Lexx aesthetic.

But there's a lot that simply misses the mark. For one thing, in an episode all about dreams and nightmares it simply suffers in comparison to **Lyekka**. The truth is, **Lyekka** exactly hit the mark in taking us into the surreal world of dream logic. **Patches in the Sky,** try as it does only occasionally hits that target. Too often **Patches** dream sequences feel forced and artificial.

And, for that matter, why have an episode about dreams and nightmares, and exclude a creature like Lyekka. She appears only for a few seconds in stock footage earlier on. Wischermann wasn't available? Who knows?

Patches goes right off the mark from the beginning, with an opening dream of Stan floating surrounded by psychedelic images while a brassy overpowering horn score blares out. Sorry, that resembles no dream I've ever had. It's closer to the psychedelic dance sequences in **House of Frightenstein**, a low budget 70's children's TV series.

For those who don't remember **Frightenstein,** it was a cheesy Saturday morning show based on badly made up renditions of the Universal Studios monsters, halfway through the show, there'd always be this dance scene were Igor or the Werewolf would shimmy and bop to cheap elevator music while psychedelic kaleidoscope colors filled the blue screen. It was bad, very bad.

The opening dream/nightmare comes across as harsh, loud and patently artificial. The scene calls for the eerie sounds of a Theremin, rather than the raucous notes of a trombone in a burlesque house.

Giggerotta's return is welcome. But the Giggerotta of Stan's nightmares seems an oddly diminished figure. In **I Worship His Shadow** and **Supernova,** she's larger than life, voluptuous, amoral, unrelenting, a woman of selfish, carnivorous appetites. It makes sense that she's the figure of Stan's nightmares, after all, she ripped his hand off, she almost ate him several times, she tried to seduce him, and is generally associated with really bad experiences. And of course, she's a lot of fun for the audience.

"It's important that she's fun," Ellen Dubin says of her character, Giggerotta. *"She's such a crude character, that if you don't combine it with tongue in cheek and fun, it can be nauseating. Men can get away with it more. If you combine it with a twinkle in your eye, sensuality, it works. I wanted people to love her. She might be awful, but I wanted there to be something appealing in her."*

But she seems too confined in her role as Stan's judge and executioner, for the most part, there's not enough glee. The predatory sexuality isn't there; she's just a woman with bad hair in an ugly suit, not a human vagina dentata. She doesn't even speak in third person.

True, this isn't the original Giggerotta, but merely a dream reflection, Stan's conception of her. But he'd heard her talk often enough that her peculiar way of speaking should have made as much of an impression as her wardrobe.

"Paul and I talked a lot," Ellen Dubin said, *"which was really a treat. In* **Patches in the Sky***, Giggerotta got smarter. The audience got to see her as a sly fox, rather than a dumb cavewoman type character. Paul and I discussed it."*

Speaking in the third person reflects self-absorption. The original Giggerotta thought only of herself. This dream Giggerotta is extroverted; she's not focused on herself, but on Stan. A third person monologue would undermine that focus.

This seems to have been a deliberate choice, but I think it was a mistake. Giggerotta's tendency to refer to herself in the third person was part of a larger than life quality, a massive, lusty, self-absorption and gusto. Losing that trait diminished her.

Another thing that diminished this new Giggerotta was the costume. The original costume had disintegrated during the final shots of Supernova, in the scene where Dubin crawls from the LEXX's belly. The original costume had been stiff latex rubber, which gave Giggerotta a sense of mass and bulk, and made her movements sweeping. The new costume was made of buckskin suede. Giggerotta seemed smaller, less massive, less of a physical presence.

In a way, the role seems generic. It's easy to imagine Giggerotta's role in Stan's nightmares being played by Wist, or Grand Prosecutor Jihanna, or even Aulk from **Luvliner** or the Cyborg from **791**. It's almost as if the role was written generically and the Giggerotta character was simply slotted in because Dubin turned out to be available, without making much of an effort to customize it.

Fruitcake's dream seems to be an attempt to show a sort of static moment of bliss and adulation, as if he'd simply bought into a perpetual frozen orgasm. Nice idea, but visually, the way it's presented, it's simply dumb and off putting. Maybe it needed a close up of him in continuous orgasm.

David Lewis, who plays Fruitcake, seems wasted, he has this soft, androgynous, doe-like quality which is very odd to find in male actor, but the episode doesn't really do much with him, and perhaps there was more that could have been done.

Lyekka previously, as well as **Garden** and **Apocalexx Now** later, would be suffused with the timeless amorality of dreams, in contrast, **Patches in the** Sky, though its subject matter is dreams is really about mortality and morality, two aspects of life which are fairly antithetical to dreams.

Interestingly, the story boards for these scenes hit just the right note, with Stan floating through a dark tunnel out into a vast star field, images that are both strange and compelling. The storyboard's for Stan's dream in the Narco Lounger are just as fascinating. Stan gliding over still waters, gigantic droplets falling in slow motion around, characters morphing into hundreds of little rubber balls which promptly fall apart, tiny comets at play around

Stan. There's images of a miniature LEXX the size of a sparrow floating around, which even on a storyboard seem visually remarkable. The story boards and presumably the script are actually more successful than the finished product in evoking the surrealism of dreams.

So what happened? A lot of the weirder CGI was probably too expensive. Some of it comes down to bad decisions. The opening dream starts off too loud and too over the top, it jars the viewer rather than seduces. We're lost right at the start, and the episode never quite wins us back fully.

Part of it probably comes down to simple exhaustion. This was the 14th episode in series, and perhaps the brutal pace is simply beginning to show. They've been working five or six days a week, putting in sixteen hour days, churning out at a pace of roughly an episode every seven or eight days, and they're just about to approach the sequence of the 'end game' episodes.

Given that pace, it's understandable if a judgement call misfires like a punch drunk fighter swinging wildly. More, they just don't have the time or energy to go that extra distance: A sparrow sized LEXX, giant raindrops, hell with it, it'll cost too much, take too much time, etc. They just don't have the time or the energy or the resources for the visual surrealism of **Lyekka,** they've got a story to tell, points to make, plot points to drop and they just want to get the damned thing in the can.

Thematically, **Patches in the Sky** is really a follow up to **Stan's Trial,** and a predecessor to **The Beach.** All three explore questions of guilt and responsibility; they're examinations of an ordinary soul. Some of the most effective scenes in Stan's nightmare are the robot complaining about its murder and Giggerotta's speech about Stan's true fear. In this case, they're better at telling than showing.

What the main plot of this story is really about is Stan's continuing and unresolved sense of guilt over the destruction of the 94 reform planets and over his own continuing screw ups. This is first referred to in **I Worship His Shadow**, referenced again in **Gigashadow**, dwelled upon in **Stan's Trial**, mentioned again in **Wake the Dead**, and even alluded to in **The Beach**.

It's an ambiguous guilt, because obviously, he didn't destroy them. But on some lower level, that doesn't help. Stan has survivor's guilt. He survived, they didn't, and more, he's truly aware that if he'd died, they would have lived.

Stan's constantly plagued by nightmares. We see him waking up from one in **Supernova**. We glimpse another one in **Lyekka** and again in **Garden**. So far as we can tell, his dreams start off well and then mutate. His gardens of Eden are always suddenly crawling with poisonous serpents.

In **Stan's Trial** he consciously confronted and acknowledged his guilt, and seemed happier and calmer for it. But people aren't like machines, you can't just throw a switch and everything is better. His guilt still haunts him at lower levels, he feels guilty and deserving of death. This guilt perhaps drives some of his more childish behavior. It's expressed in his conversation with the robot he's destroyed. Sadly, most of the dream simply degenerates into a chase by the bogeyman, and while we've got the generic dream fears, like falling, not nearly enough of the dream imagery or subtext reflects this deeper guilt.

At the end of the day, **Patches in the Sky** has enough good bits going for it to make it an acceptable episode, perhaps even a good one. By the standards of a normal television series it's perfectly fine. But the bits fail to coalesce into a whole and too many times the episode simply misses the mark. But the thing that must really hurt about Patches in the Sky is that while they missed targets here, in other episodes, they proved that they could hit those same targets spectacularly, that they had the reach to match their ambitions.

CREDIT

Creators: *Director - David McLeod; Writers - Paul Donovan and Lex Gigeroff; Production Designer - David Hackl; Creative Producers - Norman Denver and Willie Stevenson*

Main Cast: *Brian Downey (Captain Stanley Tweedle); Michael McManus (Kai, Last of the Brunnen G); Xenia Seeberg (Xev Bellringer, Rejected Wife/Love Slave/Cluster Lizard); Jeffrey Hirschfield (Voice of 790); Tom Gallant (Voice of LEXX).*

Guest Cast: *Wayne Robson (Gubby Mok); Ellen Dubin (Giggerotta); David Lewis (Fruitcake); Lee Anne Lowe (Dream Girl); Laura Cason (Dream Girl); Amy Lundergan (Dream Girl);*

Lost LEXX, The Clizzards of Woz

Story

On the Bridge of the Lexx, Zev is feeling grumpy - and a little twitchy. She has a splitting headache, and not even 790's love poetry can cheer her up. Stan says something stupid, and in an unpremeditated attack she bites him. He is not seriously injured, but the bite is proof positive that something is very wrong with Zev. Zev passes out.

A sorrowful 790 diagnoses her as having a case of "Clizzard wastage", a symptom well known to the inhabitants of the Cluster who imported the Cluster Lizards from an outer planet called Woz. The obvious solution is to go to Woz where Zev may be able to recharge her Clizzard batteries. Stan is not exactly delighted at the prospect of landing on a whole planet of Cluster Lizards. Getting there is no problem since 790 has stored the co-ordinates of Woz, like all the other 20,000 planets of the League, in his memory.

Woz is a planet covered by what seems to be white iron railways leading via several outposts to an emerald colored center. It is warmed by a yellow sun, which causes countless white dunes to look like yellow brick runways.

Kai, Stan, 790 and a groggy Zev descend in a Moth to the surface. The Moth is caught in a twister, and tumbles toward the surface…

…where an obnoxious, loud-mouthed teenage girl ("Theodora") is at a podium, ranting and raving to a curious assemblage about

"Clizzard rights" and "direct action" and "killing the Bitch", when the Moth drops out of the sky and lands right on top of her.

The crew emerges to see two feet sticking out from under the Moth - and a motley crowd of "Clizzard Rights" protesters staring at them. It seems that on Woz, the chief export (even after the Cluster's fall) is Cluster Lizards, who are horribly exploited in an inhumane harvesting operation run by The Black Lady, CEO of the Corporation that controls the planet.

Theodora was the leader of an environmental group that staged periodic "freedom raids", setting Clizzards loose so they could return to their natural habitat. Kai explains that Zev is part Clizzard, and is in need of some urgent genetic repair. The protesters advise them to see The Wuzzard, a kind of new-age ecological guru who lives in the mountains. He might be able to help.

The Wuzzard informs them that he can fix Zev, but that they must perform a task first. Since they are responsible for crushing Theodora, the Crew must carry out the next planned action, namely the assassination of the Black Lady, who lives in a gleaming emerald corporate skyscraper. She is the root of all evil. He points up to the sky, where dark patches have begun appearing lately. "That's her fault too," the Wuzzard tells them. Kai isn't so sure.

Our heroes head for the Black Lady, but along the way are confronted by a pack of Cluster Lizards. Kai puts up a strong defense, but the Clizzards manage to abscond with Zev and roll away.

Kai, Stan and 790 eventually manage to sneak into corporate Headquarters, and once inside the Executive Suites they find - Zev, chatting happily with The Black Lady. It turns out that she had heard about Zev's problem, and dispatched some Clizzards to retrieve her. Now she is all fixed up (a key DNA sequence had been corrupted on the Cluster).

The Black Lady explains that her so-called "torture farms" are actually models of humane Clizzard management, that until the

Corporation came along the creatures had almost become extinct because they had exhausted their food supply. The real problem facing the Clizzards are these enviro-weirdos up in the mountains who keep releasing them back into the wild, where they promptly die from heat and starvation.

At that point the Headquarters are disrupted by an all-out guerilla attack from the Wuzzard (who secretly monitored the crew's "betrayal"). Total panic and chaos immediately reign supreme. Kai, Zev, Stan and 790 manage to escape and somehow find their way back to the Lexx.

The Lexx leaves orbit and heads off into the stars. Back on Woz, the revolution is at its bloody apex. The Wuzzard looks up, and sees the patches in the sky fill up with millions of bright dots, all streaming down toward the planet.

From space, we see the planet Woz being devoured…

(December, 1997, Series Outline, special thanks to Lex Gigeroff)

Commentary

Let's just start off by saying that the word 'Clizzards' out loud a few times. It just sounds so naughty. Clizzards of Woz, by the way, is one of three stories proposed by the German executive producer, Wolfram Tichy.

This makes a fascinating companion to the episode that was eventually produced, and the two of them bookend neatly with the versions of **Girltown** in the third volume.

Essentially, Clizzards of Woz, eleventh episode of the December 1997 treatments, is a perfect example of the way an idea would 'ripple' through the whole script.

Here, the idea was a simple production decision. Cluster Lizards were too expensive and troublesome to do again, especially at the level of interaction with the live cast that the treatment seemed to require. They'd done them in the first movie, **I Worship His**

Shadow, with puppets, it had been costly and a huge pain in the ass, they'd done them with CGI in **Terminal** it had been costly and a huge pain in the ass. This time, it was going to be worse, the story called for more Cluster Lizards than ever before, and it called for them to interact with the cast and do more complex things than they'd ever been called to do before. Wisely, they decided to leave them alone this time.

But, if you take the Cluster Lizards out as the basis for Xev's illness, then what are you left with? Her malady then has to come, by default, from the other side of her nature, the love slave side. If it's a love slave illness, then certain consequences have to flow from that. Love Slaves are engineered to be perfect, so whatever is wrong with Xev has to have been deliberately engineered. Planned obsolescence, an expiration date, follows naturally. The whole focus of the episode quite naturally becomes one of sexual politics and radical Dworkin/McKinnon style feminism.

If the Dark Lady has the cure, then it makes sense, story wise, for the Dark Lady to be deeply involved in the love slave business. And let's add another wrinkle, if the Dark Lady is in the business of transforming ordinary girls into perfect beauties, why wouldn't she use the machine to perfect herself. Unless she can't. And if she can't use the machine on herself, why not make her hideously deformed instead of merely ordinary. But then, we have to give the Dark Lady more screen time, to develop this more elaborate character. She can't just show up at the end.

Conversely, the position of the Wuzzard, by default, has to be that spiritual beauty is all. So, we need more screen time for him too, to develop that character, and to develop his conflict with the Dark Lady.

All of which crowds poor Theodora (Dorothy) completely out of the picture, and of course, there's no room left for the 'Hey! There are **Patches in the Sky**!' subplot, a bit of surplusage which is then dumped in with Gubby Mok and the broken drone arm in **The Salesman**, to form a new episode..

See how it all flows quite naturally? One production decision, and it ripples out to create a completely different episode, and even creates ripples affecting other episodes. It's quite elegant.

And just for the record, for once Lex Gigeroff confirmed that this was exactly what had happened. Cluster Lizards were out of the question, and so they'd followed the other path. For once, I got something right.

Overall, Clizzards seems inferior to Woz. The simple truth is that Clizzards attack on the animal rights activists movement is like smashing kittens with sledgehammers, sure it's fun and easy, but you just don't get that satisfying splat. No one really takes animal rights activists all that seriously, they're a peripheral group in public consciousness. The whole episode feels fairly light and insubstantial, which isn't necessarily a bad thing.

The ideas in Woz, on the other hand, are much more lively. Every time you look at a magazine rack, you're confronted with artificial beauties, and the debate or argument between inner and outer beauty, over sex and desire, and women's place in society, takes place everywhere on levels from the personal to the political. Essentially, Woz simply has more meat to it, more ideas, and it invests more time in developing its points of view. It skirts the edge of being heavy handed and ponderous in doing so, but it does the job.

LEXX 2.15, Woz

Story

On board the LEXX, 790 shocks everyone when he mentions Xev is going to die. It turns out that Love Slaves are created with an expiration date and Xev is coming up to hers. He thought everyone knew.

Xev isn't thrilled at the thought. The only thing that can save her is a Lustikon machine, like the one that originally transformed her. But they were all destroyed on The Cluster, except for one. That one had been assigned to the remotest planet in the Divine Order for use by the clerics there, the planet Woz.

The LEXX heads to Woz. Landing in a moth, they crush a young woman. They're met by other beautiful women who lead them to the Wozard. The Wozard has a Lustikon, but he blackmails Kai and Stan into doing his bidding before he will use it. Their mission is to kill the evil Dark Lady. They reluctantly agree.

As Kai and Stan go on their mission, the Wozard restores Xev, transforming her back into her original fat form from I Worship His Shadow. As she weeps, he leaves, putting on a video of dancing vegetables to entertain her.

Stan and Kai invade the Dark Lady's sanctuary, capturing her guards. Kai encounters the Dark Lady and learns that the Wozard has been lying to them, and that she's a good person. She possesses a deformity that the Lustikon cannot fix. The Wozard shows up with a suicide vest, having exposed himself for a misogynist cult leader. Kai and Stanley flee as the Wozard blows up the Dark Lady's tower.

790 uses the Wizard's Lustikon to restore Xev and reset her expiration date for 79 years, and the crew fly off together. As the LEXX leaves, Mantrid's drones arrive to dismantle the planet.

Review & Commentary

Danny Peary, in his book **Cult Movies** writes about the **Wizard of Oz** and says that this harmless little children's film has become a cultural touchstone which so profoundly affected subsequent generations that practically every film made since 1939 has snuck in a reference to it somewhere. And it's true. It's one of those meaningless little insights that, once it's pointed out to you, you can't stop seeing everywhere you look.

All right, so here we've got our hapless crew caught in a Tornado. The moth, making a forced, landing winds up crushing poor Dodo, who was off on a quest in her red and white stripped stockings, recalling both Dorothy and the Wicked Witch of the East. They follow a yellow stone path to meet the Wozard of Woz. Stan and Kai journey to the Dark Lady's tower where they're told 'no one's home.' Meanwhile the Wozard says *'The Wicked Bitch is dead.'* and Xev finishes up with *'There's no place like home.'* And in the end, it turns out that neither the Wozard or the Dark Lady are what they were seen to be.

Do you think?

'Dodo' by the way, might possibly be a **Doctor Who** reference. 1960's **Doctor Who** had a companion named Dodo. The chances of that? Probably zero. 'Dodo' is more likely a fusion of 'Dorothy' and 'Toto.'

LEXX's skewed adventure is more than just a take on the **Wizard of Oz,** however. In fact, a lot of the **Wizard of Oz** stuff is just fun. It's not essential to the story at all; it merely adds a layer of humor and meaning to the story.

Past this, the episode also functions as a surprisingly thoughtful meditation on beauty, self-worth and sexual politics in the tug of war between the Wozard and the Dark Lady over women's bodies. Being LEXX of course, it's got its gritty off kilter undertones as the Wozard rambles obliviously on about the "Sick male need for penetration" while deprived love slaves force Stan to undress, clearly enthusiastic about the sick male need themselves.

The Wozard takes his followers on a journey from Oz to Jonestown as a cult leader gone bad. In some ways, he's reminiscent of Jim Jones, or perhaps closer to Marshall Applewhite, leader of the Solar Temple suicide cult, an idealist gone horribly wrong. The episode also plays off misguided idealism versus superficial pragmatism.

"Wozard as an idealist?" says Walter Borden, the actor who played him, "I think he was a manipulator. He didn't believe it, or if he did believe, he simply didn't care much about people. At the very least, the Wozard was just another personification of the Divine Shadow to accommodate a certain set of circumstances."

LEXX has had actors return before this. John Dunsworth and Robert Sigl showed up in multiple roles in **Gigashadow**. Holger Kunkel appeared in **Eating Pattern** and reappeared as a new character in Mantrid. Hirschfield, Gigeroff and even McManus showed up in different roles, but they were always unconnected.

This makes Borden idea interesting, if the Wozard is really a personification of the Divine Shadow, or essentially the same character, then this is the first time that we've had the sort of continuity of characters that would become a staple feature of the third and fourth seasons.

"Woz is heavier, than you'd think, it's a deceptively heavy piece. It's rather like the old classic fairy tales, like **Alice in Wonderland** *or* **Gulliver's Travels** *or the* **Wizard of Oz**, *or* **Cinderella** *for that matter,"* he continues. *"These stories were far deeper than we were lead to believe, of course, we know that now, though many people don't realize it, when one can really analyze* **Gulliver's Travels** *or* **Alice in Wonderland**. *It's great mind food. To some extent this was written into the series and I like that, I like the mental exercises it would give."*

The Wozard, is of course, Walter Borden, a local Halifax actor, who made a living working as a parking lot attendant. I remember back in 2000 some fans were shocked to find His Divine Shadow watching over their parking lot. This certainly wasn't a reflection on Borden as an actor, he'd studied and performed in New York, and he'd acted across Canada on stage and television.

But the fact is that, very few actors can make a full time living at it, and Halifax was a small place. So one week, guest star in a television series, another week working at the parking lot. It's a testament to the hardships that many actors go through to do something they love.

Borden was one of the interviews I'd genuinely looked forward too, for his roles as ultimate evil in the Divine Shadow, and his performances as the Wozard and Doctor Longbore. He was an absolute pleasure to talk to, like so many of the people involved with LEXX he was warm and engaging, very open and full of genuine affection for what he was doing. He spoke enthusiastically and provided an eloquent picture of what the experience had been like.

"I loved the Wozard! I got to have body and soul together!" Borden laughs, in the first season on LEXX, he'd played body and voice of two separate incarnations of the Divine Shadow. *"Paul and Lex always said they wanted to find characters for me to do. But they'd just say it and go on with their conversation. When the Wozard script was there, I went and auditioned, which was a scary bit. But I found out later that they wrote it especially for me. It was immensely flattering."*

"I had to do a lot of greenscreen. The first time around it's extremely disconcerting. We hear about it as actors, but when you've never experienced it, especially if you're a trained stage actor, it blows your mind. Greenscreen isn't like working against a blank wall. Green is such an aggressively florescent color; it's almost like being yelled at. After a while, it's fun. You have to follow so carefully what the director tells you, and do exactly that, because everything has to be done precisely in small bits and pieces, and it has to be filled. It is a most peculiar type of acting; because you do exactly as the director tells you and you work in only small bits."

"It was a great time," Borden recalls, *"we were constantly laughing. And of course, I'd known my co-star, Lenore Zann (who played the Dark Lady) for years, she's my buddy. She's from Nova Scotia as well. I got to know Lenore as an actress, I knew her family, we followed each other's careers. That was the first time we'd ever acted together, that was why we were so happy together. We'd always planned to do something together. She had to do a lot of prosthetics, But she never complained. David McLeod, the director, was wonderful, we just clicked from the get go. It's a wonderful thing when you can work with your director like that. He made it so easy. We just had the attitude that we wanted to make this work and do whatever it took."*

"I just remember so much laughter that there had to be crazy things happening. Even intense moments, when things come up, suddenly you'll get some mini-confrontation between the first AD and the sound person, little things, people get testy. As the actor, you're sitting there going, oh I wonder what's going to come out of this. Then some kind of diffusion would come in, some light, someone would say something and it would switch everything into a laughter situation. There was a great deal of laughter. Working with those people, there are some incredible wits flying around there. It comes in handy. They'd throw in those zingers. It was everybody taking care of everyone. I don't like to make it sound like Oz, it had its bad moments, it had its ups and downs, but it was like a family situation."

The episode isn't quite perfect. There are spots where it just doesn't go far enough over the top, where it's too restrained. The scene between Stan and the Love Slaves for instance. The sets are a bit too stark and barren, and at times the thinness of the budget shows through a little bit too much. I know that a few people balked when they saw that the Wozard's atomic vest was made of simple commonplace glow sticks. That goes beyond shabby, that's just sad and a little pathetic.

And there's an oddly stiff quality that seems to recur through the episode, a sort of theme. It shows in the emptiness of the sets. And it shows in the almost rigid costumes and flared skirts of the Love Slaves. Alex Busby called them **Jetsons** costumes, and there's something to that, but there's more. They're completely unnatural, they don't move, the skirts don't swing around the legs, they're lined with foam padding to make them stiff and keep this artificial flaring shape. It's like those two dimensional wardrobes that you get for paper cut out dolls.

The pacing and delivery of the lines, particularly in the scenes where Kai confronts the Dark Lady has this formal, wooden quality. The characters don't really talk naturally, rather, they announce, they orate, they make speeches at each other. This isn't just the delivery, this is in the writing.

The dialogue on **Woz** has this odd, stentorian rhythm, a kind of steady cadence which isn't at all natural. It can be off putting, you sit there and watch it, and it is completely unnatural. It's not smooth; it's kind of like going over a log road, steady rhythmic bumps.

It's not what people expect. But then again, if you allow yourself to accept the rhythm, it works. What it is, is theatrical. Think of **Woz** as a small stage play and the look and rhythm start to work. It's a deliberate decision, I think, it runs too consistently through too many elements of production and writing to really be accidental.

Let's face it, this is the **Wizard of Oz**, for God's sake. They know it, we know it, everyone knows it, no one is fooled. Naturalism, treating this in normal cinematic ways just isn't going to work. Instead, they've upped the artificiality and reduced the scale to go for a more theatrical look and feel. I'm prepared to go with that.

In this sense, I think we can see **Woz** as a forerunner to the even more deliberately theatrical **Brigadoom**.

On the other hand, I'm not really prepared to go with the handling of Xev and Zev. I've complained about this before, but the writers seem to have this difficulty dealing with all the characters at once. They keep propping one up in a closet while the others go off and do something. This time its Xev, who gets to lay on the Wozard's table while Stan and Kai go off. Why does she lay on the table? Who knows?. Why is she tied down to the table? Who knows? They just don't have anywhere for her to go, or anything for her to do. It's weak.

Lisa Hynes returns as the all but forgotten original Zev. This was almost certainly a sort of joke. They'd advertised that Zev would return, leading people to expect Habermann, and they delivered Hynes again. Okay, well, all's fair. On the other hand, having brought Hynes back, they don't actually give her anything to do except lay on the table and blubber. I don't know, it just feels unnecessarily cruel and pointless to go through the trouble of bringing an actor back and then having them effectively be not much more than a prop. She could have had some decent lines.

But then again, this is sometimes an actor's lot. There were a lot of women in this episode playing love slaves, and pretty much most of them really didn't have much more to do than be scenery. On reflection, that may be a little unfair, two of the Wozard's followers show friendship, the Love Slaves are implied to have a point of view. But not a lot is done with it.

By the way, look for Laura Cason as one of the Dark Lady's guards. Why does she look familiar? She was just in **Patches in the Sky** as one of the dream babes clinging to Fruitcake. I guess the love slaves of Woz really were hard up.

Of course, having deliberately established the subliminal look and rhythm and cadence of a theatrical production, the creators gave us a complete visual whiplash with the fruit scene.

The fruit and vegetable animation scenes in simply defy description. Tasteless, obscene, bizarre? No word seems to adequately describe the surreal strangeness of this piece of work. It's just amazing, especially combined with the catchy yet irritating *'Brightness sisters'* jingle. It's completely antithetical to the almost relentlessly grim visual style of the episode. It's one of those classic loopy touches that makes LEXX so visually inventive. It makes you wish **Patches in the Sky's** dream sequences were as similarly loopy.

"The dancing vegetables?" Borden laughed out loud when I asked him about it, *"I don't know about that scene. I sat down and watched the finished product, some of the stuff we see. We had no idea it was going to be there.*

None. Glorious stuff. It wasn't even in the script. Somewhere in post-production, this is what happened. We finally got to see what we did, and we'll go, oh wow, they wrapped it in this package! It was always such a hoot to do a scene. You're told to hit this button and hit that button. But nothings happening until you see it in post-production. When you're hitting those buttons and things are popping up, it's great to see. (Laughing) because you didn't see it while you were doing it. You had so little appreciation of what the eventual result is going to look like. That's the thing with greenscreen and post, the show you watch is just so different from the show you remembered working on. There's so much that's added to these shows afterwards, it's really quite stunning."

I loved the dancing vegetables, but no one seemed willing to take credit for it. I asked Dave Albiston, who'd done the stop motion sequence for Bugbomb **in I Worship His Sh**adow, but he denied all responsibility. Cordell Wynne also pleaded not guilty. Production designer Mark Laing confirms, *"the dancing vegetables were thrown in long after we finished."*

The best information I've got is that it was a brainstorm of Lex and Paul, shot ad hoc with a video camera.

CREDITS

Creators: *Writers - Paul Donovan and Lex Gigeroff; Director - David MacLeod; Designers - Mark Laing and Tim Boyd; Creative Producers -Cordell Wynne and Norman Denver;*

Main Cast: *Brian Downey (Captain Stanley Tweedle); Michael McManus (Kai, Last of the Brunnen G); Xenia Seeberg (Xev Bellringer (Rejected Wife/Love Slave/Cluster Lizard); Jeffrey Hirschfield (Voice of 790); Tom Gallant (Voice of LEXX).*

Guest Cast: *Lenore Zann (Dark Lady); Walter Borden (Wozard); Lisa Hines (Original Zev); Kerry McPherson (Skye); Stacy Smith (Calico); Robin Johnson (Dark lady's guard); Laura Cason (Dark lady's guard); Adrienne Horton (Dark lady's guard); Lori Heath (Dark lady's alarm voice.)*

Lost LEXX, Dorkadia

Story

The LEXX and crew arrive on Dorkadia, a planet rife with mousy computer geeks, Trekkies and D&D fanatics... In short, all those odd kids in school with thick glasses, dandruff and ill-fitting shirts. The bulk of their time is spent playing all manner of elaborate involved games, mostly with fancy computers. Much of the interior of the planet resembles a kind of cheesy casino.

(Handwritten notes - Maybe not computer games, but very strange mechanical games. Something never seen before anywhere else, like sticking your nose in something like a light bulb socket and measuring how long you can continue with some other function while being really pre-occupied. Bets are taken against activities. So these dorks are involved, perhaps not with computer games, as much as quasi-scientific experiments that have mutated into a degenerate form of amusement. Sort of a "Hitler just wants to have fun" episode.)

Desperate for some kind of action, Stan quickly gets involved in one of the big games. He loses his shirt, Kai and Zev, the LEXX and finally the Key in his 'magic hand.' Stan is thrown into 'receivership.'

Zev is, ironically, sentenced to be turned into a love slave, but in Dorkadia, the looks of a love slave are even more pumped up than she already is.

The LEXX takes umbrage at the thought of being turned into a giant theme park/paintball arcade, but the ship is subdued with drugs and computers.

One of the Dorks ("Flort") likes Zev just the way she is – and with the aid of 790, manages to rescue her... But Flort is only using her to get access to Stan's hand, as he really wants to steal the LEXX...

Kai saves the day when he invents a completely new game – an esoteric intellectualized cross between Chess and Go – that takes the Dork totally by surprise. They get so hooked on it that he wins the ship back... and the crew are able to high tail it out of Dorkadia...

.....just as the planet eating force rolls through and gobbles it up....

(Special thanks to Brian Downey)

Commentary

Episode 17 on the June 28, 1996, promotional series outline, **Dorkadia** actually seems like it might have been doable. I'm speaking loosely here, some of the episode ideas, particularly from the 1996 outlines but even in the 1997 outline seem like such obvious dogs it's a wonder why they were committed to paper.

This would have taken extras and actors, and a lot of work for the props department, which suggests in the realm of tight budgets, it might not have been all that doable. But it's definitely got a LEXXish feel, and seems primed for the madcap invention that sometimes characterized the series.

Unfortunately, **Dorkadia** seems to have simply died on the operating table early on. It doesn't appear in the mid-1997 promotional brochure, or the December 1997 series outline. A bit of a shame, really.

Lost LEXX, Prison Planet

Story

The time has come once again for the LEXX to eat, so the great ship lands on a planet rich in vegetation and apparently abandoned. Zev, as is her proclivity, wants to go explore in a Moth while they wait for the LEXX to fill up. Remembering their experience in Eating Pattern, Stan decides to stay on board.

Hours later, Zev has not returned. Then Stan receives a distress call from Zev that is suddenly cut off. He rouses Kai and the two of them go off in another Moth to find her.

Zev's exploration leads her to a massive prison complex on the planet. From spying distance, she is able to see that this is an all-female prison; an all hot female prison. The guards are all female too, but they are burly and sadistic.

Unfortunately, Zev has landed in the middle of a jailbreak, and she is soon swept up in the events. She is able to get a distress call off to the LEXX before being recaptured along with the inmates. The convicts complain that they are not criminals, merely wrongly convicted victims of a cruel and unfair justice system.

Stan rouses Kai, who goes to the planet to rescue Zev, but he too is captured and neutralized.

It's up to Stan to save the day. Luckily for him, Wist is beginning an active cycle. He takes her down to the planet and unleashes her. She eats most of the prison staff. Kai, Zev, and the lovely inmates are all freed.

Stan feels that, because he was the mastermind of the successful rescue mission, its pay-back time and the freed convicts should show some sexual gratitude. They all proclaim that they would too, but the problem is that they are all dyed-in-the-wool lesbians. In fact, that's why they were all put in jail in the first place.

They claim that they would happily display their gratitude to him through the women in the crew, but Zev's not quite yet willing to go down that road and Wist has no compatible sexual organs.

Stan is out of luck once again.

(December, 1997, Series Outline, special thanks to Lex Gigeroff)

Commentary

Although it never made it into production, there's a reference in the third season opener, **Fire and Water**, which seems very suggestive. The crew is looking for a place to go, and Kai suggests:

"Nimbus 9 is a prison planet rumored to be entirely populated by naked naughty nymphomaniacs."

Well, I think we all know that if Stan went to Nimbus 9, then all those naked, naughty nymphomaniacs would turn out to be very butch lesbians. Let's face it, that's just the way things turn out for Stan.

There may also be a slight shade of **Prison Planet** in **Girltown**, because in this lost episode, the prisoners' only crime is that they're lesbians, as is the case of the gay prisoners and lesbian guards of Girltown. Of course, Lyekka's eating her way through the guards here, is flipped over into her eating her way through the prisoners in **791**.

And finally, the 'Girl's Prison' shows up in **P4X**, there's no lesbian action going on, not even in the shower sequence, and there's no prison uprising. But at least the guys got it out of their system.

Like Kai's protoblood, the LEXX's need to eat was occasionally alluded to, as in **Love Grows** or in **Brigadoom,** and amounted to an ongoing plot point that was never really addressed in the series that was made.

Interestingly, an earlier, less developed version of this 'lost episode' originally appeared in the June, 1996, series outline, where it was titled **Planet of the Ultra Savage Vixens in Cages**, and where the writers, dreaming in technicolor, announced that the episode *"should feature Angie Dickinson, Morgan Fairchild, Linda Blair, Joey Heatherton, Tanya Roberts, Diane Thorne, Marilyn Chambers and Traci Lords as guest stars."* In that earlier version, it's Stan who sneaks into the prison in drag to score with the inmates, and Zev and Kai (also in drag) who go in to rescue him, but all the basic plot elements and twists are there.

The persistence of this episode in outlines and series plans between June, 1996, and December, 1997, where it was listed as the 18th episode, suggests that they were fairly serious about it, unlike other potential episodes like **My Bonnie** or **Passion Flower**, and they may well have been genuinely committed to it. But it never made it as far as a finished script.

This seems like a perfectly workable episode, undercut by what seemed to be fairly substantial production costs. All the expensive markers are there, a crowded cast, multiple sets, a lot of effects.

On the downside, it seems like they were taking on the 'women in prison' genre of films like **Caged Heat**. All the elements are there, sadistic guards, abused prisoners, probably shower scenes, an innocent girl caught up in circumstances, and the big bust out at the end. The trouble is that **Caged Heat** and its genre are fairly obscure. Everyone knows Alien, everyone knows the **Wizard of Oz**, everyone knows **Friday the Thirteenth** and its slasher film descendants. On the other hand, a satiric take off of the **Big Bird Cage** or animal rights activists is more likely to result in 'huh?'

Still, there was a lot of potential here for magnificent, charming sleaze. Scheduled for the last quarter of the season, this position in a rapidly evaporating production budget probably meant that the episode was DOA.

LEXX 2.16 & 2.17, Web and Net

Story

Kai reveals that in 31 days the Universe will be gone. The LEXX crew respond to this news with the decision to run like hell. There's another universe, the Dark Zone, so they decide to escape into it. But it turns out that Mantrid has eliminated all the gateways to the other universe. Kai reveals that there's one left, an uncertainty region at the center of this universe. They decide to go there.

A giant space web pursues the LEXX. The crew detect it just as they crash into it, and everyone is knocked unconscious. Tentacles from the Web slide into the LEXX and infect Stan, but when they reach Kai, his undead nature, causes lethal feedback to the creature, paralyzing it. Xev and 790 wake up and rescue Stan, together they detach Kai. They discover that the LEXX is still caught, and Stan orders the LEXX to blow up the Web.

Stan is acting strangely, and weirdly aggressive. This reaches a peak when he attacks Xev. Kai stops him. It turns out that Stan has been possessed by a piece of the Web creature. All it wants to do is escape Mantrid. It leaves Stan and Xev crushes it with her boot. The Lexx proceeds on to the center of the Universe.

Review & Commentary

The first time I saw **Net**, I didn't know what to make of it. It looked just like **Web** the episode that had played the week before: The LEXX runs into a giant spider web in space, the crew are knocked out, they wander around for a while until they figure out they're still in the spider web, then they break free.

Was something wrong? Were they just repeating themselves? Had the TV station made a mistake and accidentally rerun last week's episode, instead of this weeks? I was getting upset.

I started to notice differences in the first few minutes. So was footage from the previous episode being used to set up the new episode? No, it was the same episode, sort of. Except that it was different.

There were more special effects, more creature stuff. Was it the previous week's episode that had been defective? Had they simply rushed it through, incomplete, and now we were getting the proper version, or perhaps the Director's cut. Or were we watching a show edited for some other market, the British version, perhaps? I almost called up the television station. I even went on the internet quizzing chat rooms about what the hell was going on.

For the first half hour I watched it, getting steadily more confused and annoyed. In the end, I was just pissed off. I'd been swindled! I'd gotten the same episode twice, with only minor differences. I wanted my money back. I expect this kind of irritation from avante garde experimental film makers; I don't put up with this stuff on my television. It was clear what had happened, they were running out of money, so they decided to pull this ultra-cheap-O sneak.

Web and **Net** have gotten some of the most hostile reactions in a series which has ruffled more than a few feathers. A lot of people, walking into it without warning, simply reacted to it like I did and felt abused and ripped off. The US Sci Fi Channel, when it aired LEXX for the first time decided to air **Net**, but not **Web.** Instead, **Web** was cybercast.

This is probably the cheapest pair of episodes. There's no guest cast at all, simply the principal actors, there's no new sets to speak of, there's minimal special effects (by the standards of LEXX), and at least two thirds or three quarters of each episode is overlap. It's literally two episodes for the price of one, a cheap on one at that. Of course, they freely admit that being able to save money was a big motivating factor.

"Web and Net was a bottle show," Norman Denver acknowledged, "Everyone does a bottle show. Simply because, you tend to maybe see an episode you want to spend a lot of money on, and so you spend money on another one."

In this case, they'd already spent a lot of money, and they wanted to spend more money on Brigadoom and End of the Universe. They needed to cut a few corners somewhere. Money was always a concern; if you watch the series carefully you can see here and there where they really stretched their budget to the breaking point. Given that the show's per episode budget was only a fraction of a comparable American TV series budget, it's remarkable that they did so much with so little.

Web and **Net** weren't originally part of the plan. They don't appear, for instance, as part of the December, 97, outline. Rather, they were created at the last minute in answer to the crunch.

Paul Donovan admits, *"We were behind schedule, we didn't have enough days left to do all the shows. We wanted to do a* **Rashomon** *kind of thing. Conceptually it worked. In execution it didn't work as well. It's one of the things, we're behind schedule. The thing was we didn't want to do a typical bottle show. We didn't want to have the characters sitting around going 'remember when....' so we tried to do something different."*

"I think the idea was a good one," Brian Downey said, *"but the trouble is, they were trying to do it cheap and fast, and you just can't do it that way."*

Director Chris Bould, on the other hand, is an adamant defender of the episodes. When he spoke of it, he was so kinetic and animated; you were practically there with him.

"Norman Denver came to me, and he said, ' Chris, you've got to get us out of a hole.'

"I said 'Sure, Norman, what is it?'

"He said, 'You have to do two episodes back to back.' Then he coughed and fidgeted around from foot to foot. 'And you have to do them in ten days.'

" 'That's fucking suicide,' I told him. 'Are you telling me the truth?'

"'I'm telling you the truth,' he tells me.

"'Because if you aren't, Norman, I'll find out...'

"'It's the truth.'

"'All right, I'll do it.' I said.

"Then he coughed a bit more. 'That's nine days principal and one day second unit.'

"We did two hours of television in nine days. No second unit. It was the bottleneck show. There was no money, no more sets, no guest stars, no extras, even the CGI was minimal. My god, there was a challenge. People laugh at me, but I'm proud of those shows."

As time has gone on, I've come to really like **Web** and **Net**. For one thing, the two episodes aren't quite as identical as it seems at first blush.

Web starts quite differently. Its first nine minutes are unique to it, where Stan loses his hat, the crew finally realizes the danger they're in, and decides to make a run for it. There's a whole prologue here that's an essential part of the greater **Mantrid Arc** that's absent from **Net**. This is the episode where the crew finally come to understand that Mantrid is destroying the Universe.

Their response?

To run like hell, which is completely unheroic, but very sensible.

There was, by the way, another plot point that didn't make it. *"I had fights with Jeff about this,"* Chris Bould remembers. *"Irrelevant dialogue. He wanted these lines where the LEXX was getting hungry and starting to slow down as it neared the center of the universe."*

It's a shame that those lines didn't make it in. In the beginning of the third season, LEXX has stopped moving, it's run out of food. It's an abrupt development, jarring because it's so sudden. The LEXX had been fine through the entire second season. Perhaps an extra line or two here or there, foreshadowing this development might have made it a little easier to swallow.

For the most part, however, **Web** feels odd. It's as if they hired Ingmar Bergman to do an LEXX. The episode seems filled with meaningful pauses and significant glances, awkward silences. The episode is all about mysteries without solutions and questions without answers. It's an odd episode, stark and alienated, almost existential in its outlook. Again, that's one of the show's strengths, to be so radically different and experimental from one episode to the next.

The crew struggle with the mystery of what happened to them when they hit the Web, finally unraveling the mystery and killing the monster. But it's an oddly unsatisfying victory. In a normal TV show, figuring it out and stopping the creature is the whole point. Here, it almost feels like a sideshow, a meaningless distraction.

And that's exactly what it is.

It's just a monster.

They don't learn anything about it, or about themselves. They just deal with it. Destroying the Web creature changes none of their existential dilemmas. The Universe is still being destroyed; they're still running for their lives to an uncertain safety, Kai is still dead, Xev still unsatisfied. The affair of the Web creature means almost nothing in their lives. It's just grim.

You almost feel like cheering when Xev goes off to see Stan, to move on from Kai, and abandon the unattainable man for a real chance at a relationship, and we hear 790's scream. It means Stan and Xev may finally be getting it on, a human gesture of need and compassion, that adds life and warmth to a very bleak episode.

The thing that makes these episodes unique is that they've literally gone beyond **Rashomon**.

Rashomon for the record is an old Japanese film by Akira Kurosawa. Essentially, it tells the story of a murder by a bandit in the forest, from four different viewpoints, including the bandit, the hero and even a ghost. Each viewpoint showing a dramatically different encounter. The Rashomon style of storytelling purports to tell the same tale from different points of view. Even for Kurosawa, this meant showing radically different versions of the same scene.

Web and Net, however, literally show the same scenes. The differences are literally all in the points of view, it's not about the scenes playing out differently depending on who is telling it, rather, the meaning of the same scenes differ depending on who the camera is watching. This is a remarkably subtle point.

Watching **Web and Net**, we come to realize that it's all about point of view. In **Web,** the story is told from the subjective point of view of Xev. We see what she does. We know what she knows only when she learns it. The viewpoint is never so crude as to look out through Xev's eyes, or listen in on her thoughts, but the entire story is told through the framework of her perception.

The point of view of **Net,** on the other hand, is more omniscient. We see all, we hear all. Now we get to see the monster. Perhaps this is monster-cam, the story told from the creature's point of view, or perhaps from Stanley's. Or perhaps it's a neutral overview.

"We had to do scenes where Brian goes psychotic," Bould remembers. *"I'm quite proud of him. We had to use distorted lenses. Brian had to go right into the camera. We were all laughing. The cameraman Les was laughing so hard the camera was shaking. They said, 'Chris this is stupid.' But no, we pulled that off, Brian looked evil. I was the only person on the set that knew we'd pull it off."*

It's also an interesting comment on storytelling. The two episodes are literally all about what to tell the audience and when. In **Web,** information is parceled out, the whole thing is treated as a mystery with clues accumulating and resulting in a discovery.

But if our scope was limited in **Web** and we had to solve the mystery, with **Net** it's all laid out in front of us, from the beginning. There are no surprises in Net, we know who the bad guy is. Not just two different points of view at work, but two different ways of telling a story. I'm sure if Kafka were alive today, these would be his favorite episodes.

"*I talked about objective and subjective cameras a lot,*" Chris Bould confirms. "*It was about the way you lens it. The audience doesn't understand it, but they feel it.*"

One thing identical in both episodes is Xev's anguished conversation with Kai. The relationship between Xev and Kai has been one of unrequited love. Of Xev pining away for a man incapable of returning her feelings. Over the course of the season, she's grown as a person, a slow growth, unremarked upon, but it's been there.

Of the characters occupying LEXX, Xev has been the only one who actually spends time reflecting upon her experiences. Kai is incapable of change, and Stan is trapped in a loop of his own guilt. But Xev grows. She's no longer the petulant child who threw a tantrum over Kai's failure to satisfy her in **Love Grows**.

This is an older, wiser Xev. A woman who still has to go back one last time to ask if there's a chance, but one who accepts the sadness of knowing it isn't there. The emotions of this scene are handled with remarkable insight and honesty, full of the bittersweet poignance we see so often in life and so seldom in television. The relationship between Xev and Kai was always one of unrequited love, and to their credit, the creators and characters never took the easy way out.

"*When you watch a show like **Web & Net**, it looks easy peasy,*" Bould reflects. "*But the amount of anguish that went on, to make it different, to make it interesting. It was incredibly difficult. People watch TV shows, they're sandwiched between commercial breaks. Some of those commercials cost more than the episode. The audience should never know that. It should look as good as the commercial. Watch carefully, there's a lot in there.*"

CREDITS

Creators: *Writer - Jeff Hirschfield; Director - Chris Bould; Designer - David Hackl; Creative Producer - Willie Stevenson.*

Main Cast: *Brian Downey (Captain Stanley Tweedle); Michael McManus (Kai, Last of the Brunnen G); Xenia Seeberg (Xev Bellringer (Rejected Wife/Love Slave/Cluster Lizard); Jeffrey Hirschfield (Voice of 790); Tom Gallant (Voice of LEXX).*

Lost LEXX, Lexxstasy

Story

Stan keeps up his gardening responsibility, watering Wist regularly. That is, until the LEXX itself is thirsty and needs to drink. Stan gets worried because the plant that is Wist starts to shrivel. His worries increase as a weak Wist takes human form and says she must drink soon or a very nasty version of herself will have no choice but to drink their blood.

Our heroes then stumble upon a ship drifting through the cosmos with no signs of life. Boarding it, they discover that its crew are two young women, Tura and Dot, in frozen cryostasis. Upon being wakened, they explain that the reason they were sent into space is that on their planet, no one has any concept of music, and their society has become morose and stultified. Their mission was to find a mythical musical planet, but their ship malfunctioned and has been drifting aimlessly.

They want the LEXX to transport them to this legendary planet of music. Its water has an isotope balance that imparts musicality to those who drink it. Hearing that the planet is entirely water, Stan soon has the LEXX set down on it. The big ship immediately starts singing as it slakes its thirst.

As the crew enjoy the tropical sun, huge creepers with trumpet flowers appear out of the water. And the music begins. The company then engage in some very hip singing. In the end Tura and Dot will head home with their newfound musical talent and special water supply.

The mysterious, amorphous cloud that passes by after the LEXX departs approaches, but does not consume the planet of water.

(December 17, 1997, Series Outline, special thanks to Lex Gigeroff)

Commentary

What the hell were they thinking? The search for the legendary planet of music? That isn't LEXX, that's **H.R. Puff n' stuff**! This is children's quality educational programming! This was planned as the 15th episode of the December 1997 treatments.

According to Jeff Hirschfield, this almost episode came from two inspirations. Two disparate bizarre ideas from Paul Donovan and Wolfram Tichy brutally welded together.

Paul Donovan wanted to do an episode on water, sort of like **Jaws** or **Waterworld**. Normally, doing a film on water is both expensive, time consuming and technically challenging. This seems bizarre, but it's actually the sort of quirky technical challenge that seems to appeal to Paul Donovan.

The idea of setting an episode entirely on or around a water planet may have been consciously or unconsciously recycled in the concept of the water planets in **Nook** and the third season **Fire and Water** series. Certainly the idea of a planet or city of music seems to fit in better with the monomaniacal cultures of Fire and Water, and one can almost imagine circumstances where, if third season had went a bit differently, some variation of this episode might actually have been made.

The other inspiration for this episode came from Wolfram Tichy who wanted to do an episode about a '*band.*' **The Spice Girls**, the latest in a long line of all girl bands going back to **the Supremes** or the fictional **Josie and the Pussycats**, were huge at this time with Sci Fi themed videos. Wolfram seemed to want to have an episode where a band comes together and belts out some soft rock tunes, and perhaps a few salable LEXX music videos that might play on the German equivalent of MTV.

All right, that's demented but not necessarily unreasonable. Music videos may have been an excellent cross promotion for LEXX. Xenia had prior experience as a pop singer, Brian had played with blues and jazz bands, and Michael had musical training. So it wasn't out of the question.

What I suspect that was happening here, was that this was Wolfram Tichy's take on the idea of a musical, which had been in Donovan's mind from the start. Perhaps it was to be their *"back up musical"* just in case **Brigadoom** didn't come off and became a *"backstage"* episode. Interestingly, this episode was originally scheduled to follow immediately after **Brigadoom** as the fifteenth in order. It seems peculiar to place two musical episodes back to back.

Let's face it, as a straight episode, it seems like a non-starter. The motivations seem arbitrary and non-existent, the wafer of a story is pulled out of their butt. The premise is thin, the plot nonexistent and the whole thing seems entirely unrealistic. On the other hand, none of that ever stopped them before.

LEXX was doing riffs on **Alien** in **791**, and on the **Wizard of Oz** in the Clizzards of Woz, and would go on to do riffs on zombie films and teen slasher films in **Wake the Dead** and **Twilight.**

So it doesn't seem out of the question that they might take a stab at a classic musical like Hammerstein's **South Pacific**, a musical set in an idyllic paradise against the backdrop of the second world war. Interestingly, Paul Donovan's first film was named **South Pacific, 1942,** which seems to be at least a conceptual echo from the musical. So I can see Donovan and Tichy's ideas fusing together into this strange hybrid.

In fact, the treatment, what there is of it, seems geared towards the format of a musical, with a kind of irrational story geared to setting up the songs and a patently non-realistic setting. This concept of a 'non-natural' or rather a sort of 'stage' set may have found its way into **Brigadoom** and he deliberate staginess of the production.

And, if this episode idea was actually based on **South Pacific**, another crucial concept might have been imported into **Brigadoom**. The backdrop of the war, in South Pacific, would have translated into a backdrop of the Mantrid story arc. What we may have here are the last crucial elements for the final version of **Brigadoom**.

In the end, **Lexxstasy** would have probably been an extremely costly and difficult episode to write and produce, and **like The Last Days** of the Brunnen G, it simply became unnecessary, as Wolfram Tichy confirmed, **Brigadoom** made it redundant. Still, it would have been genuinely interesting to see what it might have turned out to be, if it had gone forward. If **Brigadoom** was a heroic epic, this might have been a magical sensual romance, or perhaps a journey into MTV surrealism.

Lost LEXX, The Days of the Brunnen-G

Story

Kai is staring at the stars deep in contemplation one day when Zev approaches and asks him, *"What are you thinking about?"*

"My past", he answers.

Zev requests that he tell her about it. Kai says that he will more than tell her, he will show her. They set up the proto-blood memory screen originally seen in Gigashadow and we return visually to Kai's planet when he was alive.

We discover that the Brunnen-G advanced from the triumph of defeating the insects to the triumph of immortality, having learned to manipulate their genes so as to stop the aging process. Many of the Brunnen-G are therefore hundreds or even thousands of years old, yet youthful in appearance.

This race of once great warriors have over time degenerated into a society of religious fanatics who, in conquering death, have become infatuated with it. To them life itself has become a prison and they see defeat by His Shadow as 'the great joyful release'. Therefore they have made no attempt to resist, as His Shadow's power has grown more and more threatening.

Kai is genuinely young in years, and he has joined a group of similarly young hotbloods who see this lack of resistance as a collective madness.

They try to organize a secret counter attack against the fantastic power of the Fore Shadow, the huge tentacled ship that is moving towards their planet to destroy it. But they are thwarted at every turn, finding that all Brunnen-G military capacity has been intentionally sabotaged.

Kai and his comrades manage to find a small group of experimental insect craft. They install small stinger missiles and head out to attack the immense Fore Shadow in the hope that their tiny craft will be able to thread the needle and strike at a vital point.

Meanwhile the Brunnen-G planet enters into an orgiastic feast, celebrating its destruction. This soon turns into terror and panic as reality strikes in the form of His Shadow's black sheets raining down upon the planet's surface.

One after another of the small insect craft is destroyed by the defenses of the Fore Shadow and soon Kai is the only fighter left.

He makes a kamikaze attack on the control pod, but to little effect, as we have already seen in the first part of the mini-series.

Kai is killed by His Shadow and we see the process of his body being turned into an assassin for His Shadow but Kai spares Zev images of the human destruction that he caused since that distant time.

(December, 1997, Series Outline, special thanks to Lex Gigeroff).

Commentary

It's hardly a leap to say that this episode would be consolidated into **Brigadoom**, which even in its original version, back in December of 1997, also dealt with Kai's final battle. The surprise is that the two episodes were ever separate.

It's easy to see why this was abandoned. Essentially, it's awkwardly structured, merely an extended flashback with no real application to the characters present situation. They're not fleeing, they're not pursuing, they're just wandering around, like any other episode. Dramatically, it seems quite unsatisfying.

More than that, it just seems expensive. Unlike the final version of Brigadoom, which takes place on a clearly artificial single stage, this episode would have called for 'realism.' They would have had to literally recreate the illusion of Brunnis, which would call for sets, CGI, costumes, and literally a higher level of production costs. It's hard to see how they could have afforded it.

There are a few interesting things in this treatment. What was left out, and what was put in. There's no reference to Kai's trip to the Time Prophet, or of his trial. The coming of His Divine Shadow seems inevitable and ordained, rather than being blamed on 'this newborn who has brought doom to us all.' The effect is again, curiously distancing. There's no personal component to the tragedy, so it's harder to become involved in it, especially since we're seeing a flashback.

A major difference from their portrait in **Brigadoom**, the Brunnen G are described as fanatical death worshipers, rather than decadent wastrels.

In **Brigadoom**, the Brunnen G are indifferent and apathetic, their mania for death only comes at the end. Here, it appears that Death Worship is a tenet of their society. In Brigadoom, Kai is a motivated character in an apathetic society, without focus on him, the society itself has to become more motivated.

A consequence of this 'Death Worship' is that rather than simply being vulnerable, the Brunnen G literally invite death. They sabotage their own weapons systems and refuse to defend themselves.

A minor difference is that the insect craft are not museum pieces, but experimental craft that the newborns arm themselves.

The interesting thing that is actually in the treatment is that we would have seen Kai's dead body being transformed into a Divine Assassin. Again, this is an odd decision. It seems anticlimactic within the episode, perhaps of interest to special effects artists or gross out junkies. But who knows, perhaps it could have been used to effect. We might have seen a brief echo of this in Kai's 'nude' scene in K-Town, or Vlad's birth scene in the episode of the same name.

Overall, expensive, unnecessary, redundant and lacking focus, **The Final Days of the Brunnen G** were doomed almost from the outset.

Lost LEXX, the Original Brigadoom

Story

Out of nowhere, a most peculiar environment appears where everyone sings all day, all the time. Even the LEXX is affected, charging ahead and singing, rather than blowing up the place. Our Crew find themselves in the middle of a very strange, Off-off-off-off Broadway musical, with big production values, heavy choreography, and a sweeping majestic score. Our crew really like this and get into the whole singing thing.

Even the most casual acts are put to song and the only crime seems to be speaking normally. Everyone seems to be under the sway of the Mayor/Director/Great Composer, who is looking for the greatest story ever told. Thousands of years ago, a stray Brunnen G had come to their world, warning of his people's impending fate. Kai fills in the rest, and before you know it, they've decided to produce it as their play.

But Stan, of course, grows weary of having to belt out a tune every time he wants to talk. Among the inconveniences, pretty girls would rather sing about sex than actually do it. He gets fed up and stops.

As punishment, he has to play the special walk-on part in the big musical they are planning, based on the battle between the Brunnen-G and the forces of His Shadow. Not really that much of a punishment, so Stan does not really care. He just wants to get the whole thing over with so he can get away from the incessant show tunes.

Kai realizes that Stan is destined to play Kai during the scene where Kai dies. So he tries to stop the music. But this was expected and Kai is constrained from helping, placed in a dungeon until Zev rescues him.

But Pa (from White Trash) has been burning with jealousy over Stan's getting a role when he could not. So just before Stan is to go on, Pa manages to push Stan aside and steal the big grand finale (and also death) scene for himself. And that is the end of the music as well as the last waltz for Pa.

And then the environment disappears as suddenly as it appeared. And our crew is relieved that Pa has finally exited the stage.

(March, 1997, special thanks to Jeff Hirschfield)

Commentary

This version of **Brigadoom** actually came fairly close to getting made. Unlike many of the other treatments which fell by the wayside without even getting making it to script, this **Brigadoom** was one of three series scripts completed by Jeff Hirschfield in the interregnum between the movies and the first series, the others being Luvliner and Love Grows.

Copies of this script remain in Salter Street's archives and Jeff Hirschfield's trunk. Hirschfield let me have a copy of his, and other copies may well be circulating through the fan community. The loss of this version must have hit Hirschfield hard, after all, every script represents a fair bit of blood, sweat and tears and it can't be easy to simply see it brushed aside.

The Last Days of the Brunnen G was scheduled to be the twelfth episode. Following that, the original version of **Brigadoom** was planned as the fourteenth. **Love Grows** would have been the sandwich between them.

A big surprise here is the inclusion of Paw Golene from **White Trash.** In both of the original series outlines from 1996 and 1997,

Paw Golene actually survived **White Trash**, to appear subsequently in **Sniff the Bliss**, then later in **Love Grows** and even this version of **Brigadoom**. I suppose he was intended to be a kind of ongoing lurking menace, or possibly a comic foil in the background, a counterpoint or alternative to Wist.

Perhaps the most interesting thing is the way both this treatment and **The Last Days of the Brunnen G** are divorced from the Mantrid storylines. Instead, dramatically, they're forced to stand or fall on their own internal resources. And in fact, this version of **Brigadoom** seems to be a repetition of **The Last Days of the Brunnen G** which makes you wonder what they were thinking.

This treatment manages the job a bit more effectively than **The Last Days of the Brunnen G** by placing Stan squarely in a position of crisis. The trouble is that once you do that, the whole story turns to revolve around Stan's problem, Kai is forced to intervene, he has to be neutralized, and then you have to find a solution, which brings us Pa Golene. It all takes a bit away from the Brunnen G musical plotline.

If **The Last Days of the Brunnen G** tell the story of events leading up to the final battle, then the musical has relatively little backstory to delve into. Perhaps they were thinking of a **Rashomon** style retelling, contrasting what really happened with the version of legend that comes after. If so, a variation of the **Rashomon** idea was recycled in **Web & Net**.

On the other hand, they may have chosen to emphasize the backstage aspect, people rushing back and forth, practicing, putting on makeup, building sets and costumes. This does seem to be implied in the treatment. One could imagine that if they hadn't been able to put together the musical score, they might well have cheated their way out by taking this route and confining themselves to a handful of songs and pieces of songs.

In which case, they wouldn't have actually re-enacted **the Last Days of the Brunnen G** merely quoted it. Which means they might have actually had to do the previous episode, for the audience to actually make sense of the 'play' in this story.

Still, it does seem like having the same subject matter in two episodes so close together was going to pose structural problems that I don't think they ever quite worked out.

This actually might have made a fun episode in and of itself, the idea of LEXX actually exploring a backstage environment is fascinating and was lightly touched in **Lafftrack**. In some ways, I'm sorry we never saw this version of the episode, it could have been wild.

A couple of important things happened to transform this treatment and **The Last Days of the Brunnen G** into the **Brigadoom** we know.

One was that the dramatic focus was shifted from Stan being in trouble within the play, to the Universe being in trouble outside of the play. Framing the episode within the crux of the **Mantrid** story arc actually solved a lot of problems. You didn't need an artificial internal crisis. Without that crisis, you had nothing to distract from the musical itself, which could literally take center stage rather than act as a backdrop.

On the other hand, that meant you actually had to have a musical, which resulted in the devouring of the rest of the story from **The Last Days of the Brunnen G**. And of course, actually having a musical meant you had to have music and songs, on which the whole thing depended.

Ultimately though, as with **Back to the Cluster**, I think it's likely that this version of **Brigadoom** was simply shouldered out of the way by another idea. Paul Donovan had his epiphany, a way to actually make the full musical, and once that fell into place, the whole 'backstage' of this version simply became redundant.

LEXX 2.18, Brigadoom

Story

Fleeing Mantrid, on the way to the center of the Universe, the LEXX flies into a mysterious cloud. Inside the cloud is a strange building. They hear 'Yo Way Yo' the battle song of the Brunnen G and decide to investigate.

Inside they find a theater, and a cosmic race of eternal beings that perform a musical version of Kai's life. Kai and Xev are invited to step up onto the stage, becoming characters in the story.

After the great Insect Wars, the Brunnen G turned inward, making their world an impregnable fortress and discovering immortality. But humans were not made for immortality, and so they became narrow and mad. Among the Brunnen G were a handful of newborns, Kai among them. Restless, Kai ventured beyond his home, visiting the Time Prophet, learning of His Divine Shadow, and that His Shadow would destroy his people.

Kai returned with the news, but was instead punished for this. As His Shadow approached, the aged Brunnen G began to welcome death. Only Kai and a handful of newborns were prepared to fight, taking museum pieces and attacking. Kai is killed, bringing us to the beginning of the events of I Worship His Shadow.

The players offer to let the crew of the LEXX join them, so that they can live outside of time and space, and perform again and again. Stan declines. The play has taught him that it is better to fight than to run. They return to the LEXX and the playhouse fades away.

****

Review & Commentary

What makes **Brigadoom** work is the staging.

On the face of it, a musical shouldn't work. Novels, movies, television are all about that willing suspension of disbelief. We have to stop thinking it's just a book or it's just a movie, forget about where we are, and just believe in it. To do that, to make that work, can be a little tricky.

So, the idea that they'd take a sci fi drama comedy, where credulity is stretched thin on general principles, and add singing and dancing.... People just don't do that. That sound you hear is the suspension of disbelief snapping like a twig.

But it works.

Why?

Because **Brigadoom** doesn't play like movies or television. If it did, if it had scene changes and realistic sets, snappy editing, background music and naturalistic acting, we'd wake up the minute someone belted out a song. In real life, in the kind of natural world that movies and television often try to emulate, people don't belt out songs to each other. It just doesn't happen. That's why **Cop Rock** failed so spectacularly.

But **Brigadoom** doesn't try to play like movies or television.

It does at first, just long enough to get us to buy into what's going on. We see Stan and Xev on the bridge. We see the LEXX shuddering, the whole tilting camera effect we've seen and accepted since **Star Trek**. We see them investigating an anomaly in space. Up to this point, what we're seeing is what we've come to expect from LEXX, and from endless adventure series before it.

But then, suddenly, LEXX becomes Theater. Now, this is a very clever little thing. Because as I've said, in real life, in natural life, we don't expect people to go around bursting into song.

But we do accept it in Theater. This is how **Brigadoom** sells itself to us and keeps our suspension of disbelief, we have certain expectations of film and television, we have different expectations of theater. By shifting gears, by presenting itself as theater, Brigadoom also shifts our expectations, and tricks us into going along with something we'd never buy into otherwise. Like **Woz** before it, **Brigadoom** takes a patently unreal premise, and rather than trying to present it realistically, which would fail, persuades us to watch it in another way. They reinstate the suspension of disbelief by detouring us onto another road, into other conventions.

The artificiality of **Brigadoom** becomes its strength. The fact that the Master of Ceremonies, heavily made up, bewigged, stentorian and decadent as a French aristocrat works, because we expect that sort of falseness from the stage. There's no disguising the fact that the set is a stage, both artificial and abstract, or that the clothes the players wear are merely stage costumes.

But it isn't actually theater, it's still television. Watch it, and there are still edits and cuts, close ups, camera movements. All the artifice of television is still at work. It's just the illusion they're trying to cast has changed. Instead of presenting naturalism, which we buy into, it presents theatrical artificiality, which we also buy into, without quite realizing it.

It's a very deliberate choice. To reinforce this sense of the artificiality of the stage, the costumes of the 'Brunnen G' players are made drab in comparison to Kai's scorching 'life uniform' originally made for **I Worship His Shadow**. The message is that he's real, and the others are simply players, shadows. Even the space battle we saw in **I Worship His Shadow** is rippled and faded, deliberately an image projected on a screen. It's an immensely clever bit of craft.

Stanley Tweedle becomes the audience, watching the proceedings along with us, and drawing us in. He knows it's a play, and accepts it, and so we do too. It's a subtle trick. We identify with the leads, and when Stan goes 'oh come on now,' in annoyed disbelief, we go along with him. He becomes the audience's avatar, and as he's drawn into it, so are we. It's quite cunning.

Thematically, **Brigadoom** is one of the pivotal episodes of LEXX. At its heart, it's about all the big things in life, about youth and age, innocence and guilt, living well and dying bravely, it's about courage and convictions, about true love and making decisions. It literally is operatic, the stuff of tragedy. It unifies the series on several levels, and it has an emotional core.

"Brigadoom is my personal favorite," Paul Donovan told a question and answer session for fans. *"For a stupid reason but legitimate: I personally find myself emotionally involved. I'm kind of proud of that episode."*

"Brigadoom, I get a tear at certain points," Lex Gigeroff said at the same session.

"I know why people liked it," Hirschfield asserts, *"Because its sincere. Often Lexx can be very tongue in cheek, but Brigadoom, whatever else it was, was sincere."*

It's also a fan favorite for the same reason. Because on an important level, **Brigadoom** is sincere, it's emotionally real and it's about something that matters. The setting and structure may be self-consciously artificial, but then again it makes no bones about it. But beneath the stage/set and the grease paint, there is a real live heart beating.

Most obviously, Brigadoom fills in the beginning, showing us where Kai comes from and who he was, giving us a window into the prophecy, the history of LEXX before LEXX. It ends with Kai's final battle and death, the point at which I Worship His Shadow begins.

But, it's also the turning point for Stanley Tweedle. In a way, Brigadoom mirrors what's been going on in the second season. The Brunnen G were shown to be self-absorbed, oblivious to the danger that is gathering, just as the LEXX crew have been up until recently. When the danger becomes apparent their response is literally to flee, blaming Kai, slipping into suicidal madness, anything but facing the problem. The LEXX crew has also chosen to hide from or flee their danger. In both cases, the response is obviously futile.

It's also an episode that sets up a strange sort of mirrored history between Stan and Kai. Both men left their homes. Both men were reviled as traitors by their own people. Both men were put on trial and convicted. Often, it's as if the words Kai sings are intended to have special meaning to Stan's life.

And it does, because in the end, Stan makes his decision. Offered a chance at safety and survival as a sort of living ghost, Stan rejects it. He makes the decision to stop running, stop fleeing; he turns his back on cowardice and repudiates cynicism. He chooses to fight Mantrid, and in a strange way, in choosing almost certain death, he's also chosen to truly live for the first time.

*****

Brigadoom is very loosely inspired by the 1947 stage musical, **Brigadoon**, with an 'n,' by Alan J. Lerner and Frederick Lowe. It's about a village in the Scottish Highlands which appears magically for one day, every hundred years. Two American hunters stumble onto the village, romance ensues, also a lot of singing and dancing.

Over the years, there have been nineteen or twenty productions of **Brigadoon**, notably the original Broadway production, starting in 1947, that ran for 581 performances; a British West End production starting in 1949 that ran for 684 performances, a 1954 movie starring Gene Kelly, Van Johnson and Cyd Charise, and a now forgotten 1966 television version featuring Peter Falk, Sally Ann Howes and Robert Goulet that won five Emmy Awards.

* * * *

For an episode that is so clever on so many levels, **Brigadoom** was actually pulled together relatively late. *"It was put together in a whirlwind, and the result is a little disappointing, but it was a thrill,"* Michael McManus *commented in a magazine interview.*

The first public mention of **Brigadoom**, or that they intend to do a musical episode, comes in the April, 1997 issue of **SFX Magazine**, in an interview with Dave Golder:

"Oh yeah," says Donovan, completely matter of factly, *"and for anyone who did like the song and dance routine in the second movie, there's an episode next season that's based on Brigadoon. It'll be the whole show, basically a one hour musical."*

"It'll be so great, it'll make Evita look like a Madonna vehicle," backs up Hirschfield.

"And that's Brigadoom...," Donovan informs me, "with an 'm'."

Given the contingencies of magazine publishing, it's entirely possible that interview actually took place in 1996.

Brigadoom was also alluded to in the Contender LEXXtras which dated to 1997. My own guess is that **Brigadoom**, or at least the idea of doing a musical, goes back to the early concept development of the series in 1994 and 1995.

Indeed, the *'Fantasy Dance'* sequence in **Supernova,** in particular, but also the *'Pattern Song'* in **Eating Pattern** and the *'Singing Brains'* in **Gigashadow,** may have been, in part, moves to test out the idea, testing the waters, seeing how viable it is in the studio and how well the audience responds.

LEXX has always had a musical bent though, although usually only in snippets. Stan sings in the shower in **Gigashadow,** Zev sings a dirge in **Terminal,** Pa Golene is overcome with emotion sings for his lost world in **White Trash,** the *'Brightness Sisters'* song plays in **Woz,** Xev sings a cluster lizard song in **Texx Lexx,** trees sing in **Midsummer's Nightmare** and *Yo Way Oh* is sung off and on through the series, most notably in **The Rock.** I think that this may be in part because culture in the Maritimes, where LEXX is produced, and particularly entertainment culture, has a musical bent. Almost anyone involved in the arts plays or sings, it's simply an inherent part of the repertoire, and the region has always had a vibrant tradition of folk music and song.

The origins of Kai, originally a rococo decadent, set out in **Brigadoom** are inherent in **I Worship His Shadow,** in the failed attack and His Divine Shadow's dismissive reference to the Brunnen G. Again, this goes back to the early concepts of the series.

But I don't think there was any clear notion as to who the Brunnen G were in the years before they died, until this episode. The ancient Brunnen G world had been shown in **Supernova,** a baroque and empty world. His Divine Shadow in **I Worship His Shadow** had cursorily dismissed them as a race of romantic dreamers. Frankly, given that they'd been extinct for over two thousand years, it wasn't a question that seemed to need a lot of answering. As another example, we've had constant references to the Insect Wars, but I'm not sure if anyone has any idea what they were about. Paul Donovan may, but he isn't telling, so he could change his mind and rewrite at a moment's notice.

The notion of the Brunnen G as a civilization of warriors fallen into decadence, of a people who had in the end, chosen to flee the risks and joys of life for a sterile immortality, certainly wasn't around from the beginning. Instead, that seemed to arise from discussions and suggestions made in the second season. Michael McManus notes that it wasn't until around the time of the musical that ideas for what the Brunnen G culture was were being generated.

McManus' own contribution was to conceive Kai in life as a bit of an ideological prick. An idealistic, even obnoxious young firebrand at odds with his society. In life, McManus' Kai was a revolutionary, not a hero, and perhaps not all that fun. McManus had played a similar character, a young revolutionary, in **Donovan's Squamish Five.**

Although Paul Donovan as early as the movies was talking about doing a musical, there's no indication that the episode took shape that early.

Quite the contrary, **Brigadoom** appears in the June, 1996, outlines as a place that the LEXX comes to where everyone sings, this outline has a rough idea, but it's not really hammered out in any detail. An early publicity flyer from mid-1997 for the second season refers to an episode called '**Broadway in Space**' where the crew must '*sing or die!*', which seems to have merely been an alternate title to **Brigadoom**, but which reveals where they were going with the idea. In that same flyer, another episode, **The Last Days of the Brunnen G** is planned as the backstory of the Brunnen G. Clearly, early on, the two ideas were separate, or at least, not automatically fused.

Meanwhile, Jeff Hirschfield, during the interregnum period, in March, 1997, wrote a version of **Brigadoom**, based on the **Broadway in Space** idea, using the players recreation of Kai's final days as the plot device But that meant that they would be almost obliged to go back and revisit Kai's final days in a previous episode, it had been a long time since the opening scenes in **I Worship His Shadow.**

The December 1997 series outline, contained Kai's final days, not only in Brigadoom but also in **Last Days of the Brunnen G**. Now they were wrestling with redundancy.

On top of everything else, Wolfram Tichy suggested a completely different musical, **LEXXstasy**. They were definitely heading there, but they were also all over the map. What we're seeing is less a plan or vision, but rather, a kind of 'feeling their way' toward the goal.

Even then, the concept hardly seemed feasible. A song or two, sure. To compose and score seventeen of them? That's the work of a season. Marty Simon, the series composer, told Donovan flatly that it was impossible.

Donovan found a way....

"German children's songs, except a Schubert piece, adapted, rearranged, cut up, stamped and licked," Lex Gigeroff confessed.

"The evolution of the tunes was quite something," Bill Fleming, the director told me. *"We'd taken a bunch of old nursery rhymes, some of them German, but basically old traditional folk nursery rhymes. Some of the German ones were done by relatively well known German composers. We rearranged them.*

We picked four or five and said 'these are the ones' and we did them in major or minor keys, different tempos. By doing that we constructed the 14 or 15 songs in the show. That was done a while before the show."

Even if you had the music, you still needed the lyrics. Lex Gigeroff enlisted his brother Andre Haines. Haines and Gigeroff had come from a family of performers. Andre once told me how his parents had built a stage outside their cottage for him and his brother to perform shows, and, *"If we hadn't rehearsed them well enough, our parents would get up and they'd finish the show...."*

That sounded quite traumatic, actually.

Both had gone into the arts, Haines had studied music formally and played several instruments. Haines was no stranger to LEXX, he'd appeared as a fighter pilot in **Lafftrack** and played a larger role as Doily in **Girltown.**

So, every night, the brothers would go over to Paul Donovan's house, playing the music, free associating about what it might mean, what might be said, painstakingly putting the lyrics together on Paul's piano. It's one of those images that just won't leave me, the idea that **Brigadoom** was created in someone's living room.

"We had thirteen days to write it," Andre remembered fondly, *"We would play themes... I would do improvs, what was coming to me about what the theme would be. I began writing a set of variations on each theme. TV is such an interesting and wonderful thing. The rest of the world kind of escapes you. I like that kind of stimulation. To work with Lex it was like being kids again."*

The German language lyrics were mostly done by Wolfram Tichy, which was tragic when you think of it. It was no easy task to translate song lyrics credibly, where in normal dubbing all you have to do is translate the concepts. But for songs, you had to not only translate the concepts, but interpret them for rhyme and meter. It must have been a lot of work. But unfortunately, LEXX was cancelled in Germany long before **Brigadoom** had the chance to air.

The whole episode was shot in about eight days at the breakneck schedule of television. Donovan assigned some of his most brilliant people to the project. Bill Fleming was the Director, series Production Manager Andrea Raffaghello came in for his first and only gig as Creative Producer.

"Brigadoom was a good experience," Fleming reflected, *"it ran very smoothly. We managed to get a day of staged dance rehearsals with a choreographer, just to get a rough idea. It went really smoothly. Everyone had a lot of fun doing it. For the most part everyone enjoyed the music."*

"Bill was the real star," Raffaghello claims. *"He brought that to life. It was a unique show because it was a musical. Not many people have the chutzpah. Great director, Bill, I can't say that enough. We talked together, worked on choreography. The show was a lot of people's collaboration. My contribution was some casting, issues with the script, who should be there and what. It's hard to pinpoint. A successful show isn't based on one particular person or element."*

For the most part, the show went smoothly, with only a few minor hitches, as in sets.

"I wanted to create something like a baroque theater," Fleming said. *"I'd have liked to have gone even further with backdrops. We got a few nice set changes in, the jail bars, the judge. I wanted to do some in camera effects."*

"We did build a stage from scratch," Raffaghello noted. *"In that particular case, the production design was a little more (cough) elaborate than we needed, more than was called for. It was a beautiful set. We did use elements from* **Celtic Electric***, flats and backdrops; we used the big Stonehenge pieces."*

Celtic Electric had been a one hour folk and Celtic music special that Salter Street had done the year previously. It was produced by the same Allan McGillivary who had small roles in **I Worship His Shadow** and **End of the Universe**. The set components were still around, so Donovan had the great idea of saving a ton of money by recycling them, rather than building a whole new set. It didn't work out that way...

"We'd go so far down the road sometimes on sets, there was just no turning back," David Hackl, the production designer, told me. *"A perfect example was on Brigadoom. At script stage, it hadn't been considered how grand a set was needed. Paul had mandated we had to build the entire set out of existing set pieces we had in stock, mostly Celtic Electric. But certain script points, elements of blocking, needed us to build more of a set.*

"We had to build the entire set on a three foot riser. Paul walked in and said "What the hell is this." We said, 'Paul, you'll notice the script says 'walks up onto the stage.' Well, this is a floor, not a stage, so we either have to build it or cut a hole in the floor so he can come up.' It was one of those moments of epiphany where you'd walk into a set and go 'oh.' It takes one line to say, but three weeks to build and shoot."

Best laid plans of mice and men and all that. **The Game** was also born as a great cost saving scheme. That was a consistent thing with LEXX, they were terrible schemers. They were always coming up with diabolical stratagems to save a few bucks on production costs, and half the time, it just wound up costing them more. Of course, frequently it leads to interesting looks or effects, so on the whole, it's a positive thing. I'm sure, though, that at least a few people must have cringed whenever Paul came up with a great new cost saving idea. Ah well....

"We wanted to do another scene," Fleming said, *"where the newborns raid a museum for their stinger ships. We actually created it, but no one was happy with it, we created a model or backdrop painting of a sort of Brunnen G museum where one of the Brunnen G fighters was hanging, it was more of labyrinth, with staircases, and shafts of light, and suits of armor. I was wanting to do it with more an artificial backdrop kind of feeling."*

That would have been an interesting scene, perhaps it or production stills will show up, on some DVD or future documentary someday. Of course, chronicling the running fight over sets is interesting, but everyone really wants to know how the music worked.

"We set up a little music studio in one of the dressing rooms, Michael and Xenia would come in and work on the music," Fleming revealed.

Both McManus and Seeberg had musical training. Xenia had sung and done vocals for a Goth band in Germany, and belted like a rocker. McManus had done stage musicals. Brian Downey decided to sit this one out, *"I told them if I couldn't sing like Barry White, then I wasn't going to do it."*

"We did it like a rock video, prerecord the stuff and sung to playback on the set. I wanted to create something like a baroque theater," Fleming explained.

"In production," Andre Haines told me, *"what happened was, I laid down a track, a piano track, I sang all the vocals, except for Xenia and Michael and Lorraine Segato. Then when they were filming, they would lip synch to the vocals. I was on set all the time. Then once the filming was done,, I went into the studio, we recorded full voices."*

"Later on, one of our actors, the tall guy in dull dull dull, he wasn't available" Haines revealed, *"so I sang his part. I'm him all the way through. I wrote all the harmonies and put all that together, the whole tracks were sent off to Marty Simon, who made sense of my mess. Put it all together and orchestrated it. It was fast and very exciting and a really interesting time. I don't have any regrets, I'd love to do another one."*

Patricia Zentilli was also one of the featured singers and principle voices. *"I knew they were doing a musical episode,"* Patricia Zentilli said. *"So I went down and met Bill Fleming. 'Hi, I can sing, I want to be in the musical,' I gave him a tape and the next thing I knew I was in* **Brigadoom***. It was really fun. It took about 8 days. We were lip synching and then we'd go in and re-record. When everyone's singing, it was actually my voice, me and the other girl, it was actually the two of us and they just multiplied our voices over and over and over. I was disappointed that I didn't get a big solo number, but it was a lot of fun."*

Another familiar face was John Dunsworth, making his fifth or sixth appearance in LEXX. *"I was one of the Brunnen G elders. One of the guys in robes, the dancing singing guy with the wig. I had a lot of background in musical theater, I'd directed a dozen Gilbert and Sullivan's,"* Dunsworth laughs, *"I remember I auditioned for Bill Fleming down in the basement of their sound studio singing Harry Belafonte."*

Among Dunsworth's prior roles had been the voice of **His Divine Shadow**. There'd been two Divine Shadow's in the first series: The modern one voiced by Walter Borden, and the one who'd killed Kai, voiced by John Dunsworth. Now, because Dunsworth was already in the show, they had to bring in Walter Borden to voice the His Divine Shadow role. Lex Gigeroff, so far as I know, was in the costume.

Lorraine Segato of the 80's band, **Parachute Club** appeared in a singing role as the **Time Prophet**. *"Where'd she come from?"* I asked Kim Boyd, one of the assistant directors. *"She was in Halifax a lot. Everyone in our industry hangs out at the Economy Shoe Shoppe. I think that's where the association first came to mind. She did* **Brigadoom***, it was an interesting experience."*

I suspect that she was probably cast through Toronto. Still, I find the idea that they may have gotten one of their singers from the Economy Shoe Shoppe is entertaining. **Brigadoom** plays as a community musical, and behind the scenes, there was more than a little of that flavor.

* * * *

No discussion of music on LEXX can take place without discussing Marty Simon. Simon is a Montreal session musician who has been playing drums for over 25 years. Some of his collaborators have been Mylon LeFevre, The Sharks, Leslie West, Wilson Pickett, Brian Eno, and the Liquor Giants. He has appeared on over a dozen albums of other artists.

He's also scored well over a dozen movies, including four of Paul Donovan's pre-LEXX films. **George's Island, Paint Cans, Life With Billy** and **Buried on Sunday**. He also did the musical scoring or composing for all four seasons and 65 hours of LEXX. He's also credited as Brain #14 in **I Worship His Shadow**, by which I take it to mean that his voice and not his actual brain was used.

In 1997 he released a CD of his instrumental music for the first season of LEXX. Sadly, it lacked the *Pattern* song or the '*Singing*

Brain's' songs, but it's a wonderfully diverse and fascinating collection, ranging from faux Gregorian chants to whorehouse jazz to thrilling guitar riffs. This is probably the one single successful piece of LEXX merchandise from the first season.

One piece that is included on the collection, is "*Yo Way Oh*" the Brunnen G war chant. McManus and Simon pronounce Brunnen G differently, but over time, Simon's version has prevailed. The word's to '*Yo Way Oh*' are not based on any particular language. It's just a heroic martial death song, the sung in an unknown language with pride and conviction.

It was sung by a choir of five, mixed in with Michael McManus' voice. He told an internet chat that, *"The words just flowed quickly in a burst of maniacal creativity, but I will reveal that the Yo-Ah-O is influenced by the munchkins song in the Wizard of Oz."*

Nevertheless, in different renditions, through **I Worship His Shadow, Gigashadow, Terminal, Tunnels,** and **The Rock**, it's become the anthem of the series, and for the fans. In some very inexplicable way, it's a catchy tune.

Much of the music from the first year was recycled in the second year, except for a bad-porn sequence from **Patches in the Sky** which was recycled from Donovan's earlier film **Paint Cans**. He also did some additional original music. The second season also contained a few little snippets from elsewhere, Pa Golene's lyrics from **White Trash** by Gigeroff, or 7**90RobotHead's** funk music, and of course, **Brigadoom.**

For **Brigadoom**, the melodies were children's songs, the lyrics were Haines and Gigeroff's and much of the recording took place in Halifax, but Simon did the final mix and fill-in's at his studio in Toronto.

There isn't, and likely won't ever be an official Brigadoom CD Apparently, there are issues with rights and voices. They don't have the rights to issue a CD with the existing voices or lyrics without resolving these issues, and re-recording would be a waste of effort.

Essentially, Simon worked on his own out in Toronto or Montreal. He'd receive production VHS tapes, with lots of greenscreen or videomatics, and simply develop the musical score or composition based on those. Occasionally, as in 'Wild Wild LEXX' he'd do pieces and keep them in reserve until an appropriate episode, in that case, Apocalexx Now.

Original music from the second and third year was collected into Simon's second LEXX CD, released in 2001. So far, there hasn't been a third CD for the fourth season.

"We're entering our 60th hour of music for LEXX," he told a group of fans during an internet chat, *"and I really can only remember three or four times where there was any real conflict, so I must say that the freedom for me to write has been a constant.... The one law laid down by Paul D. was that the LEXX NOT sound, like Star Wars or John Williams. My rule was to create music that seemed as though it came from a very distant place, but yet sounded very familiar."*

* * * *

Brigadoom (1999) is unique in television as the only musical sci fi episode. Its only peers are the **Bitter Suite** (1998) episode from the fantasy series **Xena**, and horror series **Buffy: The Vampire Slayer** episode **Once More, With Feeling** (2001). Oddly, all these productions came within the same general time frame, suggesting perhaps a more experimental, more idiosyncratic era. Or perhaps simply idiosyncratic creators – Whedon, Raimi and Donovan all march to their own beat.

Among fans, **Brigadoom** is legendary, the most offbeat, cultish, series, and has its own rabid following. It appears in any poll of favorite episodes, either near or at the top of every list. Lyrics have been transcribed and put up on the web; pages from Andre Haines sheet music are circulated and treasured like holy relics. Fans have even made and traded their own CD's, downloading the music onto CD-ROM from MP3 format.

During the 2001 LEXX Un-Convention, a gathering of fans in Halifax held while the shooting of the fourth season was taking, the cult reached new heights with a spontaneous re-enactment. What happened was that Salter Street gave away a hundred props and costumes to fans, including one Brunnen G costume from Brigadoom. Later that night, Brian Downey sponsored a party at the University, people showed up in costume. Someone gave the disk jockey an unofficial Brigadoom CD.

Then suddenly, spontaneously, over a hundred people were singing Yo Way Oh, along with the CD. As the songs started, one young man wearing a Brunnen G costume stood up and began miming the words. Other dancers followed him, until suddenly, spontaneously, the episode was being re-enacted to the music. As in the original episode, Brian Downey sat watching, amazed once again. Patricia Zentilli got up and danced for a song. Other LEXX crew and cast members were astonished. One woman appeared wearing a home-made Xev costume. Even His Shadow's role was performed by another fan in a Divine Cleric costume. What the performers lacked in polish, they made up in heart and spontaneity.

Since then, high school students have performed it in local productions, and in whole or in part, in mime or actually singing the parts, Brigadoom has been re-enacted by fans on many occasions. It goes on and on.

CREDITS

Creators: Writer (Lex Gigeroff and Paul Donovan); Lyrics (Lex Gigeroff and Andre Haines); German Lyrics (Wolfram Tichy); Director (Bill Fleming); Production Designer (David Haackl); Creative Producer (Andrea Raffaghello)

Main Cast: Brian Downey (Captain Stanley Tweedle); Michael McManus (Kai, Last of the Brunnen G); Xenia Seeberg (Xev Bellringer, Rejected Wife/Love Slave/Cluster Lizard); Jeffrey Hirschfield (Voice of 790); Tom Gallant (Voice of LEXX).

Guest Cast: Jeremy Webb (Master of Ceremonies); John Dunsworth (Brunnen G Singer); Sharron Timmins (Brunnen G

Singer); Paul McQuillan (Brunnen G Singer); Joe Wynn (Brunnen G Singer); Patricia Zentilli (Brunnen G Singer); Richard Sircom (Brunnen G Singer); Lorraine Segato (Time Prophet); Walter Borden (Voice of His Divine Shadow); Lex Gigeroff (His Divine Shadow); Andre Haines (Voice of singer).

Lost LEXX, Fly Trap

Story

"The LEXX being thirsty, lands on a hydro-planet. It is completely landless, just a big ball of H20 except for all sorts of huge, delicious looking flowers sticking out of the water. The flowers turn out to be fly traps, but after that...."

"..... we do not know what happens, because we have not fully developed the story. We think it has possibility, because we want the character of this episode to be the planet itself– a giant life form– that has different moods, depending on whether its day or night. We also want to shoot an outdoor episode for a change, and have promised the crew that one show will be shot in the Caribbean at the end of the long Canadian winter, before we relocate to Berlin."

(June, 1996, Series Outline, Special thanks to Brian Downey)

Commentary

Well, at least they were honest. This is barely a note or two, isn't it? To call it a lost LEXX' is something of an exaggeration. After all, the point of the lost LEXX chapters is to chronicle alternate plans, episodes or movies that were actually planned, or which might have been made, had not time or budget or some other restriction or problem intervened.

Or it's to trace the origins and evolution of the show's creative ideas. To identify where an idea comes up, or an episode is proposed, and how it morphs into something else. Or to trace a particular gag or idea, proposed for an episode that's eventually abandoned, but then plucked out and recycled in some other time or place.

We can't actually say that there is much more here than a 'notion' that under other circumstances, might have gone on to become something.

This 'potential' story dates from the June 28, 1996, outlines, and it never really got further than that. A lot of the stories in the June 1996 outline seem thin. I think that what this amounts to, more than anything, is that they were reaching hard to come up with at least a premise for an episode to round out their outline, and that's all.

That premise seems to have broken down entirely; some of its ideas were cannibalized and showed up elsewhere.

The idea of a planet completely composed of water evolved into **LEXXstasy,** which itself died on the operating table. But a similar world appears in **Nook,** and in the third season as planet **Water.** The 'Fly Trap' element seems to echo **Passion Flower** and it may be that the two are related.

And of course, the Caribbean shoot, probably wishful thinking at the time, finally happened in the fourth season, in **Xevivor.** Careful what you wish for.

Lost LEXX, Passion Flower

Story

790 observes while scanning different systems in the Light Universe that many of the planets he had stored in his memory seem to have disappeared. Based on this and other evidence, Kai begins to wonder if Mantrid is still alive and at the center of this mystery. But his more immediate concern, which he reveals to a distraught Zev, is that his proto-blood reserves will soon be gone.

Another problem for the crew is that Wist is once again active and needs to eat. If she does not find some food soon, she will be forced to eat our heroes.

Suddenly the Lexx veers off course and rushes toward the florescent glow of a volcanic planet. Being part insect, it is drawn to the light as a moth is to a flame. The crew decides that they should take the opportunity to bring Wist to the surface so that she may look for sustenance. Kai and Zev go with her.

Wist does indeed find food, and the three of them stumble across a village of plant people; people that share similar genetic properties with Wist. Wist falls in love with their leader, 'Kloro', and they go off to consummate their relationship in an entanglement of leaves and branches that grow out of them.

Meanwhile, Zev and Kai go off to have a closer look at the many volcanoes, but are set upon by creatures who make their home in the hot ash and lava. Kai kills one of these creatures in a confrontation, and is surprised to find that its vital fluid is none other than a form of proto-blood. He starts to gather up some of this fresh reserve.

Wist's entanglement with Kloro grows dangerous. It turns out that he is a type of predator. He spins Wist in a web and starts to consume her, while the other villagers set out to attack Zev and Kai.

Kai defeats plant people, rescues Zev and Wist, and the three of them get back to the Lexx just as the shadow of the awesome living insect machine Mantrid is cast over the planet. Stan breaks the Lexx out of its 'moth around a flame' trance and they hightail it away from the planet.

Mantrid lets them go without chase, more interested in devouring the planet and the proto-blood filled insects that live there. Kai wonders if Mantrid spared them deliberately, saving a confrontation for a time when he is stronger.

But for the time being the crew are overjoyed that Kai had abundantly replenished his proto-blood supply and that Wist found something to eat besides them.

(December, 1997, special thanks to Lexx Gigeroff).

Commentary

Episode number seventeen of the December 1997 treatments, this was one of four story ideas contributed by Wolfram Tichy, the German Executive Producer for TiMe. The other three were the **Clizzards of Woz, Twilight**, and **Lexxstasy**.

Small bits of **Passion Flower** show up in finished episodes. For instance, Wist's re-emergence and request to go looking for food, "or else," is transposed to the opening of 791, where it becomes a subplot.

790's observations of stars and solar systems having vanished and Kai's speculation that Mantrid is responsible shows up in **Web**, and provides the motivation for that episode.

LEXX's hypnotic fascination with flame is borrowed from a moth from the original version of **Love Grows** and returned to a moth in **Texx Lexx** (which, I suppose just goes to show you that even a really dumb idea never goes away completely).

One interesting item is the reference to the *"awesome living insect machine Mantrid"* casting a shadow over the planet, which sounds like a holdover from **Back to the Cluster's** Giga-Shadow insect machine. Despite this, it's clear that by December, 1997, the concept of Von Neumann machines had taken hold, and the other episode descriptions refer to 'clouds of specks.'

The core story, however, was abandoned entirely. The village of treacherous plant people and Wist/Lyekka's ironic romance with a predator intent on eating her is abandoned entirely. This is one of the only times where the Wist/Lyekka character would have taken center stage. In fact, Wolfram Tichy's original idea was to have a love story involving Wist.

But then again, Wist/Lyekka is fundamentally an inhuman character with extraordinary abilities; would it work to write her in a typical soap opera boy/girl situation? It's an interesting conceit, but you wonder where it would have gone?

In any case, this aspect, I think, was doomed by the cast change. Doreen Jacobi's Wist might have been good for this, but Louise Wischermann's Lyekka always had this thing going on with Stan, that might have precluded this sort of story.

The secondary story, of exploring the volcano, encountering the proto-insects and their proto-blood, is so obviously tacked on that you can see the staples. It really seems to have nothing to do with what's happening in the village with Wist/Lyekka.

One imagines the writers sitting around and Lex Gigeroff going *"Well you know, man, his proto blood is running out, we should do something about that?"* And then Jeff Hirschfield saying *"Ok, how about this...."*

It seems like an awkward attempt to address a plot issue, Kai's protoblood supply that they simply wound up ignoring.

As it is, the story seems awkwardly fractured and without any real kind of focus. In **The Salesman** for instance, there's a radical shift from Gubby's shop to the slave market, but that shift is part of the plot of the story. Here there seems to be no strong reason to go from the village to the volcano.

Perhaps if this treatment had made it into a script, or been considered further, there might have been an attempt to establish some kind of relationship between the plant people and the volcano creatures. Perhaps they'd have been symbiotes, or different life stages. Essentially, the flaws in the story seemed repairable, with a few drafts and a bit of thought.

Having said that, however, this also seems like an expensive episode, heavy on cast, special effects and sets. The production budget for this one would have been high. The story was weak. In the end, they passed and simply cannibalized a few ideas. This was just about dead on arrival, and never made it to script.

LEXX 2.19, Brizon

Story

The Universe is within its final weeks, much of it has been devoured. Having decided to fight Mantrid, the crew has no clear idea how to go about doing it. Stan decides to broadcast for help, inviting anyone left in the Universe to join them in the battle.

On an obscure planet, a man dressed as a Divine Order Bio Vizier unplugs himself from a human host, and after thanking him, climbs into a Stinger ship, much like Kai's old ship, and flies off, escaping as Mantrid's drones devour the planet.

The man makes it to the LEXX where he passes out. On waking, he identifies himself as Brizon, Mantrid's teacher. He was the one who originally designed the machine that holds Mantrid's soul or essence. Brizon is dying, his organs failing, but he easily takes control of Kai and takes over the LEXX. He has a plan to stop Mantrid by kidnaping a drone and using its data stream to shut Mantrid down by infiltrating a secret command.

Kai and Stan are sent out to capture a drone and bring it back, which they do successfully. To keep himself alive, Brizon hooks himself up to Xev, using her organs to sustain his body.

The plan seems to work, the Mantrid drones through the universe cease to operate. Brizon takes the LEXX into the center of the swarm, to Mantrid's machine. He announces his intention to destroy Mantrid, and place himself in the machine. Mantrid destroyed the universe; Brizon intends to put it all back.

But it turns out to be a trap, Mantrid was never incapacitated. Brizon is destroyed as the LEXX crew flees. Mantrid appears on the screen and tells them that he is saving them for the last.

Review & Commentary

Brizon feels very much like a fill in episode before the big crunch. It's as if the story logic demanded at least one episode between **Brigadoom** and **End of the Universe** so that the decision to fight Mantrid could sink in. At the same time, they needed a failed battle against Mantrid to raise the stakes just that much more. It's an episode motivated entirely by mechanical considerations.

It certainly wasn't in the original plans for the season. The 19th episode was originally going to be **Norb.** Moving **Norb** earlier into the season and the loss of several other planned episodes left a hole that had to be filled. The first draft of **Brizon** was originally written by Jeff Hirschfield in a brutal 72 hour period, after which Donovan, who'd run up against a wall trying to write **End of the Universe,** took over.

It's an episode motivated by costs. This is primarily another '*Ship in the Bottle*' episode, minimal guest cast, no new sets at all. Almost everything we see is either an existing set or prop, the Bridge, the Cryochamber, the galley, or it's all CGI. In terms of CGI, I'm not sure what extra cost was incurred, it looks like the Mantrid arms are nothing new, and even Brizon's ship is recycled. For that matter, so is Brizon's hat.

We've seen this fairly often, most notably in **Web/Net**. It's a sign of how tight the budgets were, and it's impressive that they could stretch it so far to this point. These guys were squeezing the nickel until the beaver shit.

In this case, there are a couple of new sets. Brizon's home, right at the start, CGI assisted and Mantrid's false lair, seen at the end. They're both extremely minimal places, about what you'd get if you swept out a big janitor's closet.

The opening scenes, considering the limitations of the budget, are creepier than they have any right to be. In particular, the guy in the pod, or more accurately, half a guy in the pod, is downright disturbing. There's a subliminal discomfort in expecting there to be a lower half to Brizon's victim, and it not being there. The man in the pod may be a kind of visual reference to another man in a pod from the beginning of the season, Mantrid himself.

David Lewis has the uncredited role as the guy in Brizon's pod, or half of him anyway. David Lewis had previously appeared as Fruitcake, in **Patches in the Sky**.

The images of Brizon puttering around, his encounter with a Mantrid arm, the giant insect behind his door have a haunting quality, enhanced by Marty Simon's musical scoring, which belie the nonexistent budget.

The CGI scenes also come off well, particularly in the interactions with the crew. When Kai and Stan fly into the drone swarm to capture a Mantrid arm it works, they look like they're going into danger. There's actually a sense of awe when we encounter Mantrid's immense drone constructs, when the drones dismantle worlds, or when the LEXX tries unsuccessfully to fight them. We've seen it all before in other episodes, of course. But that's why it works, because we've seen it all before, because all those prior episodes, the hints, the earlier encounters have educated us as viewers to see the drones as dangerous and dramatic.

The most 'cosmic' special effect goes right by us though. Towards the end, Mantrid uses literally trillions and trillions of drones to form a giant disembodied head hanging in space and talking to them. When you stop to think about that, it's awesome. This isn't a face on a screen; this is actually a structure in space. How big is it? Miles across? Light years across? It's undoubtedly cosmic in scale, but because we never get a reference point to realize how huge it must be, it only comes across as a face on a screen and not a particularly good one.

We never see the giant Mantrid head in space, only on a screen. There's no exterior shot with the giant head and the LEXX to reveal that the LEXX is a tiny speck in comparison. It doesn't do anything that might signify its true size, like gobbling a star or rolling a planet around on its tongue. Even a few lines of dialogue might have sold the effect and provided an *'ooh' 'ahh'* factor.

The weakest part of the episode is the transparently linear plot. Brizon comes on board. Brizon takes over. Mantrid gets him. That's it?

There's no subplot, there's no extraneous characters or details or developments of any sort. Brizon doesn't even get a henchman. The entire weight of the story rests on Earl Pastko, and it's a testament to the actor that he bears up under it so well.

The episode belongs, without a doubt, to Earl Pastko's character, Brizon. Literally from the start, he's completely assured and completely in command. Brizon's an engaging character; he's visibly disintegrating, carrying around the high tech equivalent of a colostomy bag, sucking up food or disgorging goo onto the floor, all to really grotesque noises. He's so disgusting it's fascinating.

Yet, at the same time, he's endlessly cheerful and polite. Even friendly. He's a well-mannered monster, unhooking himself from his victim in a pod, he takes time out to say "thank you."

One of the fascinating things about Brizon is how easily he outclasses the crew of the LEXX. Literally from the moment he arrives on the LEXX, he's in control, artfully manipulating them. It's a pleasure to sit back and watch him as he promises salvation... after lunch... after a tour of the ship. In contrast to the simmering desperation of the crew, he's completely relaxed and enjoying himself.

For their part, although the crew deciding to fight Mantrid, and having no idea how to go about it. Mantrid is trillions of drones devouring galaxies. How do you fight something like that? The original decision to run for it makes more sense. Stanley Tweedle, despite his resolve, remains confused, ineffectual and impotent, in marked contrast to the suave Bio Vizier.

Is Brizon really a villain? Sure, he takes over Kai, plugs himself into Xev and almost does bad things to Stan. But then again, he's dying and clearly struggling to save his life. He doesn't make his move to take over until literally the last minute. He could have zapped Kai right from the start. Even then, he still seems somewhat benign. He apologizes to Xev before he plugs her in. He's genial and friendly, even when in power.

Throughout the episode, Brizon is smiling constantly, and his dialogue is peppered with little jokes *"so there is a heaven after all,"* after he kisses Xev. He seems almost hurt when Stan and Xev don't trust him, but then he recovers and gives an unctuous smile *"then consider me untrustworthy."*

In contrast, Stan and Xev are thoroughly hostile to him from day one. Their conduct verges on insulting. They threaten to toss him out into space. He's got reasons not to trust them or rely upon them any more than they trust him. Although they're our protagonists, the fact that they act with such motiveless hostility, especially in the face of Brizon's friendliness and droll japery unconsciously tends to slide the audience over into his camp.

We recognize he's the designated villain, but he hardly seems like a bad guy, at least not bad enough to merit the treatment he gets. It's an interesting tightrope to walk, to try to seduce your audience towards the villain, in part by making your heroes act like jerks.

Even his motives, if not wholly benign, at least seem acceptable. He wants to live, and does what he has to in order to stay alive. He's fairly subversive in putting his position across.

"Wouldn't you save a dying man, if you could?"

"I'm a dying man."

In the Moth, when he can afford to be, he's honest and fairly open. No, he can't bring Kai back. His ultimate goal, to replace Mantrid in the machine.

"Mantrid takes pleasure in destroying the Universe, "

"I will take pleasure in putting it back."

If Mantrid is the ultimate enemy, Brizon, by default seems to fall under the side of the good guys.

But then again, here's a man who we saw consume and abandon one victim, who was prepared to do something weird and sexual with Stan and Xev against their will. This is a reminder that however genial Brizon is, he's still a monster. A friendly Nazi concentration camp guard is still a concentration camp guard. His true colors show clearest when he confronts his bitter enemy Mantrid. There he becomes a hysterical raver, a childish screaming maniac.

Earl Pastko previously starred in **Highway 61**, a movie produced and directed by Bruce MacDonald, a cult movie maker and the director of third season episodes **Garden** and **Tunnel**s.

Pastko stole that **Highway 61** with his performance as the devil, or as a man who believes he's the devil, and goes around buying souls from drum majorettes and cleaning up at church bingos. So, I guess it's a small dark zone after all. He's a regular working actor with a long IMDB record.

Later on, Pastko would go on to be the main villain in Jeff Hirschfield's children's series, **Zixx.**

In terms of the regular cast, Xev's estrangement from Kai crosses a threshold after Brizon so easily turns him off. In the third season episodes that follow from this one, she simply doesn't sport the same kind of attraction and affection for Kai that she did in this season. Apart from that, she's shown to good effect, and her finger sucking scene with Brizon is both sick and erotic.

Stanley shows himself reformed but not really changed. He's less afraid, or at least braver as in going out with Kai to get a drone, and more willing and able to stand up to people, including Brizon.

But he's no more decisive. When they return with the drone, it's Xev that has to tell him to fire the LEXX, he doesn't think of this himself, and when she tells him, he doesn't actually question whether it's a good idea or not.

CREDITS

Creators: *Writer -Paul Donovan; Director - Paul Donovan; Production Designer - David Hack; Creative Producer - Willie Stephenson*

Main Cast: *Brian Downey (Captain Stanley Tweedle); Michael McManus (Kai, Last of the Brunnen G); Xenia Seeberg (Xev Bellringer, Rejected Wife/Love Slave/Cluster Lizard); Jeffrey Hirschfield (Voice of 790); Tom Gallant (Voice of LEXX).*

Cast: *Earl Pastko (Brizon); Dieter Laser (Mantrid); David Lewis (Guy in pod)*

Lost LEXX, Big Bertha

Story

The stars are still visible, their light, thousands of years old is still traveling, even though Mantrid has devoured the stars that made them. There are no stars left in the Universe. There is only a final celestial body which has not been consumed. LEXX races towards it.

The body turns out to be a giant planet orbiting a black hole at nearly the speed of light. Its surface is littered with crashed spaceships. Prominent is a fancy restaurant with a huge neon sign high above it that reads "The Last Stop."

The restaurant is run by Lescheff, a dark black man with a broad smile and a Caribbean accent. Dana, a mysterious pale woman dressed entirely in black is in charge of keeping everything peaceful. A ship of armed rebels crashes on the planet and the dazed crew invade the restaurant, waving their blackpacs. Dana decapitates one with a brace; they decide not to make trouble.

The LEXX, arriving, is trapped by the gravitational field of the black hole and crashes on the planet, badly damaged. One by one, the bridge pylons are falling over. Forced to abandon ship while LEXX tries to repair itself, Stan, Kai, Lyekka and Xev make their way to the restaurant. 790 calculates that the planet has two days left before Mantrid drones destroy it.

The crew walk in as Dana imbibes her special protoblood up her thigh. The protoblood contains a special sauce which makes the undead assassin sensuous and fun loving. After some preliminaries, Stan settles down to a sumptuous meal and Kai gets into kinky undead assassin dismemberment sex with Dana, the LEXX sinks slowly into the planet and Xev hooks up with the rebels.

You see, the rebels have a plan to resurrect the greatest heroes of the past. This is why they've come to this planet, Bertha, the fabled 'resurrection planet.' They've got the knife that His Divine Shadow used to kill Kai with thousands of years ago, with his ages old dried blood and genetic material. Unfortunately, they're one woman short. Xev jumps at the chance to help create a living Kai.

Mantrid begins his final attack, finally amassing enough drones to overwhelm the gravity of the black hole. But Bertha is a living, sentient planet. She throws off Mantrid's drones, as a result, all the matter in the universe begins to coalesce around the black hole and Mantrid's construct.

After a mystical ceremony, the planet impregnates Xev and the others with the seeds of the heroes. Unfortunately, it turns out that the heroes will be born full grown, a process which will be fatal to the mothers. Luckily for Xev, Lyekka shows up to save her with her plant powers. Kai and Stan go off in search of Xev, and a new live Kai is born.

Bertha is ripped apart as the two irresistible forces implode, creating a new light universe. The reborn heroes escape in the revitalized LEXX, while our crew escapes in Lescheff's flying saucer. Eventually, our crew makes it back to the LEXX, the heroes go off with Lescheff, and the living Kai, overwhelmed by memories, flees.

The LEXX rocks on, daddy.

Commentary

It is perhaps a slight exaggeration to call this a lost LEXX. It was never part of the original storyline. Rather, it's the wacky brainchild of a couple of members of the production crew, Dennis Murphy, the videomatics supervisor and Sven Bergman, 790 operator.

Why? Youthful enthusiasm basically. I remember that when I first contacted Bergman, he sent me a whole bunch of JPEG's of Lexx scenes and characters done in playmobil. I thought to myself, 'this guy way too much time on his hands.' So of course, we hit it off right there; he was my kind of nerd.

Talking to Sven about LEXX, his exuberance and love for the material rings through. It wasn't just a nine to five job, he had a great time doing it, he and Dennis were at the center of things, on a first name basis with everyone from writers and stars to carpenters and makeup artists. Of course, it was like that for almost everyone then. LEXX was a great wild ride.

It was the kind of place where two happy go lucky kids could take it upon themselves to write a LEXX script.

"We wanted to help them out," Bergman recalls. *"Paul, he was doing everything, producing, directing, he had no time. Lex and Jeff were on the set every day. There was no time to write, the end of the season was coming up, and they would be complaining they didn't have an ending yet. So Dennis and I decided to write one for them, because they were so busy."*

By the last quarter of the season, the original plan had pretty much fallen apart. Many of the planned episodes were no longer feasible because of limits of time and budget, new episodes, **Web & Net** and **Brizon** were written literally on the fly. Despite this, the conclusion of the Mantrid arc had already been worked out. They knew where they were going to go, even if the road had gotten bumpy.

Still, I can imagine Lex and Jeff bitching at the lunch tables about too much work and too little time, having to pull rabbits out of their hats, and Dennis and Sven getting this sudden inspiration to help them out.

Big Bertha is an interesting take on where the crew thought the series was going, or could go, and doubtless they had a lot of fun writing it.

"We wanted to do stuff, we thought well... food on the LEXX is terrible, that spout thing, so let's treat them to some really good meals, for a change," Bergman recalls. He freely acknowledges the inspiration of Douglas Adam's **Restaurant at the End of the Universe**.

"We wanted Kai to have sex," he continues, *"we wanted Xev to get her live Kai, we wanted to deal with Mantrid, basically we wanted to have a lot of fun."*

One particularly interesting wrinkle is Dana, a brace wielding undead female assassin who has a thing for Kai, an interesting forerunner of Vlad. Is Dana the inspiration of Vlad? Sadly no. The notion that the LEXX might have an undead female nemesis/adversary is a fairly inevitable idea.

I can show you stacks of fanfiction written before and after this which feature Kai encountering female Divine assassins or executioners, and the two of them merrily start slicing off each other's limbs. Vlad is almost certainly an independent creation, although she springs from the same well as Dana and all her sisters.

Of course, as it stood, the episode was unfilmable given the budget and shooting days left. It called for at least four or five significant guest stars, a dozens of extras, a lot of effects, and all kinds of new sets. Of course, it was designed as a two-parter, which might have amortized some costs. But there were other problems - German censors would have torn their hair out at Kai and Dana's recreational dismemberment, for one example.

In the end, Paul Donovan didn't even read it.

"We tried to give it to Paul," Sven recalls. *"But he threw up his hands and said 'no, no, I can't even look at it!' Legal reasons. He was under contract with the writers. So then we put it in a sealed envelope and gave it to the finance people, and we said, 'we renounce all rights, this is yours now.' But they wouldn't even open it. So eventually, we just gave it to the cast and crew, just for the fun of it."*

Big Bertha never had a serious shot at making it on screen as a LEXX episode, at least, not in a rational world. On the other hand,

LEXX's backstage history was often hardly rational, so who knows. Perhaps in some parallel universe, this is how the season ends. Nevertheless, it's a fun and interesting bit of LEXX history.

So rock on, daddy.

.

LEXX 2.20, End of the Universe

Story

Ninety three hours to the end of the Universe.

A DJ in a satellite witnesses the destruction of his world by Mantrid Drones.

On board the LEXX, Mantrid drones attack the various members of the crew. Xev fights hers off with a club. 790 and Stan hide in Kai's cryopod. On the bridge, the drones attack Lyekka's pod, destroying it. Kai and Lyekka destroy the bridge drones. But with Lyekka's pod destroyed, her life will end shortly.

The drones are breaking through the cryopod, when Stan attaches 790 to a drone arm. 790 destroys the other drones and attacks Stan. Stan convinces it to rescue Xev instead, which it does handily. A 790 drone is superior to Mantrid drones.

Xev gets the idea to create an army of 790 drones to fight and convert the Mantrid drones, which seems at least partially successful.

The LEXX exhibits confusion, the entire mass of the universe is moving as Mantrid brings it to bear. The LEXX attempts to fire on the mass of drones protecting Mantrid, but it fails to have any effect.

Lyekka tells Stan she is dying, but will live on in his dreams. She shape shifts into a Mantrid drone infiltrates her way to Mantrid's machine and attacks him, but is killed. Still she disables Mantrid long enough for LEXX to renew the attack.

Mantrid recovers and the LEXX has no choice but to flee. Mantrid follows with everything he's got, literally the mass of the entire Universe. Mantrid taunts the crew, announcing when he's finished eating this universe, he will create a door into the other universe and eat that too.

But Mantrid has made a mistake, by coming after the LEXX, moving too much mass too quickly, he's begun the big crunch, and the mass of the Universe is now collapsing towards a single point.

The LEXX escapes into the Dark Zone universe. If they haven't won, they have at least defeated Mantrid and survived.

That evening, on Board the LEXX, we discover that Mantrid has survived, mounting the cube containing his essence on one of the drones and infiltrating the LEXX. Disabling 790, the final Mantrid drone attacks Xev, but is disabled. The cube containing Mantrid ends up on the floor, and as Mantrid's voice rises to a high pitched scream, she crushes it under her boot.

Review & Commentary

The **End of the Universe** didn't come easily. The fundamental notion, as we've said, dates to the original abandoned first season ending movie, **Back to the Cluster**, and one of the earliest second season outlines, from June, 1996, which refers to a planet eating force which seemed to be intended to be resolved in the third season.

But by December of 1997, the essential elements and title had been worked out. Briefly, the story at that time was going to be: Mantrid eats the time prophet in a prologue scene. Meanwhile the crew finally noticed that Mantrid is eating the entire universe. Seeing no way to stop him they realize that after he eats the Light Universe he'll eat the Dark Zone next. They decide to find a really big super-quasar to blow up or destabilize, which will cause the Light Universe to implode, in order to save the Dark Zone. Hopefully, they'll be able to escape to the Dark Zone in the nick of time.

Meanwhile, Mantrid figures out what they're up to and tries to stop them. Then some plot things happen, what exactly, we're not sure, but they're working on it. The Universe collapses, they escape, blah blah blah.

It's mostly there, as we can see. The 'super-quasar' angle was dropped, probably because it was really stupid, in favor of the 'center of the universe' angle, which was arguably just as stupid but unquestionably more mysterious and portentous.

The plot development of Mantrid figuring out their plan was dropped, and somewhere along the line, the 790 drones came in. But overall, the conclusion of the story arc had been established in general terms.

So far so good.

But behind the scenes things weren't working out so well. It was the end of the series and in the final block of shooting, resources and time had grown painfully short. People were exhausted; tempers were short, yet here

End of the Universe had originally been Paul Donovan's project to write. As the endgame was rethought, **Norb** was moved from the second last episode to an earlier point to heighten drama and a new character for a new penultimate episode and character, **Brizon,** was devised.

Meanwhile, a schism opened up in the creative side. As Willie Stevenson, the creative producer, recalls *"The last two episodes.... It was an insane writing process, trying to figure out how to write this up. We were at loggerheads, Lex, Jeff and myself with Paul, we were pushing for another direction: A big showdown between Brizon and Mantrid, which would have been more interesting."*

In the end, Donovan won out. It's good to be the supreme bean.

Lex Gigeroff still isn't entirely comfortable with the whole thing.

"It all just happens too fast," he said, *"and the thing is, why does the Universe collapse? The total amount of mass hasn't changed?"*

Actually though, the concept that if you could just put enough of the Universe's mass into one spot you might be able to reverse the big bang seems sound, at least in theory. It isn't so much a question of the amount of mass, but where you put it. Black holes, after all, are nothing more than admittedly large quantities of mass tucked away into teeny tiny spaces so that the fabric of space time gets all wonky.

But he's got a point in that it does seem to happen too quickly. Even doubling in number every few hours, it should take millions or billions of years to reach the point of devouring some significant fraction of the Universe, although after a certain point, things would go quickly.

But there are a number of things best left unanswered. What's powering those Mantrid drones in the first place? How do they manage to travel around between stars so quickly? How do they convert basic elements, such as pure hydrogen into drones? These things don't seem to bear close examination, the attitude of the Beans is simply "they just do, okay!"

This, of course, gets us into those dodgy areas of suspension of disbelief. The audience can be lead to believe the most outrageous things, at least within the story. A flying boy in never-never land, a giant chandelier from outer space arriving at Devil's Peak, a crew going boldly where no man has gone before, a dashing young Jedi trainee out to save a Princess, a fifty foot ape, a five hundred foot radioactive lizard, all these things and more have been swallowed whole. The audience can be asked to swallow just about everything, but they can't be insulted. Once you lose them, you don't get them back. Knowing where to push and where to give in terms of the audiences credibility is less a science than an art.

So yes, there are all sorts of problems with these Mantrid drones, problems that aren't addressed in any detailed way in the series. So, the question is do they need to be answered, or can we lightly skip past them and get on with the story? Overall, I think we can skip lightly past.

The resolution of the second season story arc is breathtaking in its scope and ambition. Our heroes defeat Mantrid finally. They only had to destroy the Universe to save it. It makes Vietnam look almost quaint. This Pyrrhic victory has a weird riff off Nook where Brother Randor destroys his own world because he believes it's irreversibly poisoned.

There's an odd bit of repetition. Xev's final crushing of Mantrid's cube is a visual echo of her crushing the web creature in Net only a couple of episodes back. The two come so closely together that it must be taken as a deliberate reference. The series is replete with mirroring, with lines, gestures, images and even sequences seeming to go in pairs. Stan, for instance, is trapped in a cryostasis pod again while doing mechanical tinkering, just as in **Gigashadow**.

The physical constraints on the episode are apparent. Almost all of the live action takes place on the LEXX itself, there are only two rudimentary sets built, one for Lyekka's confrontation with Mantrid, another for the Disk Jockey. There's also practically no guest actors, series regulars Dieter Laser and Louise Wischermann are back to reprise and conclude their ongoing roles. To their credit though, they're each given their meatiest roles since the creation of their characters.

But apart from that, there's only a cameo from Alan McGillivary as the disk jockey. We all remember Alan as the ill-fated pie maker, Argon Protopi, from **I Worship His Shadow**? McGillivary was one of the original members of Salter Street, and appeared in small roles in early films such as **DefCon 4, Siege** and **South Pacific 1942**. He also acted as a producer for Salter, with Producer credits for Paul Donovan's **Life With Billy**, and with **Celtic Electric**. And of course, set pieces from Celtic Electric were used in **Brigadoom**, it all goes in circles, you see.

The musical clip he plays, is from the band **790RobotHead,** a mid to late nineties funk band lead by Kenny Seay. Their name was obviously inspired by LEXX and Hirschfield's character, and the beans were so tickled, they threw in a nod. Seay's band eventually broke up, but he retained the name and reconstituted a new band.

Exhaustion was also showing up in the CGI post production. *"That was really difficult in terms of the demands on CGI,"* Alex Busby recalls. *"We recycled stuff from other episodes, particularly* **Norb** *and* **Brizon.** *"*

But then again, the fact that we've seen this in **Norb** and **Brizon** makes it effective here. Those two episodes not only help sell the visual, but the tension. Those episodes have taught us to accept just how dangerous the drones are. So sometimes these things work simply because the scripts have put the effort into selling the idea to us. Sometimes 'telling' works better than 'showing.'

Much of the final CGI, the image of giant cones and pyramids comes across as curiously flat. The images often fail to do justice to the immensity of the ideas.

But, on the other hand, these are mind boggling ideas. How do you effectively show the mass of the universe being moved in to create a gigantic black hole that will reverse the big bang? That's a mind boggling challenge in itself. Short of retaining a whole bunch of Nobel prize winning physicists and Academy Award winning effects technicians and locking them in a room for a few years, it's hard to see how you'd meet that challenge. But then again, the old sci fi trope holds... The audience can't actually know how this would look, so they're willing to be tolerant... We've never actually seen the end of a universe, so we're prepared to make allowances.

As in **Gigashadow**, the script of **End of the Universe** makes the difference by selling its ideas to the audience. Frequently, special effects more and more are simply left to stand on their own. Big explosions, big CGI, giant monsters, amazing light shows, or racing space ships become an end in and of themselves, all but unremarked on in the script. Possibly, Hollywood is buying in a little too much to the writers' old adage of 'show don't tell.'

But the thing is, sometimes you've got to tell. Without some exposition, some build up in the script, the Death Star in **Star Wars** is just a runaway globe, no big deal.

Gigashadow, quite possibly because things had gone so badly wrong in production, spent a great deal of time setting up and selling its monster before it actually showed, and that was very effective.

End of the Universe takes the time to explain and elaborate on the significance of its images. Two colored blobs up on the screen? That's a star being eaten, Kai explains and this is how it's being done. Suddenly, the image takes on new significance; it's at once more grandiose and more frightening. Suddenly, the dismantling of the Universe isn't just patches of grey, but an actual process, the mechanics hideously clear.

Pyramids and Sphere's heading in, all by itself, that's not too scary. Who's afraid of idealized Platonic forms?

These are titanic accumulations of mass, galaxies worth of Mantrid drones, so many that the LEXX is less than a speck. The geometric shapes, impersonal and primal, are deceptively unthreatening. They don't achieve their real impact until we're told what they are.

In a sense, the entire season has been devoted to subtly selling the whole concept of the final episode, attempting to lead us to the point where we'll accept, yes, this really is the end of the universe they're showing.

This isn't to sell the effects short; the CGI is far more impressive on its own terms than it has any right to be, given the time and budget available. But the concepts are so mind boggling, most writers would hesitate to even use them in a novel, to show them up on a screen speaks of breathtaking chutzpah, and both the script and effects are in service to it, when either, on their own, simply weren't up to it.

Overall, I think it works.

Modern physics suggests that our Universe is not cyclic. There will be no big collapse as its exhausted energies fold in on itself, to eventually explode again in a big bang. Instead, it appears that our Universe will simply age to death, expanding endlessly, the stars going out one by one, even the particles of matter and energy breaking down with time, until there's nothing left but an endless cold gray void.

This, I suppose, was the potential fate of the Light Universe, but Donovan and his friends have found a way around it. Instead of expanding forever, the big bang will be reversed and the big crunch will take place because of the machinations of intelligent life. Rather than free agents, we're all just part of that endless cycle of cosmic birth and rebirth.

In some ways, the **End of the Universe** is almost optimistic. The Universe isn't so much dying as being brought to a point of rebirth. The big crunch leads to the big bang, and the whole thing starts all over again.

Towards the end, as Xev races through the LEXX, she stops to notice a butterfly spreading its wings. It's a quiet beautiful moment, a promise of renewal in the midst of destruction.

CREDITS

Creators: Writers -Paul Donovan, Lex Gigeroff, Jeff Hirschfield; Director - Paul Donovan; Production Designer - David Hackl; Creative Producer - Willie Stephenson;

Main Cast: Brian Downey (Captain Stanley Tweedle); Michael McManus (Kai, Last of the Brunnen G); Xenia Seeberg (Xev Bellringer, Rejected Wife/Love Slave/Cluster Lizard); Jeffrey Hirschfield (Voice of 790); Tom Gallant (Voice of LEXX).

Cast: Louise Wischermann (Lyekka); Dieter Laser (Mantrid); Alan McGillivary (Disc Jockey)

Apocryphal LEXX, the Second Season Documentary

The second documentary, on the making of the television series, was on the table shortly after the confirmation of the second series of LEXX itself.

Mark Asquith was a documentary producer at CITY-TV/Space. He came by his love of Science Fiction honestly. After a short career working for a literary press, he'd managed a comic book store in Toronto called the **Silver Snail** for six years. From there, he'd gone on to produce, with Ron Mann, the documentary **Comic Book Confidential**, and after that, had done an award winning half hour television series about Science Fiction and Science Fiction writers for TV Ontario called **Prisoners of Gravity** for five years, producing 137 shows.

Things happened very quickly. The Canadian Science Fiction network, the Space channel, had only come into existence on August 15, 1997. Asquith came on board the Space channel as a producer only a couple of weeks later.

"LEXX was already part of the picture at my first meeting," he recalls. *"Jay Switzer, of CITY-TV, the parent company of Space had booked it even before we had the license. He was taking a risk, but it paid off. It was perfect timing for Space, the movies were done and it was set to go to series."*

"I looked at everything, watched everything. When they decided to go to series, I pitched a documentary and got involved."

Asquith and his crew went up for almost a week, principally during the shooting of **Twilight,** although another episode was being shot at the time, and **Woz w**ould be going into production. He watched rushes for **Lafftrack,** and post-production on **Lyekka.**

"One of the things that struck me about LEXX was that it was very relaxed, the set was full of humour, there was so much green screen, so much really technical stuff. A lot of the blocking was technical, stand here, do this, a lot more technically demanding than I expected. A weird combination of technically stringent and loose."

From this evolved the through line, the underlying unifying theme of the documentary.

"It was a very friendly, very positive set. There was no hierarchy at the crafts table, people would come up and talk to you. You'd see Michael in a corner playing chess with some extra or grip, Lex Gigeroff would be hanging out, it was very different."

"We came back with fourteen tapes," Asquith said. *"You see a lot of 'making ofs and it's very corporate. You don't usually see the kind of access that we had. We shot production meetings, we shot cool stuff."*

Like the series itself, the second documentary is saturated by beautiful and startling images. They devote minutes to the field of heads from **Lyekka,** visually startling in its own right and fascinating in its execution. Equally memorable is the compositing of the Eagle One from **Lyekka,** and a quick shot of a green ninja walking around with a crude model of the LEXX.

The best scenes in the documentary are with the zombies of **Twilight.**

"The two zombies were great. There were quite a few zombies. But there were the two who would have zombie eyes. I wanted to shoot them having their eyes, the contact lenses, put in. I wanted to celebrate the fact that it was a community, and the best way to do that was to follow some of the minor characters," Asquith recalled.

"Gordon White, the crying Zombie, was hilarious. Those two zombies would never have been in a more corporate making of documentary. They were minor characters, practically extras."

Gordon White almost stole the show, his riff on being 'the crying zombie, 'they took away my brain but they couldn't take my heart,' is one of the most memorable scenes in the whole documentary and earned him a minor cult status.

Another memorable scene features zombies from **Twilight** chatting up love slaves from **Woz**.

"That wasn't staged at all," Asquith told me. *"But they were great, they were wonderful. All the love slaves in that episode were hilarious. They all had these bimbo wigs and micro minis. They all looked like extras from the first season of* **Star Trek**. *But out of character, it was very strange, it's just as surreal on the set as on screen. I try to be as unobtrusive as possible. Don Wright, the videographer, was wonderful at being invisible. That was where a lot of it came from. It was just happening."*

It was just LEXX.

Interregnum: The Canadian Television Fund Strikes Back

The third season began with a disaster that oddly, had almost nothing to do with LEXX, but would wind up shaping the series.

What happened was, in 1998, the Canadian Television Fund ran out of money early.

A little bit of background: Film and Television in Canada, or for any market outside the United States, is a chancy proposition. It's very expensive to do, the home market is very small, and the American entertainment juggernaut is almost impossible to compete with.

Size matters. Suppose, you're running a television station in Australia? You're in it to make money. Your market is twenty five million people, and that defines the limits of your revenue, and your expenses. You have to spend money to fill your programming hours; you want to spend as little as possible.

What are you going to do? Fill it with Australian programs which cost you a fortune and look like crap? Or buy American programs which look good and are dirt cheap? On a level playing field, the answer is simple.

But then again, it isn't a level playing field at all is it? The very size and nature of the American entertainment behemoth completely distorts the field.

The gigantic size of the American market means that there's an incredible amount of money to pay for programming, and to pay for expensive high end programming, and to pay for a huge volume of programming.

And the thing with the American marketplace is that all that programming is paid for in the American market.

Which means that anything you sell it for on the international market is basically free money. You don't have to cover your costs of production, that's already covered; you're just raking in profit.

So in the international marketplace, American production has a huge advantage. It can literally undercut local programs anywhere and everywhere, because local productions have to pay their production costs locally, while American programs are paid for, so it's just a matter of squeezing the locals out of their own markets.

Alternatively, the American productions, even if they're relying on international money for their production costs, start with such a huge advantage with the American market, that literally, they're starting the race two thirds of the way to the finish line.

Local productions - Italian, French, Canadian, German, British, what have you, are at a huge disadvantage. Particularly English speaking nations. It's like sending Pele and the Brazilian national soccer team out to play against a group of schoolboys. Only an idiot would consider that a fair market.

This is why almost every Government in the world outside the United States is desperately interested in cultural programming, and in supporting local books, television and movies in a variety of ways, from tax breaks and direct funding to imposing minimum local content requirements on local channels.

Culture is, after all, intrinsically tied up with national identity. The nations of the world all have their own history, and these histories are reflected in songs, in music, in the works of writers and artists, and potentially in television and film. Most nations see a healthy indigenous culture and cultural/entertainment establishment as one of the keys to a stable, prosperous society. And besides, if their cultural creators are just as talented as American ones, why aren't we supporting the locals?

So, if American economies of scale, mass marketing and promotion, make it impossible for local writers and musicians, local film and television to compete fairly, then by and large, most Governments have felt the need to balance out the contest, at least a bit, by supporting the locals. This can be done in a variety of ways, from direct or indirect funding of arts, as in grants, subsidies, loans or tax breaks. Or by imposing national content restrictions, to limit American imports, or national content requirements, forcing broadcasters to show a certain proportion of their total air time as local productions.

This creates an interesting dichotomy between the United States, which advocates free trade, largely because they dominate the planet, on the one hand; and the rest of the world on the other hand. This includes many countries not embracing the notion of having their cultural institutions decimated just so some American mogul can siphon a few more dollars. Of course, the American ideological commitment to free trade in entertainment is not unlimited... Canada has become a cheap place to produce film and television at professional levels, so now the Americans are complaining about 'runaway production,' their entertainment jobs leaving their country.

Of course, from a television station's point of view, these government commandments are a pain in the butt. All they want to maximize revenue and aren't particularly interested in promoting local culture. So, they'll push for the cheapest local programming and show it on off hour slots, reserving the most lucrative and prime time slots for much better looking and appealing American productions, or they'll invest in a prestige production and tout it for all its worth, to conceal the fact that most of their programming is imported.

To try and level the playing field, various governments try different tactics: Reserving a certain number of movie screens or certain number of television hours for local content, tax breaks, international co-production agreements, and funds. It's different from one country to the next.

It doesn't always work as hoped or expected. In Canada one of the major outcomes of the effort to create a Canadian film and television industry resulted in what is often a Hollywood Branch plant. A lot of American movies and television series took advantage of tax breaks, production agreements, and low costs to make film and television for the American market up in the Great White North.

Or if you take a look at the miles of credits on modern Marvel Superhero movies, you'll find that these productions are sourced all over the world, with production teams and locations as far apart as India, Australia, Germany, Canada, etc., and you'll see credits signaling various provincial and state tax credit programs that have gone into them. I'm pretty sure that a multi-billion dollar company like Disney, doesn't need or rely on tax credits from the Quebec Film and Television Production Fund, or Australian Tax Incentives, and I doubt it's a large portion of the latest Avengers, but it's out there, and the American entertainment complex is quite good at hoovering up money from any and every source around the world.

So, for many places, figuring out how to fund and support a viable local film and television industry, figuring out how to support national and local culture as a live and meaningful thing, in the face of the juggernaut... that's a challenge.

The Canadian Television Fund was one such approach to the challenge, a pool of a few million dollars provided by the Government and Canadian Broadcasters to support the production of Canadian Television series, in order to meet Canadian content requirements on local channels.

Now, of course, there's usually far more projects than money. The Canadian Television Fund wasn't infinite, of course. Still, it seemed to work well enough. Projects applied, if they were eligible according to the 'Canadian Content' criteria, they got their money and went away happy. And when the Fund ran out of money, it just closed down until the next year when the whole thing started all over again.

Unfortunately, in 1998, the wrong people got all the money. You see in Canada, there's a peculiar schizoid component to the film and television industry. A lot of the Canadian film and television industry is actually American productions which have moved north of the border to take advantage of low costs. Canada is an attractive place for that kind of thing, the language is the same, the culture and lifestyle is the same, the technical crews are skilled, the infrastructure is there and of course the Canadian dollar is so low that you make a killing on the exchange rates. So, a lot of American programs, with American stars, writers, producers and directors come up here. Back in this time period the **X-Files** was shot in Canada, so was **Outer Limits, Forever Knight, Psi-Factor, Earth Final Conflict, Staargate SG1**, and **Andromeda**, among many others.

For the members of the Canadian film and television industry, it's a ready source of employment and revenue, especially in the lower level jobs, and it keeps the whole thing chugging along. But by and large, it's seen as 'peon' culture, not truly Canadian productions. A lot of Canadian workers get employed, but the stars, the supporting roles, the writers and directors all come up from south of the border. This designation isn't without merit, especially given the dramatic lengths that many of these productions go to conceal their Canadian settings, even down to changing the license plates on cars, and the signs on storefronts. There are so few real differences between Canada and the US that this meticulous attention to detail, the elimination of even vestigial national traces often comes across as offensive.

Canadian productions, by and large, were seen as Canadian owned, Canadian written, Canadian produced, with hopefully Canadian stars, and usually about significant topics of Canadian culture, history or politics: Mad lumberjacks, Cape Breton ice skaters, dynastic politicians mostly made in and around the central Canadian cities of Toronto and Montreal, with an occasional bit of quaint regional programming from somewhere else like Halifax.

Canadian television and film often makes the distinction of being 'literary' and 'relevant.' Too often it's tedious, self-referential, painfully sincere and humorless. It's not really made for a general audience, which has largely been abandoned to watch imported American programming. Rather, the driving force is an incestuous circle of bureaucrats and artists who form the self-designated cultural elite and are tolerated so long as their demands are not exorbitant and as long as they don't make too many waves (No sense upsetting the American entertainment giants).

All right, I admit I'm being a little harsh here. On the other hand, Paul Donovan made a movie called **Paint Cans** on the subject, and he was harsher than I was. But at the same time, there's a bit more truth to this than much of the Canadian film and television establishment would be comfortable with.

Anyway, in March of 1998, disaster struck. The Canadian Television Fund ran out of money, which wasn't unusual. But its grants and funding went to American imports, programs like **Stargate SG1,** or **Earth: Final Conflict.**

The ruling cultural elite were outraged. First, those programs didn't need the money. By and large, they were made for the American market, funded by networks and syndication and sitting pretty. There was also something demeaning about giving cultural money to series which bent over backwards to avoid even having a Canadian license plate in their show. Stargate was a fine show, but in ten seasons, I suspect you could count on one hand the number of times Canada was even mentioned.

If Canada has any distinctiveness, it is probably that by and large, we've surrendered the territories of popular culture to the American entertainment industry. 95% of all movies shown in Canada are foreign. 70% of all English language television is foreign, and that's mostly the stuff that people actually watch. The 30% that is Canadian or local tends to be news, community news, current affairs, sports and daytime children's fare like **Romper Room,** that's the time killing stuff.

The overwhelming mass of this foreign stuff, perhaps 99% is American, with perhaps the odd occasional British thriller or comedy series making a quick brief appearance.

To some extent, this is just natural economics. To some extent, it's a political and financial decision, it's simply cheaper to abandon popular culture and restrict support to high culture and it causes less trouble with those aggressive American entrepreneurs who might otherwise cry foul.

Like a society under siege, Canadian culture has retreated to the towers of high art, as the forces of Viacom and Disney run rampant among the lower orders. Having given up the commercial ground, the establishment clung desperately to its remaining entitlements, its grants, its subsidies, its cultural funding programs and peer reviewed juries of artists appreciating other artists. It's all very sincere and very important, and underneath it all, there's a current of desperation. American branch plant series didn't really need the money, but Canadian producers did. The needed it desperately.

So the sudden emptying of the Canadian Television Fund wasn't just annoying. To the people involved, to the cultural industry, it was a disaster. It was the storming of the last battlements. It was the Yankee entertainment machine finally breaching the final ramparts.

And of course, the loudest voices came from those Canadian cultural producers, the companies and executives whose own 'worthy Canadian cultural productions' had been left short funded.

The Cows Come Home to Roost

Oddly, LEXX was one of the shows getting money that people were denouncing as un-Canadian. Unlike **Stargate SG1** which takes place in the here and now and explicitly is about Americans, LEXX arguably had an excuse; it was off in outer space, in a time and place unrelated to the present.

The truth is, I think, that the Canadian cultural establishment was biased against Sci Fi. Canadian film critic, Geoff Pevere, has blithely argued that Science Fiction and Horror wasn't part of the Canadian literary tradition. It's a foreign concept, alien to our sensibilities, so it is seen rarely and usually not done very well...People like Margaret Attwood, David Cronenberg or William Gibson notwithstanding.

In fact, Canada, like most other western nations does have a genuine and vibrant tradition of both literary and film science fiction, fantasy and horror. But by and large, it is a tradition not acknowledged or respected, and somewhat distrusted as childish and 'American.'

And of course, the Canadian cultural establishment doesn't really have a lot of room for humor, notwithstanding people like Mordecai Richler or Stephen Leacock. Truly important art, of course, is deadly serious and painfully humorless, and apparently not just a little pretentiousness. The Canadian cultural elite, for all its pretensions, tended to be a remarkably stodgy and conservative group.

Now, to be absolutely fair, that kind of description pretty much says it all for the 'High culture' of just about any western country, from the United States to Belgium. Inbreeding and self preferentiality goes with the territory.

Ultimately, the controversy had very little to do with LEXX, and the series was only mentioned in passing, if at all. LEXX was just another 'lowest common denominator' production which had nothing to do with 'explaining Canada to Canadians.' It got lumped in with the American productions. It wasn't an American production at all, of course. However, that didn't stop the hammer from coming down on top of it.

The Hammer Falls

In December, 1998, the Canadian Television Fund rules were changed. Under the new rules the 1999 fund would consider only programs that are aimed at Canadian audiences and reflect Canadian themes and subject matter and that are shot and set primarily in Canada. From now on, for support, a series would have to be *"Clearly and Identifiably Canadian."* That is, it had to have recognizable Canadian settings, rather than trying to pass itself off as American.

Approximately 15% of the successful applicants for 1998 wouldn't be eligible under these new rules. It was generally assumed that LEXX, along with branch plant series like **Psi Factor** or **Earth: Final Conflict** would not be eligible. LEXX was specifically singled out in newspaper articles in the Ottawa Citizen and Globe and Mail. Paul Donovan still got no respect.

All right, here's LEXX, you're off in deep space. See any maple leafs around? The new rules hadn't been aimed directly at LEXX, but the effect was the same. A major source of funding for season three was in danger.

This was a real kick in the head to LEXX and the people involved knew it.

The impact can be seen in the anger felt by many people around the show. There was a clear sense that they'd been sandbagged unjustly.

"It was about the people in power, closing the wagons," Jeff Hirschfield said, *"I think it's a lot of people who haven't got what they wanted, and they were finally in a position to change the rules. So they get what they wanted and the rest of us can go to hell. It's that cynical, unfortunately."*

Lex Gigeroff was so upset he posted an angry message on the Salter Street Bulletin Board. The result was a handful of rude emails from places as unlikely as England and Russia, as angry international LEXX fans vented their wrath on a puzzled CRTC.

"Paul said something actually," Hirschfield told me, *"and he was right on. He said 'If these rules were around in Shakespeare's day, you wouldn't have*

Hamlet.' Or most of his works, because Hamlet is set in Denmark, and Othello is in Italy. You couldn't do it."

Although a major source of Canadian money had been impacted, there was still Canadian money in the series, from Salter, from Space and CITY-TV, from Telefilm and other funding agencies.

The irony was, according to line producer Norman Denver, that they did get money from the Canadian Television Fund. But there was less money for the third season, and despite Denver's assurance, I think this may have been a part of it.

"That year we had to have our production assistant standing outside the door the day before to get our applications in. We were the first at the door, the absolute first. The guy camped out for 24 hours. CTF revisions didn't have a big effect on us; we still got money from them. We were first in line, after all."

"It was like camping out for Stones tickets," Denver laughed.

Although they'd won money once again from the Canadian Television Fund, it made the future of LEXX after the third season, that much more uncertain and unlikely.

As it turned out though, another problem lay on the horizon. According to Wolfram Tichy, there was a collapse of the international television markets shaping up and just beginning to be felt in 1999. This made season three that much harder to sell, and made LEXX's future even more uncertain.

Stormy weather at home and abroad.

Apocryphal LEXX, Books Unauthorized

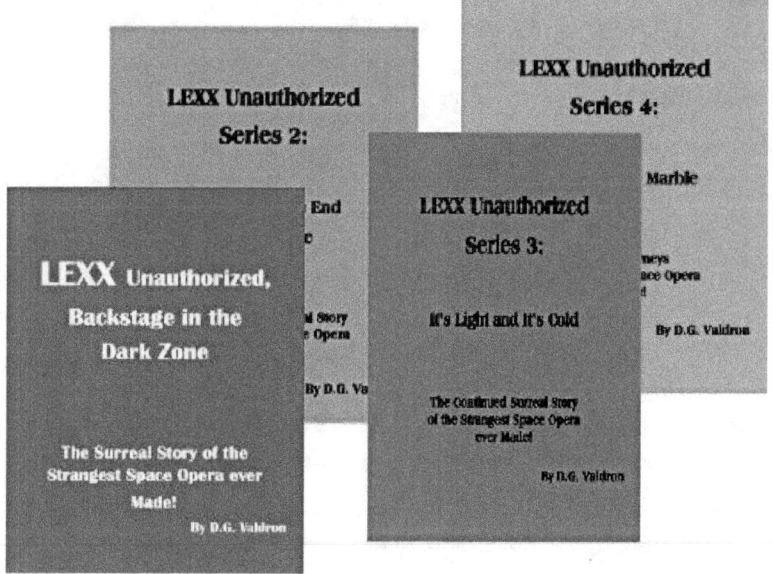

Back around 1999, Paul Donovan, the creator of LEXX, invited me to work on a book about the show. I was a major fan, wildly enthusiastic about the show, so jumped on it, traveling cross country several times to Halifax and Toronto to visit sets and locations, meet actors and crew, watch filming, and conduct a multitude of interviews. Apart from the invitation, I never had a contract with Salter Street or anyone else. It was a labor of love.

Unfortunately, the book project never took off on the business side. The merchandising guy didn't seem to know much about or put any effort into the publishing side, the project drifted through different publishers, TV Books, ECW Press, Titan Books and eventually just kind of died.

A couple of years later, I was invited down to Dragoncon, to participate in a LEXX event with the cast and fans. That galvanized me. I pulled out my notes and materials, three or four years of work, and wrote the book I always wanted to write. I printed off one copy, took it to a bookbinder, travelled across the continent and gave it to Brian Downey. If I'd been able to afford it, I would have made a dozen for cast, creators and directors. But it was just Brian. That was it, I was finished.

I admit, that was a pretty flawed manuscript, written in white heat, to a deadline, first draft stuff, and I frequently misspelled people's names. A fan down in the states asked if they could do a print on demand, and so a few copies were made of the first three parts. But it was done. I'd gotten it out of my system.

More years later, after three changes of career, two major moves, marital breakdown, a flooded basement, three hard drive crashes, and all the other trials of life, I found the manuscript again on a couple of floppy disks in a box. I decided that if it had survived all of this time, I wanted to share it with the world.

I don't know that there's a big audience left, but LEXX was a brilliant series, and it deserves to be remembered.

Volume One chronicles the rise of Paul Donovan and Salter Street films, from the early days when they were struggling to make their first films, up to the creation of LEXX. We explore the strange chain of coincidences that lead to LEXX's approval, the development of the stories and concepts, the production of the four movies, and even the stories of lost or abandoned movies that might have been, but never got made.

Volume Two you have with you.

Volume Three reveals the secrets of the third series, the original genesis of the Heaven and Hell storyline, all the way back as early as the first season, the production experiences in the second season that drove it, the location filming, the lost episode, the challenges and transformations.

Volume Four will chronicle the final desperate season, the American experience, and the fall of Salter Street.

Check them out.

A Note and More Books by the Author

If you've skipped to the end, looking for an apology, well... Sorry? Also, no refunds.

Thank you for taking the time out to read my little book. If you've made it all the way here, then I'm just going to assume you liked it.

What else do I have to offer? More LEXX Unauthorized, some kick ass Doctor Who pirates history, a trilogy of alternate history stories, a trilogy of horror collections, novels, you name it.

If you liked this, could I suggest you leave a review wherever you got it. Mention it on your blog, or your Facebook. Say nice things. If that's too much, just toss me a couple of stars. Writing is a solitary, lonely pursuit and actually getting some feedback or appreciation is a wonderful thing.

But there's more to it. It's about trying to get out there. There are a lot of people writing a lot of books, and it can get hard to get noticed. Reviews help.

And speaking of writing more....'

Check out my Website, at denvaldron.com

STARLOST UNAUTHORIZED
And the Quest for Canadian Identity

The series that was Harlan Ellison's nemesis. The most
controversial series in the history of sci fi television. This
exhaustively researched book, based on interviews with some of
the stars and writers, brings a fresh new interpretation of of the
Starlost, and a re-evaluation of the series and its themes in the
context of the 1970s crisis of Canadian nationalism.

HEARTS IN DARKNESS
A Trilogy of Horror Collections

Three Collections of Subversive Horror and Dark Fantasy.

Giant Monsters Sing Sad Songs – The connection between the author of the Necronomicon and a boy in Providence; a girl who meets the last sasquatch, a poet who shares abandoned Tokyo with a Kaiju, and more…

What Devours Also Hungers – The unkillable killers in masks are recruited into the army, vampires and their hunters, clever serial killers, monsters, ghosts and more….

There Are No Doors in Dark Places – A childlike cancer that talks to its owner; A single mother drawn into dark magic; A man who turns into a different monster each night; a vampire that twists lives; a pregnant woman finding her body being stolen from her; and many more

A Dark Fantasy of Murder and Redemption

There's a City where all the races come together uneasily, descending into civil war.

There's a Mermaid, murdered cruelly her people distraught and crying out for justice.

There's an Orc, the lowest and the worst, her mission: Solve the murder, before it all comes crashing down.

And there's something else... this world's first serial killer.

Available only as an Audiobook

ALTERNATE REALITIES
A Trilogy or Strange New Worlds
The Other books

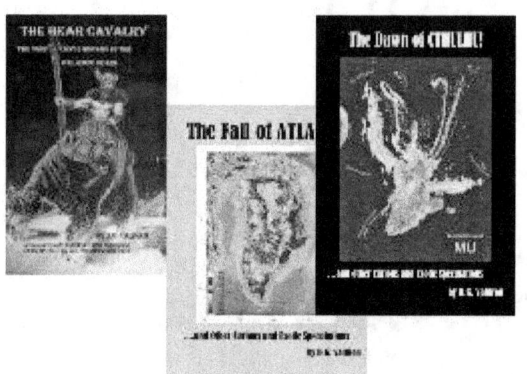

The Dawn of Cthulhu - The Secret History of H.P. Lovecraft's Cthulhu Cult; Lost Continents Found – real and legendary; The Monsters of Sesame Street, is a light hearted examination of Muppets as if they were actual animals.

The Fall of Atlantis – Retroverse, An Accidental Cinematic Universe of 50's Sci Fi movies, Greenland Without the Ice, Rome Crosses the Atlantic, and the Rise and Fall of Atlantis, an ecological catastrophe.

The Bear Cavalry, the True (Not!) History of the Icelandic Bears, an off the wall, short novel about the Viking domestication of bears, their evolution into a medieval cavalry Bonus novelette, The Sharebear Apocalypse.

AXIS OF ANDES
NEW WORLD WAR
A History of WWII in South America

Berlin, 1937, Adolph Hitler and his cabinet meet with a strange delegation from Ecuador. The delegates from the small South American nation beg for help, fearing an impending invasion from their rival, Peru. What happens at that meeting sets in motion a chain of events that sets the entire continent on fire. By the time it's done, millions are dead, nations are in ruins, and the map of Latin America will be changed beyond recognition.

A Pirates History of Doctor Who

The greatest, most professional Doctor Who fan films ever made, explorations of the peculiarities of copyright, the developments of new technologies, the evolution of fan culture, and histories of the Doctor on stage, in audio, and in animation. These books are full of new and entertaining insights and revelations that you'll love.

www.ingramcontent.com/pod-product-compliance
Lightning Source LLC
Chambersburg PA
CBHW060758120626
46557CB00001B/25